The Official®
Club Directory and Price Guide To

Limited Edition
Collectibles

The Official®
Club Directory and Price Guide To

Limited Edition
Collectibles

First Edition

Susan K. Elliott and J. Kevin Samara

House of Collectibles • New York

Important Notice. All of the information, including valuations, in this book has been compiled from the most reliable sources, and every effort has been made to eliminate errors and questionable data. Nevertheless, the possibility of error, in a work of such immense scope, always exists. The publisher will not be held responsible for losses which may occur in the purchase, sale, or other transaction of items because of information contained herein. Readers who feel they have discovered errors are invited to *write* and inform us, so they may be corrected in subsequent editions. Those seeking further information on the topics covered in this book are advised to refer to the complete line of *Official Price Guides* published by the House of Collectibles.

©1994 by Susan K. Elliott and J. Kevin Samara

This is a registered trademark of Random House, Inc.

All rights reserved under International and Pan-American Copyright Conventions.

Published by: House of Collectibles
201 East 50th Street
New York, New York 10022

Distributed by Ballantine Books, a division of Random House, Inc., New York, and simultaneously in Canada by Random House of Canada Limited, Toronto.

On the cover
"Jiminy Cricket," ©1993 The Walt Disney Company

"God Bless Our Years Together," © 1985 Precious Moments Inc. •Licensee Enesco Corporation

1993-94 "Heaven Lea Cottage," members-only piece from Lilliput Lane Collectors' Club

Swarovski 1990 Collectors Society Annual Edition "Lead Me, The Dolphins"

Manufactured in the United States of America
ISSN: 1071-0965
ISBN: 0-876-37927-7

Cover design by Kristine V. Mills

First Edition: January 1994

10 9 8 7 6 5 4 3 2 1

To my father, who taught me how to dream, and to my mother, who helped me learn the skills to achieve them.

— *Susan K. Elliott*

To my parents, Edna and George, I have always been amazed at your commitment to overcome the obstacles and your ability to excel in all of your endeavors. Thank you would never be enough to fulfill the debit that I owe. Sharing your dreams will always be a privilege.

— *J. Kevin Samara*

Table of Contents

Acknowledgments

By its very nature, a book requires the helping hands of many people, all of whom deserve special recognition for their contributions or encouragement. As we've assembled this book, we've been fortunate to receive input and suggestions from many key people in the collectibles world.

When we began developing this book, we turned for guidance to the people who know clubs best. One of the first people we contacted was Joan N. Ostroff, founding executive director of the M.I. Hummel Club, who took the time to carefully critique a sample profile.

During the initial stage, we also received ideas for direction from Bill and Sandy Bales of *Collector's mart* magazine, Cathy Bates of Duncan Royale, Shonnie D. Bilin of Enesco, John Conley of Enesco, Tony Constantino of Schmid, writer Linda Fishbeck, Roger Fitness of Lilliput Inc., Allan Flamm of Flambro, Malcolm Henderson of P. Buckley Moss, John Hine of John Hine Studio Inc., author Dick Hunt, Paul Johnson of Schmid, Ray Kiefer of the National Association of Limited Edition Dealers, D. Bruce Kollath of John Hine Studio Inc., Ken Le Fevre of Goebel Inc., Bob Martin of Gartlan USA, Betty McKenney of North Hill Gifts, Susan Peterson of Schmid, Andy Plotkin, Ph.D. of the Edna Hibel Corporation, Marge Rosenberg of Carol's Gifts, George and Edna Samara of The Shropshire Shop, Paul Schmid III of Schmid, Pat Shaw of Enesco, and Paula Sigman of the Walt Disney Collectors Society. Each one had useful ideas to share.

Later in the process, we received valuable input and assistance from Janeen Benbenek of *Collector's mart* magazine, John Bocchino of Country Gallery, Carousel Fantasy, Lorrie Church of Lorrie's Collectibles, Collectible Exchange, Sandy Forgach of Collectibles, etc. Inc., Roland Gosling of *Collector's mart* magazine, Jack T. Grant of Swarovski, Dave Grossman of Dave Grossman Designs, Diane Carnevale Jones of the Collectors' Information Bureau, Barbara Kennedy of The Bradford Exchange, John Kuck, Jr., artist Sandra Kuck, Joyce Harper of Bear's Den, Janet Gale Mauro, King Minister of King's Gallery, Pat Owen of Viking Import House Inc., Eloise Parks of Eloise's Collectibles, Duane Pullen of Duane's Hallmark Card & Gift Shop, Joan Pursley of *Collector Editions*, Herb Rostand of Rostand's Fine Jewelers, Robert C. Rowe, *Collector Editions*, Winnie Slack of The Side Door, Clif White of Swan Galleries,

Winnie Watson of Watson's Collectibles, James Wetherbee of Finishing Touch, artist Maurice Wideman, and Hal Williams of Mountain Christmas.

We owe a special thanks to the following authors and price guide experts who gave generously of their time to consult on the price guide section of this book: Ken Armke, Sr., of Opa's Haus Inc., Pat Cantrell of The Cottage Collector, Dean A. Genth of Miller's Gifts, Helga Grasher of Secondary Market Scene, Louise Patterson of *The Greenbook*, Reneé Tyler and Russ Wood of Collector's Marketplace, and Rosie Wells of Rosie Wells Enterprises Inc.

We are especially indebted to Pia Colon of the David Winter Cottages Collectors Guild, who graciously critiqued our initial survey form to clubs and, with the assistance of Kim Andrews, gave us ideas for additional questions to ask. They helped us make the book more complete.

In-house, our team consisted of the following tireless workers: Kaki Matheson who created the book's design, and who, along with Lisa O'Neill, spent many late nights and weekends formatting and refining the pages; writers Louis Marroquin and Emily Camp, who input the data from the companies and helped to tell each club's story so eloquently; copy editor Frances Knight (my mother), who added her invaluable expertise to each step of the process; Mary Gonzalez-Davis, responsible for scanning all the photos and art contained in the book; and Reed Poole and Airey Baringer for offering their technical production knowledge along the way.

For moral support, I'd like to thank Jim Beckett III, Lynne Chinn, Rex Hudson, and Fred L. Reed III, of Beckett Publications. Ray Bard of Bard Productions also gave us publishing advice.

Executive directors, public relations people and officers of many clubs helped simplify our task of gathering so much information. This group includes: Margaret Adamic, Walt Disney Collectors Society; Arlene Bae, Enesco; Beth Baer, M.I. Hummel; Leigh Barber, Roman Inc.; April Bargout, The Santa Claus Network; Nina Batson, United Design; Vic Blackburn, The Windberg Collectors Society; Chris Berry, Iris Arc Crystal Collectors Society; Donna Blaska, Collector's League; Henry Blumner, Myth & Magic Collectors Club; Tina Bourguignon, Iris Arc Crystal Collectors Society; Margret Brocks, Steiff Club USA; Cindy Brooks, Forever Friends Collectors' Club; Sharon Button, International Bossons Collectors Society; Marian E. Casey, Muffy Vanderbear Fan Club; Pat Chandok and David Woodard, Krystonia; Gail Cohen, Artaffects Marketing; Glenn Conciatori, Lladró Collectors Society; Loretta Connolly, the Lowell Davis Farm Club; Dr. Robert E. Davis, International Bossons Collectors Society; Chip deMatteo, Hand & Hammer Collector's Club; Diana Derbas, Enesco Memories of Yesterday Collectors' Society; Nancy Falkenham, PenDelfin Family Circle; James E. Farrell, Dreamsicles Collectors' Club; L. Susan Fife, Mark Hopkins Sculpture Guild; Hedi B. Fitz, Swarovski Crystal USA; Mari Forquer, Cabbage Patch Kids Collector Club; Brent Germany, Daddy's

Long Legs Collector's Club; Diane Goedkoop, Royal Doulton USA; Pam Grier, Old World Christmas® Collectors' Club; Mary Ann Guerrieri and Marlyn Ward, the P. Buckley Moss Society; Claire Golata, Pocket Dragons & Friends; Mary Lee Graham, Flambro; Gretchen Hagle, Enesco Treasury of Christmas Ornaments Collectors' Club; Nadine M. Haase, Club ANRI; Jim Hennon, PJ's Carousel Collectors Club; Debbie Hoover, Debbie Hoover Public Relations, Marketing; Pat Jahn, Stein Collectors International Inc.; Viola Janz, Great American Collector's Guild; Betty Keepin, Pedone and Partners; Patricia A. Kendall, Donald Zolan Collector's Society; Julia Kirkwood, Enesco; Lance Klass, Donald Zolan Collectors Society; Bobbi Kurani, Thomas Kinkade Collectors' Society; Maria Maynard, Belleek Collectors Society; Jerri and Jim McCloud, Jerri Collector's Society; Barbara McLaughlin, Melody in Motion Collector Society; Susan Moore, Annalee Doll Society; Cyndi Gavin McNally, Lance Corp.; Tanya McWhorter, Madame Alexander Doll Club; Lisa Murphy, Swarovski Collector Society; Real and Muff Musgrave, Pocket Dragons & Friends; Anne-Marie O'Dwyer, Lilliput Lane Collectors' Club; Jan Potter, G. Armani Society; Ronnye Peace and Rachel Perkal, Hallmark Keepsake Ornament Collector's Club; Kathy Pisano and Shelia Thompson, Shelia's Collectors Society; Don Polland, Polland Studios; Connie Ribaudo, G. Armani Society; Hugh R. Robinson, Lladró Collectors Society; Beth Benore Savino, The Toy Store's Collector Club for Steiff; Barbara J. Schrage, Maud Humphrey Bogart Collectors' Club; Linda Seyedin, Edna Hibel Society; Carolyn Snead, Marty Bell Collector's Society; Linda Smith, Lawton Collectors Guild; Marsha Smith, Harry Smith Collectors' Club; Susan Stashkevetch and Larissa Woroch, Lalique Society of America; William Stat, The Franklin Mint Collectors Society; William Swain, Diane Graebner Collector's Club; Jim Swiezynski, Chilmark Gallery; Imal Wagner, Summerhill Crystal; Townsend Thorndike, Annalee Doll Society; Patrick Wong, Little Cheesers Collectors' Club; Liz Wilkins, Walt Disney Collectors Society; Evelyn Faye Windberg, The Windberg Collectors Society; Kelly Womer, Enesco; and Alene Yarnall, Lizzie High® Society.

If we have inadvertently omitted anyone who contributed, we sincerely apologize.

And of course, we'd like to thank our editors at House of Collectibles, Stephen H. Sterns and Owen Lock, for believing in this project.

In addition, Kevin and I would like to thank our families for their patience during this lengthy writing process: Kevin's wife Phyllis, daughters Nicole and Elizabeth, and my fiancé Jerry Hamm. They know how many late nights and weekends were spent away from them and we appreciate their understanding.

Again, thanks to all who made this book possible.

— *Susan K. Elliott*

How to Use This Book

This book was written to provide a complete reference and price guide to both current and past collector clubs for collectors and dealers. In using the book, you will notice that the club profiles contain pertinent facts, information, and features about each club and how it operates. Background information on artists and company histories round out coverage.

In addition, price guide sections on club collectibles provide details about exclusive gifts and members-only pieces by year of issue, original value and current valuation.

The "In Brief..." sections of listings provide abbreviated information about other clubs that will be of interest, but which include no pricing information due to lack of secondary market activity. Some of these clubs are so new that many of their programs have not been finalized.

Current values of most collector member pieces appear as a range of prices which represent reported high and low values of pieces traded or available on the secondary market. Most prices quoted reflect actual trading prices reported from secondary market; limited edition dealers; collectible trading exchanges; and auction reports. Some prices came from specialist observers who concentrate their interest in a specific club or category. In totality, prices were derived from a national investigation. Keep in mind that prices often vary regionally. This book has not been compiled for the purpose of establishing price values, but for the purpose of reporting prices found in the marketplace within the past 18 months.

The lowest value of the price range can be termed fair market value, representative of a competitive selling situation. In most cases, higher values would be for replacement cost — the highest price that a buyer would reasonably be willing to pay. Factors such as signatures, remarques, availability of box or certificate may also influence value.

Appraisals

Use this book for appraisal purposes, as well as keeping up with the specifics of each club's structure and benefits. Appraisal valuation can meet several needs, such as for insurance coverage, estate valuation, or liquidation. When using this book to determine a value for insurance purposes, the higher value or replacement cost should be applied. These values will give you the ability to enter the marketplace with enough resources to replace your piece.

For estate valuation, appraisers would also normally apply replacement, or the highest value, but it is up to the discretion of the collector, depending on one's situation. Valuing a collection for your heirs might require different documentation than for tax purposes. Typically, when a collection is part of an estate, the executor is confronted with having to sell the assets quicky — often at the lowest values. Estate valuations also may be made in cases of divorce.

In some circumstances, collectors may want or have to sell part or all of a collection, and may need to sell quickly. When approaching a dealer to sell pieces or liquidate an entire collection, one should take into account that the dealer must resell the piece and make a profit. Typically, dealers would pay between 20 and 50 percent below fair market value.

Collectibles represent today's art and tomorrow's heirlooms — and often are one of the most fragile assets in a household. Due to their rapid appreciation and short supply, collector club pieces can be among the most difficult to replace in today's market.

Most collectors do not fully realize the appreciated value of their collection. Even if you are not interested in valuing your collection for estate or insurance purposes, accurate documentation of what you've so carefully collected is important to ensure that your family understands its value. Recordkeeping involves a certain amount of drudgery, but the reward comes in keeping up with the value of your collection.

Valuation forms appear throughout the book (see the sample below) to help you keep personal records of the value of your club pieces. Either fill out the pages in the book to use the entire volume as a record, or photocopy and store with your other financial records. Remember that values vary from year to year, so as an added benefit to this book, you may obtain a free pricing update, available January 1995. (See ordering details on the last page of this book.)

We, the authors, hope that you will find this book to be a helpful tool in your collecting pursuits.

My Personal Inventory

Club Name _____

Description	Number	Size	Issue Value	1994	Current Valuation 1995	1996	1997

Clubs Today

In the 1960s and 1970s, collectors and manufacturers began developing the concept of national and international collectors' clubs as we know them today. The first clubs were created for collectors of Madame Alexander dolls, Wedgwood porcelain, Franklin Mint collectibles, and artists Edna Hibel, Norman Rockwell, and Sister M.I. Hummel. Formed with a variety of approaches, each added their own elements to the concept of collectors' societies that has become so essential in today's world of limited edition collecting.

As the collectors' market has grown, collectors have focused on specialization to keep from being overwhelmed by the number of offerings. Collectors' clubs offer one means of accomplishing this narrowed focus.

Be the First to Know

With emphasis on collectors' clubs continuing to increase, the key ingredients that go into a successful club appear to be more and more clearly defined. First and foremost, collectors expect to become part of a group that provides inside information. Such information ranges from first release of new product announcements to news about artists' appearances, auctions, tours, and company history.

To be a devoted collector, one needs knowledge, and today's clubs recognize that necessity. Whether large or small, a successful club meets this need first. Among the few club failures of recent years (the exceptions rather than the norm), most failed to provide adequate or well-conceived publications, or to put adequate

Early clubs include: The Madame Alexander Fan Club (started in 1961), The Wedgwood Collector's Society (1969), The Franklin Mint Collectors Society (1970), Rockwell Society of America (1974), and The Edna Hibel Society (1976).

planning into their benefits. The most successful societies focus on their magazine or newsletter, making these publications worthy collectibles in themselves.

The potential value of special club gifts and members-only exclusives attract collectors and encourage them to justify their membership dues, but quality information lies at the heart of a club. Letters from artists to members help enhance the idea of closeness that a club wants to foster.

Variety of Benefits

Clubs offer a convenient and fun way to become more intimately involved in collecting. Local chapters of many national organizations and national club conventions give members a chance for personal interaction, bringing together devoted collectors who may form bonds and friendships that last for years.

Edna Hibel Society members on tour

A national club does not necessarily need to be large to sustain local clubs if individual collectors show enough desire to create and run local chapters.

Size also does not determine the quality of a club, as one will see from reading through the profiles that this book includes.

Many groups sponsor tours to European factories with interesting travel destinations in the area. Among these tours, collectors may cruise with Duncan Royale, the Precious Moments Collectors Club, the P. Buckley Moss Society, or explore various corners of Europe with the M.I. Hummel Club, the Belleek Society, the G. Armani Society, the ANRI Club, and many others. Museums in this country may be found for the Edna Hibel Society in Palm Beach, Florida, the Lladró Collectors Society in New York City, The Franklin Mint outside Philadelphia, and All God's Children Collector's Club in Alabama.

Member Profiles

Jack T. Grant, president of Swarovski America, describes the 155,000 members of the Swarovski Collectors Club as 80 percent women, average age 35 to 55, who work full time and buy six to seven pieces of Swarovski crystal a year. He reports about 15 to 20 percent growth per year in membership for the Swarovski Collectors Club, a trend that applies to the growth of clubs in general. The company's surveys indicate that most Swarovski collectors don't buy other lines or clubs, which may not be as pronounced for other clubs.

Demographics of members vary widely for clubs, depending on the type of product featured.

The Development of Clubs

Innovations in the field have come naturally as each new club tries to create better ways to serve members. In 1976, The Edna Hibel Society was the first full-fledged group formed to honor one artist. (The Madame Alexander Fan Club, formed in 1961, was still providing newsletters only until 1976, without additional benefits.) The Hibel Society was the first club to release two members-only collectibles at the same time, as well as the first to release a collectible with a pre-announced edition limit rather than a firing period or time limit. This group has travelled extensively with Hibel for exhibitions around the world, and to observe the printing of her art in Switzerland.

P. Buckley Moss Society collectors enjoy similar types of trips with artist Pat Buckley Moss, and also gather for their own annual conventions held in various American locales known for their Amish populations, subject of Moss's art. This society represents a unique focus, since it is

Local, general focus collector clubs received assistance in organizing from the American Limited Edition Association (ALEA), which formed in 1977. The group sponsored four national conventions before folding.

3

A sampling of club membership cards shows their design diversity

run entirely by collectors with the cooperation of the Moss Portfolio, and concentrates on raising money at the local level for numerous suggested charities.

The advent of the M. I. Hummel Club in 1977 (originally the Goebel Collectors' Club) and the Enesco Precious Moments Collectors' Club in 1981 each provided tremendous excitement and energy to the club field, laying the groundwork for today's well-run clubs.

Enesco now sponsors more clubs than any other company, with two Precious Moments groups, the Maud Humphrey Bogart Collectors' Club, the Enesco Memories of Yesterday Collectors' Society, Enesco Treasury of Christmas Ornaments Collectors' Club, and Sports Impressions Collectors' Club.

One interesting club launched with much fanfare in 1980, the Mettlach Collectors Society (see illustration of club medallion), closed

The Goebel Collectors' Club held its first annual convention in October 1981, and named a Local Chapter Member of the Year.

Blue-and-white phanolith Mettlach Collectors Society medallion was a giveaway when the club began. The Society had 10,000 members at one point

a few years later, but left behind interesting memorabilia. Some clubs with short lifespans have been reorganized and restarted, usually reflecting changes that the artist has made in their affiliation with a particular company. A few of the reorganized clubs have included those for Donald Zolan, Gregory Perillo, and Sandra Kuck.

Throughout the 1980s, clubs continued to form and refine their approach, with a virtual explosion of clubs in the early 1990s.

The Future

In 1993, more than a dozen new clubs formed, including four devoted to Christmas (Enesco Treasury of Christmas Ornaments, Old World Christmas® Collectors' Club, Santa Claus

*Members-only pieces for the Jan Hagara Collectors'
Society range from pins to prints, figurines to dolls*

Network, and The Christopher Radko Family of Collectors). Most major collectible companies have at least explored the idea of beginning a club. With so much competition for members, collectors gain a higher level of benefits and creativity.

Exploring the world of clubs will offer many happy hours with the bonus of receiving beautiful souvenirs for the journey. Studying the profiles on the following pages should help collectors, or would-be collectors, to discover new club possibilities while providing solid pricing and background information about well-established clubs.

We hope that you enjoy your armchair journey through the world of clubs and the many benefits of club membership.

Wedgwood Collectors Society issues feature adaptations of the company's original 18th-century jasper ware designs.

Attention Club Directors:

Marian E. Casey, director of the Muffy Vanderbear Fan Club, would like to explore the idea of forming an association for club directors. For more information, contact her at 401 North Wabash, Suite 500, Chicago, Illinois 60611, or call (312) 329-0020.

About the Market

The earliest collectors' clubs in the limited edition field were created in the 1960s and 1970s as the collecting market in general was booming.

More than a hundred and twenty limited edition collectors' clubs now prosper in a variety of formats to promote a multitude of collectible lines. The structures of each may differ, but most sponsors would agree that their clubs exist to enhance loyalty for an artist or collectible by giving collectors the most complete information available, along with a special collectible experience that comes from this added knowledge. And then there are the highly sought after exclusive pieces available only to members.

Knowing that one is the first of a limited group to begin a collection has been the impetus for creating secondary market superstars of numerous charter year club editions. "Little Pals," Lladró's first members-only piece, came out in 1985 at $95. Recent auctions record its value at $4,100, quite a sizeable increase.

Other top performers include Swarovski's crystal "Lovebirds" from 1987, up to $4,000 from $150; the G. Armani "Awakening" sculpture, now $1,200; and Lilliput Lane's 1986 "Crendon Manor" cottage, up to $1,000 from $285. (See chart on page 12 for other highly valued editions.)

The majority of collectors acquire limited editions for the pure enjoyment and pleasure they derive from collecting, but others collect for the investment and value appreciation of limited edition collectibles. Collector club pieces meet the needs of both collectors.

"For the most part, club members represent

the most avid collectors in the market, and are looking for something special," says Dean Genth, a secondary market expert on M.I. Hummel, Swarovski, and other lines. Collectors consider club membership pieces one of their most important benefits in joining a club. Once these editions are no longer available, they have proven to attain substantial appreciation on the secondary market.

Collectors traditionally redeem their certificates for members-only pieces at collectibles retailers, knowledgeable sources on a wide range of issues.

Limited production of members-only pieces, with one for each collector who joins the club in any given year, means that the edition always sells out. This fact, more than any other, accounts for the rapid appreciation of values of the members-only pieces.

"A large number of collectors are just discovering collector clubs, chasing a very limited supply of early membership-only pieces," says Genth. "This is especially true of the larger, well established clubs." The popularity of collector's clubs demonstrates the collector's desire for limited edition pieces.

Many collectors who have acquired members-only pieces are holding onto them and are not making them available on the secondary market. The supply is so short and the demand often far exceeds the number of pieces for sale at any given time, thus accounting for the high retail values that collectors are willing to pay to acquire these scarce limited edition collectibles. The age-old law of supply and demand rules the secondary market as the values for each item settle to what someone is willing to pay to acquire what another possesses.

Some collectors routinely take more than one membership in a club to obtain multiple club pieces. These tend to be speculators anticipating price appreciation. Pat Cantrell, a writer-broker who specializes in cottage and architectural collectibles, says, "Speculation in club pieces is a volatile market with no assurances of sustained value. Looking at collector's club prices is really a study in human nature. Rapid appreciation eventually slows down and meets a point of resistance."

Tracking the valuation of club pieces is extremely important when dealing on the secondary market and prices must be monitored on a regular basis.

A new collector emerging today concentrates on only club pieces and frequently takes memberships in a number of clubs. This collector could be called an acquirer of limited edition pieces — choosing pieces based not only on personal taste, but also observation of the overall collectible market.

Anyone who wishes to buy or sell secondary market members-only pieces should not confine themselves geographically. The widest search for a buyer or seller will bear the best results. Collectible publications such as *Collector's mart* magazine or *Collector Editions* are an excellent source to locate dealers and national collectible exchanges who specialize in secondary market editions.

Looking at the new clubs entering the field recently, one would expect the new Walt Disney Collectors Society to quickly join the list of top ten clubs, both in the value of its early editions and number of collectors who will join. Taking into account the careful preparation that has gone into developing this society, along with the fervor that Disneyana collectors already exhibit, one doesn't need a crystal ball to predict a bright future for the Walt Disney Collectors Society.

The more difficult question might be to figure out which other clubs now in their infancy will become tomorrow's superstars. We suggest that you review the possibilities carefully, and if you choose to speculate in club editions, perhaps you will look back in a few years to discover that you've acquired editions from one of the next mega-clubs in the field. On the other hand, if you explore the variety of new clubs available based primarily on their appeal to you, you'll also enjoy enjoy building a collection that offers benefits not found anywhere else, without having to worry about any shifts in the market.

With new clubs emerging each month, the possibilities for both personal and price appreciation are great.

International Collectible Expositions held twice a year in various cities give collectors a chance to meet favorite artists and learn about new collectors' clubs. Buy and Sell events provide a market for locating or selling club collectibles. (For more information, contact International Collectible Expositions, McRand International Limited, 1 Westminster Place, Lake Forest, Illinois 60045, phone (708) 295-4444)

A Sampling of
Top Appreciating Club Issues

1. Lladró "Little Pals," 1985, issue $95, current value: $4,100, up 43.1 times issue price

2. Swarovski "Togetherness," 1987, issue $150, current value: $4,000, up 26.6 times issue price

3. M.I. Hummel "Valentine Gift," 1977-78, issue $45, current value: $900, up 20 times issue price

4. Precious Moments "Hello Lord, It's Me Again," issue $25, current value: $435, up 17.4 times issue price

5. Annalee Dolls "Johnny Appleseed," 1983, issue $80, current value: $1,000, up 12.5 times issue price

6. David Winter "Robin Hood's Hideaway," 1987, issue $54, current value: $625, up 11.57 times issue price

7. G. Armani "Awakening," 1990, issue $137.50, current value: $1,200, up 8.72 times issue price

8. Chilmark Gallery "The Chief," 1983, issue $275, current value: $2,050, up 7.45 times issue price

9. Chilmark Gallery "Unit Colors," 1984, issue $250, current value: $1,350, up 5.4 times issue price

10. Chilmark Gallery "Oh Great Spirit," 1985, issue $300, current value: $1,300, up 4.33 times issue price

1985 Top valued "Little Pals"

1981 "Hello Lord, It's Me Again"

Terms to Understand

Anniversary exclusives
Items offered to members who achieve certain anniversaries with a club, such as five, ten, or 15 years

Annual dues
Fee paid for one-year membership in a collectors' club

Appraisal
Assignment of value to an item

Architectural designs/collectibles
Three-dimensional reproduction, scale model building or cottage figurine

Artist proof
Traditionally the first pieces produced in an edition which are set aside for the artist's corrections and/or personal use, normally ten percent or less of an edition

Authorized redemption center
Normally an authorized dealer chosen by the manufacturer to represent a product on the primary market

Backstamp, trademark
An identifying mark usually placed on the base of a collectible, or a registered logo

Brokerage fee
The cost paid to a listing service or exchange for the service of selling a piece, usually a percentage that is charged to either the seller or the buyer

Certificate redemption period
May extend beyond the club year's end

Charter member
A collector who joins a club during its first year or designated charter period

Club size
The total membership population of a collectors' club

Club year
May extend until a pre-set date anytime during the year, or one year from the time a collector joins a club

Cold cast
A casting composition used to produce figurines without firing. A material that enables reproduction of fine details

Collectible exchanges

A trading service that brings together buyers and sellers, frequently through a listing service, either via phone or printed listings, frequently charging a commission for the service to either buyer or seller, may be general or targeted to specific collectible lines

Collectors' club

An organization sponsored by the manufacturer for the purpose of enlisting collectors who want the privilege of receiving additional information, benefits and members-only pieces in exchange for an annual membership fee (although a few clubs exist without dues)

Collectors' society

The same as a collectors' club

Commission

The fee charged a collector to sell a piece by a dealer or exchange service. The same as a brokerage fee

Consignment

Placing an item with a dealer under the condition that it will be placed for sale in exchange for a fee or commission for the service, rather than selling the piece to the dealer outright

Discontinued

A retired collectible that has ceased production

Edition limit

The total number of pieces produced of an individual collectible

Estate appraisal value

Documentation for tax, or inheritance purposes

Fair market value

The value at which a piece may appear in a competitive marketplace

Fine arts floater

A type of insurance which can be purchased in addition to a homeowner's policy for the purpose of itemizing and insuring specific collectibles or works of art at predetermined valuations

Free gift

In the cases of some collectors' clubs, a customer appreciation gift given to the collector upon joining

Immediate redemption

A service provided by some large dealers who are able to sell a members-only piece to the collector upon the presentation of the redemption coupon, due to the large volume of collectors' club members-only pieces sold by that dealer. Usually, a dealer must send the redemption coupon in to the collectors' club to obtain members-only pieces for a collector

Instant gratification kits

A term for membership kits which are boxed and available in

the store for a collector to take home upon joining

Insurance appraisal value
Replacement cost

Limited edition
An item produced with an announced limit by quantity or time period

Liquidation appraisal value
Normally the lowest valuation depending on the supply, demand, and availability of an item

Local chapters
Clubs formed locally as offshoots of a larger organization, notably for members of the M.I. Hummel Club, Enesco Precious Moments, P. Buckley Moss Society and others

Membership card
The identification provided by a club when a collector joins and pays a membership fee

Membership exclusive edition
A collectible made available for purchase only by members of a club

NALED
The National Association of Limited Edition Dealers, a trade assocation for retailers who specialize in collectibles and limited editions, co-sponsor of major national collectors' conventions, headquarters at 1-800-HI NALED

New member kit
Sent upon joining to new members, usually contains the club's gift items, publications, redemption form for members-only offering, catalogs, and membership card or identification certificate

Newsletter
May take many forms among collector clubs, provided as a membership benefit to club members and may contain classified advertising as well as features about the company and artist, new issues and letters from members

Primary market
Initial sales of a collectible from retailer to collector, normally at issue price

Redemption center
An authorized dealer who will sell a members-only piece when provided with a redemption certificate by a collector

Redemption certificate
Provided to members for limited, club items, usually redeemed by returning to an authorized retailer, or sometimes directly to the club, one per club member

Remarque
A special drawing added to a collectible by an artist, normally to prints

Replacement cost
The highest valuation cost that a buyer may expect or have to pay

to duplicate a lost piece, normally applied to insurance value

Retired
When a collectible design has ceased production and is not available on the primary market

Sale of record
Auction prices from regular sales events, such as those held by Lalique, Lladró, and Swarovski Crystal

Scheduling
The listing and accurate documentation of collectibles or fine art for the purpose of insurance

Secondary market
Sales of a collectible after the original (or primary) stock has been sold by retailers to collectors, may involve sales from collector to collector, collector to retailer, or retailer to collector

Secondary market history
The tracking of the performance of a collectible after it is sold out on the primary market, usually adjusted on an annual basis or sometimes more frequently

Signed
Generally refers to collectibles personally signed by an artist and may add to the value of a piece if actually signed by the artist; many items also bear incised or decal signatures which have no special value

Special events
Open house events that are held by collectible dealers allowing the collectors to meet artists or representatives of a manufacturer. In some cases, special event pieces sold only during an open house are available for purchase

Speculation
Buying for investment with the intention of selling a collectible when the value increases on the secondary market

Supply and demand
The cause and effect relationship of the amount of product available for sale and the corresponding desire to purchase the product, thus establishing a market value for an item. The higher the demand for a collectible while in short supply, the higher its value. The higher the supply of the product while in less demand, the lower its value

Suspended club
A collectors' club that has ceased operation and servicing its collectors, with members-only pieces no longer being produced

Trading prices
The valuethat collectors are actually paying for a collectible

Valuation
The assignment of a price to a collectible based upon research of the marketplace and the actual price at which an item is trading

A

In Brief...

The Adorables Society
71-73 Weyman Ave.
New Rochelle, NY
Founded in 1982 — offers a special pin, newsletter and opportunity to purchase members-only pieces, $7.50 per year

American Bell Association
Alter Road, Box 386
Natrona Heights, PA 15065
Sponsors annual conventions around the country, issues newsletters; contact director Louise Collins for details

Aviation Relic Prints Club
8152 N. 32nd St.
Richland, MI 49083
President, Mike Lentes

All God's Children®
Collector's Club

ALL God's Children®
COLLECTOR'S CLUB

P.O. Box 8367
Gadsden, AL 35902
Director, Kathy Martin
(205) 549-0340

Featured collectible: Figurines and Christmas ornaments, primarily African-American children and adults, also historical figures by artist Martha Holcombe

Benefits: Free figurine, quarterly club magazine, opportunity to buy exclusive members-only figurine, personal checklist to keep track of your collection, club membership card, notification of Miss Martha's appearances, and invitation to attend annual All God's Children Open House and Fellowship Banquet

Year club founded: 1989

Sponsored by: Miss Martha Originals ™ Inc., founded in 1980

Membership size: About 12,000

Club publication: *All God's Children Collector's Edition*, quarterly magazine, 28 pages, four-color, with collector profiles, classified ads, dealer listings, event news and new products

Annual dues: $20 (foreign, $28 U.S. funds)

Factory tours: Club Headquarters and Museum, open Tuesday through Saturday, 8 a.m. to 4 p.m.

Club year ends: May 31, membership ends one year after joining

Local chapters: Yes, contact the club for assistance and details

Membership kits received: Four to six weeks after joining

How to join: By picking up membership forms at an authorized Miss Martha Originals retailer, or by contacting the Club directly

How to redeem certificates: At an authorized Miss Martha Originals retailer

"Mandy," 1991-92 issue

Collectors know Martha Holcombe to be soft-spoken and gentle, qualities which come through in her art. She describes her goal as being "to express the love of Jesus Christ to others through my artwork and to produce the finest quality product possible."

Holcombe's success in creating the ethnic All God's Children® Collection of figurines has come slowly, but represents a success story to inspire any aspiring artist. She originally began selling soft sculpture doll patterns by mail to raise money to help her church. Five years later, she tried issuing her first black figurine, and ever so slowly, the line became a hit with collectors of all races.

Today, "Miss Martha" — as the children in her church first called her — meets collectors at major shows such as an artists' weekend held at Walt Disney World in Orlando, Fla., or the dozen or so open houses she does each fall. Club members come to her home town in Alabama for the popular Open House and Fellowship Barbecue held in June each year, and may attend a Christmas Open House at the Club Headquarters and Museum.

Miss Martha enjoys collecting antiques so Club Headquarters reflects that love, with its location in a restored, turn-of-the-century house decorated with a variety of antiques.

Artist Martha Holcombe

Special Features

The complete line of AGC figurines, including retired pieces, is on display at Club Headquarters.

All God's Children® Collector's Club

Membership Gifts

Figurines	Years Available	Original Value	Current Value
Peek-a-Boo Bear	1993-94	$20	$20

Members-Only Items

Figurines	Issued	Issue Price	Current Value
Molly, 1524	1989-90	$38	$345-$525
Joey, 1539	1990-91	$32	$220-$270
Mandy, 1540	1991-92	$36	$135-$200
Olivia, 1562	1992-93	$36	$36
Garrett	1993-94	$36	$36

Redemptions until May 31 of each year.

Annalee
Doll Society

P.O. Box 1137
Meredith, NH 03253
Director, Townsend Thorndike
(800) 433-6557
Fax: (603) 279-6659

Featured collectible: Felt and wire dolls, many designed for seasonal decorating
Benefits: Complimentary 7-inch Logo Kid (different design each year), enamel pin, special edition sun pin, one-year subscription to *The Collector*, free admission to the Annalee Doll Museum, membership card, invitations to members-only events
Year club founded: 1983
Sponsored by: Annalee Dolls Inc., founded in 1954
Membership size: 30,000 U.S.
Club publication: *The Collector* (quarterly, four-color, 40 pages)
Factory tours: Members may visit the Doll Museum at any time. The factory is open for tours only during the annual members-only Auction & Barbeque Weekend held the last weekend of June each year.
Annual dues: $24.95   **Renewals:** $24.95
Club year ends: June 30
No. of staff devoted to handling club: Three
Membership kits received: Two to three weeks after application submitted
How to join: Applications at authorized dealers, or to join by phone call 1-800-433-6557
How to redeem certificates: Mail in registration card

12" "Mrs. Santa with Poinsettia" and 12" "Chef Santa" dolls

Annalee Thorndike's Doll Hospital is a regular Santa's Workshop. As part of the Annalee Doll Society, members can restore the beauty and value of their Annalee Dolls by admitting them to the Annalee Doll Hospital. Annalee will give each doll a thorough examination and determine just how to repair them. At a cost of $47.50 plus labor and materials, Annalee's design team will restore the doll to its original luster.

Artist Annalee Thorndike

Annalee Dolls, of course, are those unique, posable, wire and felt dolls with the cheerful expressions that often add that finishing touch to seasonal displays. As Annalee says, "The most important part of an Annalee Doll is the face."

Those contagious grins that decorate each doll's face have been bringing smiles to collectors' faces since 1954, when Annalee turned her dollmaking hobby into a business. She, her husband, and their two sons transformed their home in Meredith, N.H., into a workshop, making festive dolls for every occasion. Today, Annalee has a staff of nearly 400 people working away to meet the demand for Annalee Dolls.

The Society was founded 10 years ago to bring collectors and fans of Annalee Dolls together. An Antique & Collectible Doll Shoppe was established as a consignment service to help owners of Annalee Dolls buy and sell out-of-production dolls to each other. The dolls available at the shop are listed every other month in "The Sale List," which is sent to all members.

Members also receive a full-color, quarterly magazine called *The Collector*, which informs them of the latest happenings in club news.

The Society conducts two auctions each year, one in June and one in the fall. During the June event, the doors of the factory are opened for members to tour.

If you miss the once-a-year tour, you might be able to catch Chuck Thorndike, Annalee's son and an artist at the company, as he tours the United States signing dolls at sponsor stores and major department stores. Members are notified of

Special Features

An Antique & Collectible Doll Shoppe helps members buy and sell out-of-production dolls. And a Doll Hospital puts older dolls back on the mend.

appearances through *The Collector* and by numerous postcard mailings the Society does during the year.

In addition to making its presence known at several International Collectible Expositions, and at the Walt Disney World Doll & Teddy Bear Convention, the Annalee Doll Society has sponsored the Christa McCauliffe Ski Invitational in Waterville Valley, N.H., and Easter Parade Weekend in North Conway, N.H.

> Annalee designs each face with a sunny expression that is guaranteed to make one smile.

Annalee Doll Society

Membership Gifts

Dolls	Years Available	Original Value	Current Value
7" Cookie Boy Logo Kid	1985-86	$15.00	$240-$280
7" Sweetheart Logo Kid	1986-87	$17.50	$225-$275
7" Naughty Logo Kid	1987-88	$17.50	$225-$275
7" Raincoat Logo Kid	1988-89	$19.50	$225-$275
7" Xmas Morning Logo Kid	1989-90	$19.50	$175-$210
7" Clown Logo Kid	1990-91	$19.50	$130-$165
7" Reading Logo Kid	1991-92	$19.50	$80-$110
7" Schoolgirl Logo Kid	1992-93	$24.95	$25

Members-Only Pieces

Dolls	Issued	Issue Price	Current Value
10" Johnny Appleseed[1], ed. 2,500	1983	$80.00	$900-$1,000
10" Robin Hood[2], ed. 2,500	1984	$90.00	$800-$850
10" Annie Oakley[3], ed. 2,500	1985	$95.00	$650-$750
10" Mark Twain[1], ed. 2,500	1986	$117.50	$500-$575
10" Ben Franklin[4], ed. 2,500	1987	$119.50	$500-$550
10" Sherlock Holmes[3], ed. 2,500	1988	$119.50	$500-$550
10" Abraham Lincoln[5], ed. 2,500	1989	$119.50	$500-$550
10" Betsy Ross[1], ed. 2,500	1990	$119.50	$425-$550
7" Sherriff Mouse	1990	$49.50	$50
10" Christopher Columbus, ed. 2,500	1991	$119.50	$300-$375
10" Victory Ski Doll	1991	$49.50	$50
10" NH Conductor Doll	1991	$129.50	$130
10" Aviator Frog	1991	$29.95	$30
10" Uncle Sam[6], ed. 2,500	1992	$87.50	$145-$190

[1]$1,500 artist proof; [2]$1,200 artist proof; [3]$1,000 artist proof; [4]$2,100 artist proof; [5]$1,300 artist proof; [6]$1,600 artist proof

ANRI
Club

73 Route 31 North
Pennington, NJ 08534-0009
Director, Nadine Haase
(609) 737-7010
(800) YES-ANRI (937-2674)

Featured collectible: Alpine maple wood figurines
Benefits: Gift of Love figurine, subscription to club magazine, opportunity to purchase exclusive figurines, unlimited access to club's research services, advance notice of special events, members-only binder filled with history and production of ANRI figurines, current information and collector's log; members-only trips to Europe
Year club founded: 1983
Membership size: 6,500 U.S.; members in 22 countries including Japan and New Zealand
Local chapters available: None
Club publication: *Reflections,* published three times a year, June, October and February (four-color, eight pages)
Factory tours: Tours arranged through the Club, English-speaking tour guide available
Annual dues: $50   **Renewals:** $40
Extras: Binders with inserts $16; ANRI videotape $28.45; Sarah Kay 10-year catalog $12.50; general ANRI catalog $7.50
Club year ends: May 31
No. of staff devoted to handling club: Two
Membership kits received: Three to six weeks after application submitted
How to join: Applications at authorized dealers, or call toll-free number; club members can sponsor one to three new members and receive one to three different gift levels

A Sarah Kay carving in various stages of creation

In 1912, Anton Riffeser created the name ANRI by combining the first two letters of his first and last names. And with that name he also created a vision for the Riffeser family, a vision to produce high-quality articles for art lovers and collectors.

His son, Anton Adolf Riffeser, nurtured that vision and saw the ANRI sculptures become highly sought after collectibles. Today, Ernst Riffeser, Anton Sr.'s grandson, carries the vision into a third generation, bringing new collectors along with him.

President
Ernst Riffeser

Steeped in tradition and produced in St. Christina, Italy, these charming handpainted figurines are sculpted from Alpine maple wood that has been aged for almost 100 years.

Now in its 11th year, the ANRI Club brings the vision of the Riffeser family to the public. Each edition of *Reflections*, the club's three-times-a-year newsletter, is like a photo album of this family and its extended family of club members and collectors. From talks with the artists to looks back to how it all began, *Reflections* offers a broad idea of ANRI and its collectibles.

The Mailbox feature of each issue allows members to ask any questions that come to mind. For instance, how do you clean a figurine as delicate as an ANRI? The Mailbox happily informs you that dusting with a clean, soft cloth is best, and by all means, avoid using cleaning agents such as oils or creams. Or, in this era of conservation, you might wonder what happens to the wood chips that fall to the ground as the artist whittles away at a sculpture. Again, the Mailbox will tell you. The chips are used as fuel for wood-drying kilns and to heat the workshops. Whether by using the Mailbox or by eliciting the help of the club's free-to-members research department, members can have their every question answered.

The Club also arranges trips to Italy so that members can see where these figurines are created and visit the place where Anton Riffeser caught that first glimmer of a vision that has been delighting collectors and art lovers alike for many years.

Special Features

• A research department is available free of charge to club members. Non-members must pay a $40 fee.

• The club sponsors members-only tours of the ANRI studios in Italy.

"With All My Heart" by Juan Ferràndiz, left

"Kiss Me" by Sarah Kay, right

ANRI repre-
sents the
vision with the
personal guar-
antee of the
Riffeser family
to produce
high-quality
articles for
art lovers and
collectors.

ANRI Club

Members-Only Pieces

Figurines	Issued	Issue Price	Current Value
Welcome[1]	1983	$110	$100-375
My Friend[1]	1984	$110	$100-408
Apple of My Eye[1]	1984	$135	$340-390
Harvest Time[1]	1985	$125	$150-390
Dad's Helper[1]	1985	$135	$144-375
Harvest Helper[1]	1986	$135	$175-350
Romantic Notions[1]	1986	$135	$175-320
Celebration March[1]	1986	$165	$235-285
Will You Be Mine[1]	1987	$135	$180-320
A Young Man's Fancy[1]	1987	$135	$175-190
Make A Wish[1]	1987	$165	$200-300
Forever Yours[1]	1988	$170	$240-300
I've Got A Secret[1]	1988	$170	$200-250
Maestro Mickey[1]	1988	$170	$215-250
I'll Never Tell[1]	1989	$190	$190-250
20 Years of Love[1]	1989	$250	$250-270
Diva Minnie[1]	1989	$190	$190-240
A Little Bashful[1]	1990	$220	$220-250
You Are My Sunshine[1]	1990	$220	$220-250
Dapper Donald[1]	1990	$199	$200-250
With All My Heart[1]	1991	$250	$250-300
Kiss Me[1]	1991	$250	$250-300
Daisy Duck[1]	1991	$250	$250-300
You Are My All[2]	1992	$260	$260-275
My Present For You[2]	1992	$270	$270-300
Truly Yours[2]	1993	$290	$270-300
Sweet Thoughts[2]	1993	$300	$290-330

[1] 1 yr.-certificate; [2] 2 yr.-certificate

1992 Sarah Kay "My
Present for You"

1992 Ferràndiz "You Are
My All"

1993 Sarah Kay
"Sweet Thoughts"

1993 Ferràndiz
"Truly Yours"

L-r, charter year "Welcome" by Ferràndiz; Sarah Kay "Apple of My Eye," club year two; "My Friend," Ferràndiz, club year two; "Harvest Time," Ferràndiz, club year three; and "Dad's Helper," Sarah Kay, club year three

L-r, "Celebration March," special club figurine for club year four by Ferràndiz; "Romantic Notions" by Sarah Kay, club year four; "Harvest Helper" by Ferràndiz, club year four; "Make a Wish," by Sarah Kay, club year 5, special club figurine; and "Will You Be Mine," Ferràndiz, club year five

L-r, "A Young Man's Fancy," club year five, by Sarah Kay; "Forever Yours," Ferràndiz, club year six; "I'll Never Tell" and "Psst, I've Got a Secret," by Sarah Kay for years seven and six, respectively; and "Mickey Maestro" by Walt Disney, club year six

L-r, "20 Years of Love," Ferràndiz, club year seven; "Minnie Diva" by Walt Disney, club year seven; "Dapper Donald" by Walt Disney, club year eight; and "Daisy Duck" by Walt Disney, club year nine

G. Armani Society

300 Mac Lane
Keasbey, NJ 08832
Director, Connie Ribaudo
(800) 3-ARMANI/(908) 417-0330
Fax: (908) 417-0031

Featured collectible: Handcrafted cold cast porcelain figurines by master sculptor Giuseppe Armani
Benefits: Member gift (free) - 1993: miniature figurine by Armani, "Petite Maternity"; subscription to official club publication, *The G. Armani Review*; membership plaque, signed by the artist, Giuseppe Armani; opportunity to purchase members-only merchandise at members-only price(s)
Year club founded: 1990
Sponsored by: Miller Import Corporation, founded in 1952
Membership size (1993): 10,000 (U.S.)
Local chapters available: Three, independently organized. Free background materials on artist and other support materials provided. Executive director attends meetings when available.
Club publication: *G. Armani Review* (full-color, ten-page quarterly)
Factory tours: Possible member tour of the G. Armani factory in Italy in 1994
Annual dues: $37.50   **Renewals:** $25
Club year ends: December 31
No. of staff devoted to handling club: Three full time
Membership kits received: Six weeks after application received
How to join: Applications available at authorized G. Armani Society dealers, club application enclosed in every Armani figurine box when packaged in Italy or in collectibles publications
How to redeem certificates: At an authorized G. Armani Society dealer

"Peace and Harmony"

For more than 30 years, sculptor Giuseppe Armani has captured the human experience in his richly detailed collection of work. Best known for his sculptures of women, children, and wildlife, Armani creates a special drama in his work through the realistic expressions and flowing movement of each figurine.

*Sculptor
G. Armani*

Whether employing a festive art deco style or a more regal renaissance style, Armani draws collectors with his precise detailing.

Having lived most of his life in Florence, Italy, Armani was greatly influenced by the Italian masters of the Renaissance. He mixes that historical perspective with his personal experience to find romance in daily life.

Special Features

Look for a member tour to Italy in the near future.

"In the feverish pace of today's life," he says, "I would like to give people a poetic respite — something to which their souls can relate. If this happens, then the most profound reasons for existential journey through life is certain to be discovered and appreciated."

The G. Armani Society serves as a common network through which Armani's fans can learn more about the artist and his work. Members also are provided with certain exclusive merchandise generally not available to the public.

For those who would like to see the sculptor at work without the expense of a trip to Italy, the Society has produced a video of Armani at the Studios Florence Sculture d'Arte.

The club newsletter, *G. Armani Review*, is published quarterly (January, April, July, and December). Each edition informs members of new products, retiring works by Armani, biographical information on the artist and fellow collectors, and more. The News & Views section includes a "How To" column, which offers tips on display, lighting, insurance, and other points of interest to collectors.

Although the sculptor does not attend collectibles fairs or trade shows, he does make six to ten in-store appearances each year in the United States, plus the annual Disney-sponsored Disneyana Convention and appearances abroad.

"Venus"

"Ruffles"

Membership plaque
with "Petite Maternity"

G. Armani Society

Membership Gifts

	Years Available	Original Value	Current Value
Membership plaque	1990-93	$37.50	$38
Magazine binder	1990-93	$37.50	$38
Membership card case	1991	$37.50	$38
Armani sculpting video	1992	$37.50	$38
Petite Maternity (figurine)	1993	$50	$50

Members-Only Pieces

Figurines	Issued	Issue Price	Current Value
Awakening[1]	1990	$137.50	$650-$1,200
My Fine Feathered Friends[2], bonus	1990	$175	$400-$550
Ruffles[3]	1991	$139	$400-$650
Peace and Harmony, 7,500 ed., bonus	1991	$300	$300-$550
Ascent[4]	1992	$195	$300-$450
Julie[5], bonus	1992	$95	$250-$450
Venus[6]	1993	$225	$225

Certificate terms: [1]1/1/90 to 3/31/91; [2]2/90 to 6/91; [3]1/91 to 3/92; [4]1/92 to 3/31/93; [5]10/92 to 3/93; [6]1/1/93 to 3/31/94

Artaffects Perillo Collectors Club

THE
ARTAFFECTS
PERILLO
COLLECTORS CLUB

Box 40
Staten Island, NY 10307
Director, Liz Morsi
(718) 948-6767
Fax: (718) 967-4521

Featured collectible: Native American porcelain collectibles
Benefits: Yearly free membership piece; subscription to quarterly newsletter; redemption certificates for exclusive club offerings; *ArtaQuote*, an up-to-date listing of current values of Artaffects Perillo collectibles
Year club founded: 1991
Sponsored by: Artaffects, Ltd., founded in 1975
Membership size: Not available
Club publication: *Drumbeats* quarterly newsletter (two-color, six pages)
Factory tours: Not available
Annual dues: $35 **Renewals:** One year - $30; 2 years - $50
Extras: Binder to store *Drumbeats* and other club information; official membership card; special Club Currency, used for savings on Exclusive Club Redemption items
Club year ends: December 31
No. of staff devoted to handling club: Three
Also sponsors: Plans in the works for a Carol Roeda "Simple Wonders" club
Membership kits received: Immediately
How to join: Club applications and club kits available at authorized dealers
How to redeem certificates: At an authorized dealer

1992 black and white mini plates by Perillo

Specializing in the beauty of the Native American, Gregory Perillo captures the essence of a peoples' history in several mediums, ranging from porcelain plates to lithographs to sculptures.

A favorite with collectors for nearly two decades, Perillo's club began as the Perillo Collector Society in 1983, then reorganized in 1991 as the Artaffects Perillo Collectors Club.

The Club was established with the Perillo enthusiast in mind, providing members with the latest information on the art and life of this artist, who has received the Artist of the Year and the Collectible of the Year awards from the National Association of Limited Edition Dealers (NALED).

Members of the Club have the opportunity to buy limited edition collectibles designed and produced by Perillo exclusively for members. Dates of retirement and upcoming releases are found in the quarterly newsletter, *Drumbeats*. And they'll even get some sumptuous recipes from the Perillo family kitchen. Members also receive a subscription to *ArtaQuote*, an up-to-date listing of the current values of Artaffects Perillo collectibles. Every plate, figurine, doll, lithograph and limited edition collectible is tracked and updated to provide members with the secondary market activity of their pieces. Perillo collectors have found it an ideal source for buying, selling and insurance purposes.

In keeping with the artist's outgoing personality, the club offers contests and special activities each year, including an annual contest each Christmas season. Plus, members are made aware in advance of appearances by Perillo. The artist makes it a point to meet his fans at shows such as the International Collectibles Expositions in South Bend, Indiana, and Long Beach, California.

Says club president Richard J. Habeeb. "The Artaffects Perillo Collectors Club promises the kind of personal service and dramatic, new collectible treasures you have come to expect from Artaffects, a future full of exclusives."

Artist
Gregory Perillo

Special Features

Members receive updated editions of ArtaQuote, a comprehensive listing of all Perillo products ever produced by Vague Shadows/Artaffects. Includes year of issue, edition limit, issue price and current price.

"Chief Crazy Horse," sculpture for members only

"Little Shadow," a gift to Perillo collectors

"I would never portray the Native American in a bad or negative light. They are beautiful, proud people and I paint them in all their glory."

— Gregory Perillo

Artaffects Perillo Collectors Club

Membership Gifts

Items	Years Available	Original Value	Current Value
Perillo/Cougar (Poster)[1]	1983	$35	$50-$150
Crazy Horse (T-shirt)	1984	$35	$25-$55
Little Plum Blossom (Poster)[1]	1985	$35	$65-$100
Dolls (Figurines)[2]	1986	$35	$60-$110
Sunbeam (Figurine)	1993	$35	$35
Little Shadow (Figurine)	1993	$35	$35

Members-Only Pieces

Items	Issued	Issue Price	Current Value
Apache Brave (Bust)[2]	1983	$50	$150-$200
Out of the Forest (Litho)[1]	1984	$50	$300-$500
The Pencil (Plate)	1985	$35	$75-$150
Painted Pony (Figurine)[2]	1986	$125	$180-$300
Chief Crazy Horse (Sculpture)	1991	$195	$195
Studies in Black and White (Plates)	1992	$75	$75
Watcher of the Wilderness (Plate)	1993	$60	$60

[1]signed and remarqued; [2]signed

B

In Brief...

Bradley's Collectibles Doll Club
1400 N. Spring Street
Los Angeles, CA 90012
Offers members-only dolls for purchase and various contests

Brian Baker's Deja Vu Collector's Club
8547 152nd Ave. NE
Redmond, WA 98052
President, Michael O'Connell

The Stacey Baumgardner Carousel Collector's Society
P.O. Box 12155
Santa Rosa, CA 95406
Founded in 1992 — offers a newsletter, signings and stories of interest, free. Director is James Durgin

Boyett Collector's Registry
P.O. Box 632012
Nacogdoches, TX 75963-2012
Founded in 1987 — offers first notification of new releases and a newsletter, free membership with purchase and return of collector's card. President is Michael Boyett

Marty Bell
Collector's Society

9314 Eton Ave.
Chatsworth, CA 91311
Director, Deborah Johnson-Abughazaleh
(800) 637-4537
Fax (818) 709-7668

Featured collectible: Limited edition canvas or archival paper lithographs
Benefits: 5-by-7-inch lithograph on 8-by-10 inch archival paper with complimentary poem by Marty, four issues of *The Sound of Bells* newsletter, secondary market value survey, cloisonne pin, voucher for members-only offerings, map of Marty Bell's England
Year club founded: 1991
Sponsored by: Marty Bell Fine Art Inc., founded in 1987
Membership size: 8,000 U.S
Club publication: *The Sound of Bells* (four to six pages, parchment paper)
Factory tours: Guided tours are available by appointment to all members. Guests are guided through the 22,000 sq. ft. facilities on a tour that includes a visit to the Gallery of Limited Edition Lithographs, as well as the "private" gallery of Marty Bell Original Paintings. Reservations requested for all size groups
Annual dues: $30 ($35 foreign)　　**Renewals:** $30
Extras: $57 matting and framing of free archival paper lithograph through authorized dealers
Club year ends: One year after joining
No. of staff devoted to handling club: Three
Membership kits received: Two to three weeks after application submitted
How to join: Applications at authorized Marty Bell dealers
How to redeem certificates: At an authorized Marty Bell dealer

"Blossom Lane"

"As I paint the treasures I find hidden in the English countryside, I strive to portray the warmth of tradition, the enchantment of romance and the unique vibrant colors of England. Being able to share these cherished places with you is the joy that inspires me to paint."

With those words, Marty Bell welcomes collectors into the enchanting world of English cottages, noble castles and gentle landscapes as portrayed in her unique oil paintings. Thousands of beautiful images have been captured on canvas, and hobbyists are invited to enjoy these pastoral portrayals.

Marty, who has had her artwork featured in numerous national publications, has been commended for her diverse talent and imaginative eye, not to mention an exquisite and architectural look at detail that lends a realness and authenticity to her work.

This collectors' club combines the warmth and genuine nature of its artist with the excitement and interchange of a true collectors' forum, featuring exclusive gifts, a cloisonne collector's society pin and countless other incentives and bonuses.

The Sound of Bells quarterly newsletter always includes a word or two from Marty, sometimes detailing her most recent painting trip or the story behind her latest creation. In addition, this antique-style correspondence offers letters from collectors, tips on storing and protecting the lithographs and an agenda of visits planned by the artist. Each section is designed to keep members up-to-date and informed on the workings of the club and the artist. In recent years, she's made about 25 appearances around the country annually.

The society makes a special effort to welcome all calls from Marty Bell enthusiasts and collectors, and it does its best to assist all interested with requests, information or perhaps the name of their local authorized dealer.

The goal of this club is to enhance the collector's enjoyment and appreciation, while encouraging an open and friendly forum for the exchange of

Artist Marty Bell

Special Features

The Society offers matting and framing of free archival paper lithographs for $57 each through authorized dealers.

information and ideas between Marty Bell hobby-ists. Programs on the society's drawing board include tours, contests, conventions and chapter meetings.

"There's always a spot for them ... like that spot where you want just a touch of life on your wall," Marty Bell says about her paintings.

"Laverstoke Lodge,"
1993 members-only issue

Marty Bell Collector's Society
Membership Gifts

Various Mediums	Years Available	Original Value	Current Value
Charter Rose, lithograph	1991	$30	$30
Cloisonne Pin	1991	gift	n/a
Candle at Eventide, lithograph	1992	$30	$30
Cloisonne Key chain	1992	gift	n/a
The Chideock Gate, lithograph	1993	$30	$30
Gift boxed note pad & pen	1993	gift	n/a

Members-Only Pieces

Lithographs (Canvas)	Issued	Issue Price	Current Value
Little Thatch Twilight	1991	$288	$300-$400
Blossom Lane	1992	$288	$290
Laverstoke Lodge	1993	$220	$220

Belleek® Collectors' Society

144 W. Britannia Street
Taunton, MA 02780
General Manager, Joseph Visotski
(800) 822-1824

Featured collectible: Fine parian china, including highly glazed ivory and shamrock decorated pieces
Benefits: Full color catalog, members-only pieces with Collector's Society stamp, quarterly journal, information about local chapter meetings, membership certificate, annual member tour to Ireland, and heart dish gift
Year club founded: 1979
Sponsored by: The Belleek Pottery Ltd., founded in 1857
Membership size: About 9,000
Club publication: *Belleek Collector*, full color, quarterly
Factory tours: Contact the factory in advance (Belleek, Co. Fermanagh, Ireland, Tel. Belleek 501), or join the annual, 12-day Belleek Collectors' Tour. Pottery Tours available every 20 minutes Monday-Friday.
Annual dues: $25 (U.S. and Canada), or £15   **Renewals:** $20
Club year ends: One year after joining
Local chapters: Eighteen
Membership kits received: Three weeks after application received
How to join: By picking up an application at an authorized Belleek retailer or contacting the company
How to redeem certificates: At an authorized Belleek retailer

Collectors who share an interest in all things Irish will appreciate the distinguished history of Belleek, founded in County Fermanagh, Ireland, in 1857. Known for its delicate, translucent porcelain art — lustrous tea services, vases, flowered and woven chain baskets, dinnerware and collectibles — Belleek also knows how to host visitors.

1990 Chinese teapot

As Ireland's oldest and most historic pottery, Belleek was awarded British Airways 1990 Tourism Award for the best tourist facilities in Northern Ireland. The Belleek complex includes a fine museum and audio visual theater.

Generations of admirers have treasured Belleek porcelain. In some families, the tradition of collecting Belleek began when emigrants left Ireland for the New World. In fact, the original Statue of Liberty Museum included Belleek as the typically cherished possession of an Irish emigrant.

The society promises to serve the needs of collectors who have just a few treasured pieces to those who have "grand, established collections." In either case, the society invites collectors to become part of the Belleek family.

An example of Belleek artistry

Belleek® Collectors' Society

Membership Gifts

Items	Years Available	Original Value	Current Value
Heart Dish	1992-1993	$25	$25

Members-Only Items

Items	Issued	Issue Price	Current Value
St. Matthew Plate	1979	$97.50	$100
Belleek Bonbonniere	1980	$65.00	$70
St. Mark Plate	1981	$110.00	$120
Institute Cream & Sugar	1982	$165.00	$170
St. Luke Plate	1982	$110.00	$115
Wild Irish Rose Candlesticks (pair)	1983	$95.00	$100
St. John Plate	1983	$195.00	$200
Wild Irish Rose Bell	1984	$75.00	$75
Tassel Wall Pocket	1985	$87.50	$90
Wild Irish Rose Bowl	1985	$60.00	$65
Blarney Demitasse Cup & Saucer, set	1986	$50.00	$50
Wild Irish Rose Vase	1987	$55.00	$55
Irish Wolfhound	1987	$95.00	$100
Society Brooch	1987	$71.00	$75
Pendant & Earring Set	1988	$99.00	$100
Inspiration	1989	n/a	n/a
Chinese Teapot	1990	$195.00	$200
Chinese Cream & Sugar	1991	$75.00	$75
Crouching Venus, ed. 100	1991	$4,950.00	$4950
Chinese Tea Cup & Saucer	1991	$50.00	$50
Oak Leaf Pitcher	1992	$100.00	$100
Papillon Vase, painted, ed. 200	1993	$200.00	$200
Papillon Vase, gilt	1993	$65.00	$65

Maud Humphrey Bogart Collectors' Club

P.O. Box 245
Elk Grove Village, IL 60009-0245
Director, Barbara J. Schrage
(708) 956-5401
Fax: (708) 640-8356

Featured collectible: Resin figurines
Benefits: Personalized membership card, subscription to quarterly newsletter, Symbol of Membership figurine titled "Playful Companions"
Year club founded: 1990
Sponsored by: Hamilton Gifts Ltd., founded in1986
Membership size: 20,000 U.S.; 50 Canada
Club publication: *Victorian Times* newsletter (six-page, two-color quarterly)
Annual dues: $37.50   **Renewals:** $33.75
Extras: Gift registry binder listing all figurines in the Maud Humphrey Bogart Collection, a cloisonne brooch featuring the artwork of "Playing Mama"; charter members receive the Symbol of Membership figurine with a special understamp listing them as charter members
Club year ends: December 31
No. of staff devoted to handling club: Three
Membership kits received: 45 days after application submitted
How to join: Membership kits available in stores. In 1992, the club launched a Christmas membership drive for gift memberships. The gift-giver received a free ceramic hanging ornament from the Maud Humphrey Bogart Collection
How to redeem certificates: At an authorized Maud Humphrey Bogart dealer

"Nature's Little Helper"

The name may bring instant recognition from a whole nation of moviegoers, but Maud Humphrey Bogart was more than simply the mother of screen legend Humphrey Bogart. Long before Bogie just put his lips together and whistled, Maud had made a name for herself with her turn-of-the-century paintings of children from the Victorian age.

In honor of this pioneering artist, the Maud Humphrey Bogart Collectors' Club sponsored a special 125th Anniversary celebration of the artist's birth. The March 1993 event included the dedication of her house in Rochester, N.Y., complete with a speech from Mayor Thomas P. Ryan, a luncheon and an exhibit of the Maud Humphrey Bogart Collection.

As time goes by, it is that collection of resin figurines inspired by Mrs. Bogart's artwork that has continued to introduce today's collectors to her work during the last five years. The lovely, highly detailed figurines interpreted from her art capture the same innocence of youth and romance of the Victorian age as the artist's paintings.

As part of a yearlong celebration of the Collection's fifth anniversary, a special version of "Playing Mama" was introduced in 1993 and was exclusively available during Maud Humphrey Bogart events at participating stores. To differentiate the special edition of the popular piece, an anniversary yearmark of a quill and the number five was added, and the little girl washing her doll wears a white bow in her hair instead of the original blue.

In addition to the many events that highlighted 1993, the Collectors' Club fosters an atmosphere of friendliness among collectors of the line's figurines and accessories. The quarterly *Victorian Times* newsletter keeps members apprised of introductions of new pieces, retired items and background on the artist, and makes them aware of special events and promotions.

Artist Maud Humphrey Bogart

Special Features

In addition to receiving a Symbol of Membership figurine, members receive a cloisonne brooch featuring the artwork of "Playing Mama."

"Sitting Pretty," 1993 members-only issue for Bogart collectors

The highly detailed figurines capture the same innocence of youth and romance of the Victorian age as the artist's paintings.

Maud Humphrey Bogart Collectors' Club

Membership Gifts

Figurines	Years Available	Original Value	Current Value
A Flower For You	1990-91	$60	$60-$75
Sunday Best	1992	$65	$60-$75
Playful Companions	1993	$65	$45-$55
Cloisonne Brooch	1993	$20	$20-$55

Members-Only Pieces

Figurines	Issued	Issue Price	Current Value
Friends for Life	1990-91	$60	$140-$190
Nature's Little Helper	1992	$65	$110-$140
Sitting Pretty	1993	$65	$65

Maud Humphrey Bogart Collectors' Club

"Sunday Best"

Cloisonne
brooch, 1993 gift

"Friends for Life"

"Flower for You"

"Playful Companions"

My Personal Inventory

Club Name

Description	Number	Size	Issue Value	Current Valuation				
				1994	1995	1996	1997	

In Brief...

Colonial Village Service Bureau
1555 Merchandise Mart
Chicago, IL 60654

**Communicorp's Coca-Cola
Christmas Collectors Society**
P.O. Box 420157
Atlanta, GA 30342
(800) 653-1221
*Founded in 1993 — offers exclusive Coca-Cola®
brand ornament, quarterly newsletters, membership
card, charter membership certificate, and members-
only items such as action musical, annual dues $20*

Connoisseur Spoon Collectors' Club
P.O. Box 4096
Wilmington, NC 28406
*Free membership — offers spoons made in
Worcestershire, England*

Country Roads Collector's Club
P.O. Box 190
Menan, ID 83434
*Founded in 1991 — offers a quarterly newsletter,
special promotions and first-purchase opportunities
on all new releases, annual dues $20*

The Cowboy Collector Society
Shade Tree Creations, Inc.
6210 NW 124th Place
Gainesville, FL 32606-1071
800-327-6923   FAX 904-462-1799
*Offers free membership with purchase of Cowboy
sculptures by Bill Vernon, available since 1980, $30
each, made in United States*

Crystal World Collector's Society
3 Caesar Place
Moonachie, NJ 07074
*Founded in 1993 — offers members-only pieces for
purchase and a newsletter*

Cabbage Patch Kids Collectors Club

P.O. Box 714
Cleveland, GA 30528
Director, Nancy Pritchett
(706) 865-2171
Fax: (706) 865-5862

Featured collectible: Original Cabbage Patch Kids, hand-stitched, soft-sculptured dolls, and other collectible works of art by Xavier Roberts
Benefits: *Limited Edition* newsletter, souvenir pins, logo key chain, lithograph print, three-ring notebook binders
Year club founded: 1987 as Xavier Roberts Collectors Club, renamed in 1991
Sponsored by: Original Appalachian Artworks Inc., founded in 1988
Membership size: 4,000
Local chapters available: Numerous, independently organized
Club publication: *Limited Edition* newsletter (bi-monthly, eight pages, four-color)
Annual dues: $25　**Renewals:** $25
Club year ends: December 31
No. of staff devoted to handling club: Two
How to join: Applications at authorized dealers, available inside Hasbro Cabbage Patch adoption certificates, birthday cards and CPK merchandise
How to redeem certificates: At an authorized dealer or directly through club

Logo for Cabbage Patch Kids Collectors Club Newsletter

There probably are very few people who are unfamiliar with the round-faced, plump-bodied phenomenon known as the Cabbage Patch Kids. In fact, 85 percent of households with children between the ages of two and eight are homes to adopted Cabbage Patch Kids.

If you don't own one, maybe you tuned in to the 1992 Summer Olympics. The U.S. Olympic Team officially adopted the "kids" (dressed in Olympic garb, of course) as mascots. The Original Appalachian Artworks Inc. became an official sponsor in a gesture of international goodwill, providing each doll to be carried to Spain by the athletes and then donated to children in Barcelona.

Created by Xavier Roberts, no two Cabbage Patch Kids are the same. They are absolutely original each time, hand-numbered and accompanied by authenticating documentation.

Collectors are attracted to the fantasy that surrounds the Cabbage Patch Kids, and to becoming a part of the "kids" growing family.

Roberts works from two driving philosophies that fuel his success as an artist and the success of his Cabbage Patch Kids. First, every person is an individual entitled to individual respect and consideration. And second, if you have a dream and work hard enough, you can make that dream come true. Both of these beliefs are exhibited in the care and dedication illustrated in each Cabbage Patch creation.

And the reality of that dream is recognized in the acclaim Roberts has received from the collector's community. Enjoying the most prestigious award of all, Xavier's Cabbage Patch Kids are recognized as a "classic" and are the single, all-time, best-selling large baby doll in the toy industry.

Roberts makes rare personal appearances and currently isn't attending any "show circuits." Should Roberts be appearing in a member's local area, however, a notification is printed in the Club's official newsletter, *Limited Edition*.

This bi-monthly mailing features a wide array of articles concerning past editions of Xavier Roberts

Artist Xavier Roberts

Special Features

Buy, sell, trade classified ad section in the bi-monthly newsletter.

collectibles, details of new releases, "happenings" in the world of Cabbage Patch Kids, collector events and a special classified section. For new members, back issues are available for $2. Each issue offers a colorful glimpse into the world of Cabbage Patch Kids, keeping collectors informed and up to date.

A limited number of lucky members can attend the Cabbage Patch Kids Collectors Club's week-long convention held annually in Cleveland, Ga., home of the Cabbage Patch Kids. Attendance is limited to 200 members on a first-come, first-reserved basis.

Each independently organized collectors' group within the United States offers a wide variety of activities to interest and enthuse its members. For instance, the California Cabbage Patch Club used its "kids" to help real kids in Southern California by donating dolls to the Greater El Monte Girls Club.

The Club certainly celebrated its five-year (1992) anniversary in style, providing a series of parties and events to trumpet the success of the Cabbage Patch family. A tour of Garden Parties for members only highlighted the list. Each Party Adoption Center chose a unique theme for their event. Party games, contests, decorations, and souvenirs consistent with that theme assured that no two parties were alike.

A second event in the anniversary year boasted an Old West theme and consisted of a week-long series of seminars, workshops, contests, and banquets.

As an added attraction to hobbyists, these events usually coincide with the introduction of new Cabbage Patch Kids. Since most events are open to members only, many times, these collectors are the first, and sometimes the only, ones to have access to the special-event "kids."

In addition to cuddling up with these hand-stitched soft-sculptured collectibles, the Club has offered limited edition lithograph prints by Roberts. The prints have been given free of charge or at a discounted price as an incentive to renew and remain part of the Cabbage Patch family.

Local Cabbage Patch Chapters often assist charities in their area with doll donations.

1989 "Anna Ruby"

1992 "Baby Dodd & 'Ittle Bitty"

Cabbage Patch Kids Collectors Club

Members-Only Gifts

Cabbage Patch Kids	Years Available	Original Value	Current Value
Baby Book (logbook) renewal gift	1990	free	$15
"Xavier Discovers the Cabbage Patch" renewal gift	1992	$25	$25
10th Anniversary Key Chain, renewal gift	1993	$25	$25

Members-Only Pieces

Cabbage Patch Kids	Issued	Issue Price	Current Value
Baby Otis (first in Nursery Edition)	1987	$250	$250-$300
Xavier Roberts Print "Walk in the Garden"	1988	$250	$250
Anna Ruby (7-inch Sprout)	1989	$250	$300-$400
Lee Ann (porcelain doll)	1990	$250	$250-$300
Richard Russell (7-inch Sprout)	1991	$250	$250-$275
Baby Dodd & 'Ittle Bitty	1992	$250	$250

The Cairn Collector Society®

P.O. Box 400
Davidson, NC 28036

Featured collectible: Gnome sculptures by artist Tom Clark
Benefits: Redemption letters for Collector Society Artwork series, Society newspaper, Cairn Collector portfolio print-out of a member's Cairn purchases ($15 for non-members), creation stories on Tom Clark artwork (written and illustrated by the artist), advance notice of new issues and retirements, priority ranking on both sales and bid-to-buy offers when executing a trade on the Cairn National Secondary Market
Year club founded: 1983
Sponsored by: Cairn Studio, Ltd.
Club publication: *Cairn Collector Society Newspaper*, tabloid
Eighteen-month dues: $17.50 ($20 outside continental U.S.)
Renewals: $17.50
How to join: By picking up an application at an authorized Cairn retailer
How to redeem certificates: At an authorized Cairn Studio retailer

The Cairn Collector Society®

Members-Only Items

Items	Issued	Issue Price	Current Value
Rory (retired in 1985)	1983	$35.00	$675.00
Ernst (retired in 1987)	1984	$35.00	$400.00
Kilmer (retired in 1988)	1985	$40.00	$300.00
Hitch (retired in 1990)	1987	$47.50	$275.00
Blackie (retired in 1992)	1988	$55.00	$250.00
Mum (retired in 1993)	1990	$67.50	$202.50
Foster	1991	$57.50	$67.50
Race	1992	$150.00	$150.00
Potter	1993	$65.00	$65.00

Cat's Meow
Collectors Club

2163 Great Trails Dr.
Wooster, OH 44691
Director, Tammy Myers
(216) 264-1377

Featured collectible: Cat's Meow Village, collection of small wooden historic and architecturally significant houses and buildings
Benefits: Redemption certificate for free gift house, identification card, notebook with collectors buy list and newsletters. New members receive choice of gifts for joining (club logo tote or lapel pin offered in 1993)
Year club founded: 1989
Sponsored by: FJ Designs, Inc., founded in 1983
Membership size: 20,000
Club publication: *The Village News*, four pages, quarterly
Factory tours: FJ Designs factory and Cat's Meow Village open to the public Monday through Friday, 10 a.m. to 1 p.m.
Annual dues: $22   **Renewals:** $20
Club year ends: One year after joining
No. of staff devoted to handling club: Two
How to join: By picking up an application at an authorized Cat's Meow retailer
How to redeem certificates: At an authorized Cat's Meow retailer
Special: The company celebrated its tenth anniversary with a convention for members

Cat's Meow benefit package

Cat's Meow Collectors Club

Membership Gifts

Items	Years Available	Original Value	Current Value
Club logo T-shirt	1989-92	$10	$10
Betsy Ross House	1989	free	$130-$150
Club logo mug	1990	$10	$10
Amelia Earhart House	1990	free	$65-$85
Bookmark	1991	$6	$6
Limberlost Cabin	1991	free	$40-$55
Abigail Adams Birthplace	1992	free	$35-$50
Pearl Buck House	1993	free	n/a
Club logo tote bag	1993	$10	$10
Lapel pin	1993	$10	$10

Members-Only Items

Items	Issued	Issue Price	Current Value
Famous Authors House (4-pc. set)	1989	$37.00	$325-$380
Great Inventors Houses (4-pc. set)	1990	$37.00	$300-$600
American Songwriters Houses (4-pc. set)	1991	$37.00	$120-$220
Signers of the Declaration Houses (4-pc. set)	1992	$39.00	$100-$120
Anniversary Arch	1992	$8.50	$9
19th Century Master Builders Houses (4-pc. set)	1993	$41.00	$41

The Chilmark Gallery

The Lance Corp; 321 Central Street
Hudson, MA 01749
Director, Jim Swiezynski
(508) 568-1401
Fax: (508) 568-8741

Featured collectible: Chilmark fine pewter sculpture
Benefits: Upon registration, members receive the current issues of *The Chilmark Report* (newsletter), *The Observer* (secondary market newsletter), *The Chilmark Collection Price Guide Update* (aftermarket values), and redemption certificates to purchase the current American West and Civil War Annual Specials
Year club founded: 1983
Sponsored by: The Lance Corporation, founded in 1968
Membership size: 28,000
Club publications: *The Chilmark Report* (quarterly newsletter, black and white, eight to twelve pages); *The Observer* (quarterly update, two pages)
Factory tours: Chilmark dealer-sponsored tours available
Annual dues: None
No. of staff devoted to handling club: Four
Also sponsors: Sebastian Miniature Collector Society; Shirelings Collectors Club debuted in July 1993
Membership kits received: Two to three weeks after application submitted
How to join: Collectors are automatically enrolled in the Gallery when they register a piece of Chilmark sculpture they have purchased. There are no annual dues
How to redeem certificates: At an authorized Chilmark dealer

"Skedaddlin'"
by Lowell
Davis, edition
of 350, issued
at $2,000

When Chilmark sculpture arrived on the scene in 1975, it brought with it a totally new concept in metal sculpture. In a marketplace dominated by the great European porcelain sculpture houses and bronze sculptures, limited by number and expense to an extremely small circle of collectors, Chilmark fine pewter sculpture made art affordable and accessible to a wider range of collectors.

Sculptor
Don Polland

Many of those collectors have been further drawn in by Chilmark's detailed craftsmanship and authenticity. And those with an appreciation for American historical subject matter are dazzled by the maker's ever-growing catalog of American West and Civil War related pieces. Still others, who are looking for investment potential, are enticed by the proven aftermarket values of sold-out and retired Chilmark sculptures.

With a membership of about 28,000 collectors, The Chilmark Gallery draws segments of all of those factions of collectors together into one club, providing collectors of Chilmark sculptures with information on new releases, artist appearances and special collector events, edition status, and aftermarket updates.

Unlike many clubs which require annual dues, The Chilmark Gallery grants automatic enrollment to any collector who registers a piece of Chilmark sculpture that they have purchased. There are no annual dues.

Through the extensive research of Dr. Glenn S. Johnson and the Chilmark Advisory Council, current aftermarket values are available in *The Chilmark Collection Price Guide Update*, which is sent to collectors who register their Chilmark sculpture. Collectors can inquire via mail or by phone for detailed information regarding any Chilmark sculpture. *The Identification and Price Guide* (with annual price updates) also is available for sale to collectors either through their local Chilmark dealer or through The Lance Corporation, the founding company for The Chilmark Gallery.

According to the Introduction of *The Official*

Special Features

Registering a Chilmark sculpture provides the collector with a Certificate of Registration, which serves as a title transfer and is invaluable when insuring a collection.

MSA Identification and Price Guide to The Chilmark Collection, "In 1968, three Massachusetts men joined technical skills and formed The Lance Corporation, a tiny foundry centrifugally casting Space Age resins and metals. They machined them to tight tolerances for use in NASA sub-contract prototypes, computers and other instruments. When Reed & Barton, a silver producer in the area, placed an order for small, ornamental legs for their sugar pots, the three men got together and came up with a mold that could handle fine pewter." And thus the saga of miniature-scale bronzes began.

But the saga isn't about to stop now. Interest in American history and specifically the Civil War fascinates people today more than ever — witness movies such as *Dances With Wolves, Glory* and *Sommersby*, as well as books and public television documentaries.

The Chilmark Collection artists listen to their public and sculpt subjects based on the broadest possible appeal. They don't just sculpt to personal whim. That's why the catalog is so diverse, ranging from Native Americans to animals to fantastical images of medieval times.

The Walt Disney Company, in fact, awarded The Lance Corporation with the 1990 Best New Product honor for "The Sorcerer's Apprentice Collectors Series." Then in 1992, The Lance Corporation received the *Collector Editions* Award of Excellence (Figurines over $500) for Joseph Slockbower's "Chief Joseph" from the Great Chiefs Collection.

The artists are able to get a feel of what their audience wants by appearing at various shows throughout the year. Artists, including Don Polland, Francis J. Barnum, Anne McGrory and Joseph Slockbower, meet the public at the International Collectibles Expositions at Long Beach and South Bend each year, plus at other Chilmark dealer-sponsored events depending on each artist's schedule.

Chilmark Gallery members are mailed invitations to local events, and they can also find out

Unlike many clubs which require annual dues, The Chilmark Gallery grants automatic enrollment to any collector who registers a piece of Chilmark sculpture that they have purchased. There are no annual dues.

about appearances in *The Chilmark Report,* the club's quarterly newsletter. Each edition of the 8- to 12-page black and white quarterly features a letter from director Jim Swiezynski and information on new products, retired and sold-out products, special editions, awards, and regional shows and artist appearances. *The Observer,* a two-page addendum that covers the secondary market, is mailed with each *Chilmark Report.* In addition, all registered collectors receive color brochures on all new introductions and annual updates of the *Chilmark Collection Price Guide Update* and *Chilmark Showcase Dealer Listing.*

Just as Chilmark sculptures brought a new concept to metal sculpture, The Chilmark Gallery introduces a new concept in collectors clubs.

The Chilmark Collection artists listen to their public and sculpt subjects based on the broadest possible appeal. They don't just sculpt to personal whim.

The Chilmark Gallery

Members-Only Pieces

Sculpture	Issued	Issue Price	Current Value
The Chief[1]	1983	$275	$1,650-$2,050
Unit Colors[2]	1984	$250	$1,250-$1,350
Oh Great Spirit[3]	1985	$300	$1,000-$1,300
Eagle Catcher[4]	1986	$300	$850-$1,200
Surprise Encounter[5]	1987	$250	$700-$750
I Will Fight No More Forever[6]	1988	$350	$700-$830
Geronimo[7]	1989	$375	$700-$785
Lee to the Rear[8]	1989	$300	$550-$825
Cochise[9]	1990	$400	$575-$725
Lee and Jackson[10]	1990	$375	$415-$685
Crazy Horse[11]	1991	$295	$445-$685
Stonewall Jackson[12]	1991	$295	$400-$660
Strong Hearts to the Front[13]	1992	$425	$425-$550
Zouaves — 1st Manassas[14]	1992	$375	$375-$450

Certificate terms: [1]7/83-7/84; [2]7/84-7/85; [3]7/85-7/86; [4] 7/86-7/87; [5]7/87-7/88; [6]7/88-7/89; [7]7/89-7/90; [8]10/89-10/90; [9]7/90-7/91; [10]10/90-10/91; [11]7/91-7/92; [12]10/91-10/92; [13]7/92-7/93; [14]10/92-10/93

"Eagle Vision" by Anne McGrory

"Chief Joseph" by Joseph Slockbower

"Sorcerer's Apprentice" by Walt Disney artists and sculptors

Top Chilmark Artists

Joseph Slockbower

Anne Transue McGrory

Francis Barnum

Collectors' League

15502 Graham St.
Huntington Beach, CA 92649
Director, Donna Blaska
(714) 897-0090
Fax: (714) 892-1034

Featured collectible: Fine art limited sports collectibles
Benefits: Quarterly newsletter, members-only figures, pre-market information regarding new issues, VIP privileges at Gartlan USA-sponored events. Charter members received special signed figurines
Year club founded: 1989
Sponsored by: Gartlan USA, founded in 1985
Membership size: Members in United States, Canada, Japan and Australia
Club publication: *Collectors' Illustrated* (six-page, black-and-cream quarterly)
Factory tours: Showroom available for tours by appointment
Annual dues: $30   **Renewals:** $20
Extras: T-shirts, $14
Club year ends: December 31
No. of staff devoted to handling club: Three
Membership kits received: Four weeks after application submitted
How to join: Applications at authorized Gartlan USA dealers
How to redeem certificates: At an authorized Gartlan USA dealer

Members-only figurine of Hank Aaron in 1974 Atlanta Braves uniform

Sports collectors now have a league of their own with Collectors' League, a club which rewards avid Gartlan USA collectors with special offers and notification of offers before items hit the open market.

Gartlan USA is a leading producer of fine-art limited sports collectibles. With artwork by Michael Taylor, Gartlan USA features personal autographs of famous athletes, coaches and umpires on limited edition pewter and cold-cast figurines, collectors' plates, canvas transfer prints, lithographs and ceramic trading cards.

Collectors' League members receive the quarterly newsletter, *Collectors' Illustrated*, which informs readers of new issues, members-only offers, insights into production processes and announcements of sold-out items.

Members also have the opportunity to meet some of the top names in the sports world at club-sponsored events.

Sports and collecting. It's a winning combination every time you come up to the plate.

Special Features

Each year, members get a free plate and have the opportunity to purchase members-only figurines.

Collectors' League

Membership Gifts

Plates	Years Available	Original Value	Current Value
Pete Rose 8-1/2"	1989	$30	$85-$145
Al Barlick 8-1/2"	1990	$30	$55-$85
Joe Montana 8-1/2"	1991	$30	$55-$85
Ken Griffey Jr. 8-1/2"	1992	$30	$45-$65
Gordie Howe 8-1/2"	1993	$30	$30

Members-Only Pieces

Figurines	Issued	Issue Price	Current Value
Wayne Gretzky (mini)	1990	$75	$250-$390
Joe Montana (mini)	1990	$75	$125-$175
Kareem Abdul-Jabbar	1991	$75	$150-$200
Mike Schmidt	1992	$79	$120-$225
Hank Aaron	1992	$79	$120-$225
George Brett	1993	$79	$79-$100

(All figurines have three-month certificate term.)

D

Daddy's Long Legs Collector's Club

300 Bank Street
Southlake, TX 76092
Directors, Brent & Karen Germany
(817) 488-4644

Featured collectible: American-made collectible family of dolls by artist Karen Germany, primarily African-American subjects made of wood resin with fabric costumes

Benefits: Full-color catalog of currently available dolls, list of Star Dealers in member's area, personalized membership card, newsletters, members-only dolls for purchase, opportunity to place locator ads in the newsletter, and notification of artist signings

Year club founded: 1993

Sponsored by: KVK, Inc., founded in 1989

Membership size: 3,000

Club publication: *Daddy's Long Legs* newsletter, bi-annual, four pages

Annual dues: $20 for one year, $35 for two

How to join: By picking up an application at an authorized Daddy's Long Legs Star dealer, or by calling the club

How to redeem certificates: At an authorized Daddy's Long Legs Star dealer

"Faith"

"Faith"

Daddy's Long Legs Collector's Club

Members-Only Items

Dolls	Issued	Original Value	Current Value
Faith	1993	$50	$50

Lowell Davis
Farm Club

55 Pacella Park Drive
Randolph, MA 02368
Director, Loretta Connolly
(617) 961-3000
Fax: (617) 986-8168

Featured collectible: Cold-cast figurines of humorous and nostalgic farm subjects
Benefits: Collector's guide, dealers list, membership card, farm cap, figurine "Thirsty," coloring book, free subscription to *The Gazette*, special invitation to visit Lowell Davis at his farm outside of Carthage, Missouri, opportunity to buy exclusive members-only figurines
Year club founded: 1985 (originally called Foxfire Farm Club, name changed in 1987)
Sponsored by: Schmid, founded in 1932
Membership size: 7,000
Local chapters available: Yes
Club publication: *The Gazette*, received three times per year, full-color, eight pages
Factory tours: Contact the club, who will contact Border Fine Arts in Scotland to make arrangements. To visit Lowell Davis' farm, contact Davis and make specific time arrangements
Annual dues: $25   **Renewals:** $20
Club year ends: On member's anniversary of joining
No. of staff devoted to handling club: Two
Membership kits received: One to two weeks after inquiry, or available immediately from stores during promotions
How to join: Applications at authorized Schmid dealers
How to redeem certificates: At an authorized Schmid dealer

"The Check Is in the Mail"

Lowell Davis is a pipe-smoking artist, farmer, preservationist and basic, down-home all-American. It is through his nostalgic cold-cast figurines that he presents his message of the beauty, serenity and simplicity of country life.

The Lowell Davis Farm Club provides a link between the collector and the artist. Part of that link is created through the club newspaper, *The Gazette*. This tri-annual newsletter keeps collectors informed about new items and has a "Wanted" section to help members locate retired pieces that another member may wish to sell.

Information on the market in relation to their collections also is provided, and *The Gazette* lets members know where Lowell will be touring. Davis appears at many in-store events and annual collector shows.

In addition to collection talk, the Lowell Davis newsletter works hard to provide members with the country flavor so present in Davis' art. Each *Gazette* includes columns such as "All the Latest from the Farm," "Ozark's Tall Tales," and "Dinner Bell," a back-page recipe section ready to cut out and add to your recipe box.

Davis, a 1991 Artist of the Year, creates his pieces from real animals on his farm and derives inspiration from real-life experiences. He creates molds that are then sent to Border Fine Arts in Scotland, where the figurines are produced.

You might say that Davis is doing his best to dispel the notion that you can't go home again. He and his wife, Charlotte, have invested more than $1 million in the recreation of Lowell's home town of Red Oak, Mo.

Red Oak II, Davis' 60-acre replica, is an old-town collection of refurbished homes and buildings including a general store, a church, a one-room school house, and two bed and breakfast facilities. Davis proudly invites club members to come and enjoy some down-home hospitality.

The Lowell Davis Farm Club holds an annual barbeque for members on the third weekend of September. In addition to enjoying the country

Artist
Lowell Davis

Special Features

The Gazette carries a wanted column for members looking for particular items.

atmosphere, the weekend includes a Friday night auction, an all-day get-together with Lowell, bingo games, a swap and sell, music, dancing, and a Sunday church service.

Members enjoy a peaceful look at country life through Lowell's creations, and experience true old-fashioned flavor through Red Oak II. Using depictions of animals, country life, art, and messages of the simple life, it's truly hard to argue that you can't go home again.

By the time Davis decided he wanted to end up where he'd begun, his hometown was gone. So, he built a new one.

Coloring book and Farm Club cap — gifts

Lowell Davis Farm Club

Membership Gifts

All members receive a Lowell Davis cap.

Figurines	Years Available	Original Value	Current Value
Thirsty (FoxFire Farm)	1985-'87	$25	$60-$100
Thirsty (Mr. Lowell's Farm)	1987-now	$25	$25
Cacklcberries, renewal	1987-88	$20	$70-$100
Ice Cream Churn, renewal	1988-90	$20	$55-$70
Not a Sharing Soul, renewal	1990-91	$20	$60-$78
New Arrival, renewal	1991-92	$20	$30-$40
Garden Toad, renewal	1992-93	$20	$20
Luke 12:6	1993-94	$20	$20

Members-Only Pieces

Figurines	Issued	Issue Price	Current Value
The Bride	1985	$45	$340-$480
The Party's Over	1987	$55	$145-$190
Chow Time	1988	$65	$125-$150
Can't Wait	1989	$75	$90-$140
Pit Stop	1990	$75	$110-$143
Arrival of Stanley	1991	$100	$150-$180
Don't Pick the Flowers	1991	$100	$140-$180
Hog Wild	1992	$100	$100-$150
The Check Is in the Mail	1992	$100	$100-$150
The Survivor	1993	$70	$70
Summer Days	1993	$100	$100

*For those
who love
the simple
things in
life, member
newsletter
in its 1991
format*

Lowell Davis Farm Club

"Hog Wild" 1993

"Arrival of Stanley"

"Thirsty" — gift for new
members

Walt Disney
Collectors Society

Manager, Paula Sigman
(800) 678-6528

Featured collectible: Animation sculptures from the Walt Disney Classics Collection made of low-fire porcelain

Benefits: Members joining in 1993 receive charter member status; free annual gift sculpture; subscription to quarterly magazine; opportunity to purchase yearly members-only sculpture

Year club founded: 1993

Sponsored by: The Walt Disney Company, founded in 1923

Membership size: Charter year, not available

Club publication: *Sketches* (12-page, color quarterly)

Annual dues: $52 U.S.; $54 Canada

Extras: Folio to store *Sketches* and other Society materials; embossed membership card

Club year ends: December 31

No. of staff devoted to handling club: Nine, plus eight customer service operators

Membership kits received: Six to eight weeks after application submitted

How to join: Applications available through authorized Walt Disney Classics Collection dealers or directly from the Walt Disney Collectors Society. Gift memberships are available.

How to redeem certificates: At an authorized Walt Disney Classics Collection dealer

© The Walt Disney Company

Benefit package for charter members

Collectors of the Walt Disney Classics Collection no longer have to wish upon a star. Beginning in January 1993, The Walt Disney Company launched the first Disney-sponsored membership organization for Disney collectors and enthusiasts. But it's not just for those who collect the Classics Collection. It's a wonderland for anyone who has a Disney memory.

Manager
Paula Sigman

All members who join in 1993 receive charter membership status, which includes a gift sculpture of Jiminy Cricket, one of Disney's most beloved characters, as well as an embossed membership card, the opportunity to purchase members-only figurines, and a subscription to the quarterly magazine *Sketches*.

Each colorful issue of *Sketches* features in-depth interviews with Disney artists; a behind-the-scenes look at the world of Disney both past and present; advance notices of major Disney events and upcoming offerings; articles on the making of the Walt Disney Classics Collection; and news about the Disney Studios, theme parks, and animated feature films.

The society grew out of the Walt Disney Classics Collection, the only collectible figurines developed directly by the artists and animators at The Walt Disney Studios. The artists' common goal is to faithfully translate Disney characters from two-dimensional drawings to three-dimensional sculptures, while maintaining the same charm and personality first portrayed in the movies.

And which character is more fitting to symbolize the society than that stargazer himself, Jiminy Cricket. Appropriately, he is the subject of the charter member gift sculpture. Renowned artist/animator Ward Kimball, affectionately known as "the father of Jiminy Cricket," was consulted at length to ensure a perfect replica of his famed creation.

"We wanted to involve a character who went beyond a single story," says society manager Paula Sigman, who was a Disney archivist for 15 years and is one of the most knowledgeable sources on Disney and its creations. "Jiminy happens to be

Special Features

Member Services specializes in answering questions about the society, the Walt Disney Classics Collection and The Walt Disney Company in general.

one of the few characters the company created who steps out of his role to speak directly to the audience. Since his debut in the 1940 classic *Pinocchio*, he has reached out and touched so many of us by acting as a conscience, teacher, and friend. And it's Jiminy who sings 'When You Wish Upon A Star,' the song that represents the heart and soul of The Walt Disney Company, the Walt Disney Classics Collection and now the new Walt Disney Collectors Society."

The Society adds to the phenomenal exposure Disney already receives by participating in International Collectibles Expos in South Bend and Long Beach, its own Disneyana Convention and numerous Walt Disney Classics Collection dealer events throughout the year.

The first annual "Animators' Choice" — the Society's members-only sculpture — is Mickey Mouse as "Brave Little Tailor." Each year, the "moment" captured in the very special members-only sculpture will be selected by Disney feature animators based on animation excellence.

Prepared to help members with any questions they might have through its Customer Services and Member Services departments and shimmering with that Disney magic, the Walt Disney Collectors Society is a dream come true for collectors and Disney lovers of all ages.

"Our goal is to offer members new insight into the magic of Disney by exploring the creative processes behind various programs and events, especially those that embody the storytelling and entertainment philosophies instilled by Walt."

— Paula Sigman, Society Manager

The much-loved character Jiminy Cricket is the first gift sculpture for charter members of the Walt Disney Collectors Society

Walt Disney Collectors Society

Membership Gifts

Charter Gifts	Years Available	Original Value	Current Value
Jiminy Cricket	1993	$75	$75
Cloisonne Pin	1993	free	n/a
Bound Folio	1993	free	n/a

Members-Only Pieces

Figurine	Issued	Issue Price	Current Value
I Let 'em Have It! 7-1/4", with *Mickey Mouse Tales* ($5.95 value)[1]	1993-94	$160	$160

1- Certificate term through March 31, 1994

Selected by Disney feature animators as the finest moment in Mickey's career, "Brave Little Tailor" is the first annual "Animators' Choice," available exclusively to charter members of the Walt Disney Collectors Society

© The Walt Disney Company

Dreamsicles
Collectors' Club

5970 SW 18th St., Box 237
Boca Raton, FL 33433
Director, James E. Farrell
(800) 437-5818

Featured collectible: Cherubs, bunnies, and other figurines made of hydrostone
Benefits: Figurine, boxed club binder, guide to the collection, membership card
Year club founded: 1993
Sponsored by: Cast Art Industries, Inc., founded in 1990
Membership size: 20,000, U.S.
Club publication: *ClubHouse* (two-color, four-page quarterly newsletter)
Factory tours: Group tours set up through dealers
Annual dues: $27.50
Club year ends: One year after joining
Membership kits received: Four to six weeks after application submitted
How to join: Applications at authorized Dreamsicles dealers
How to redeem certificates: At an authorized Dreamsicles dealer

Charter year Dreamsicles benefits

"A Star Is Born"
charter year gift

Ten years ago, Kristin Haynes, the product of an extremely artistic family, turned her talents to the field of sculpture and began creating a group of cherubs, bunnies, and other storybook characters that became very popular with her fans in the San Diego area.

When the demand grew, Kristin searched out a manufacturer who could help her and linked up with Cast Art Industries, Inc., of Corona, Calif. This adorable line from Cast Art's Precious Collectible Treasures is known as the Dreamsicles.

Each original sculpture is created by Kristin in her farmhouse studio, and is then reproduced by the artisans of Cast Art Industries. Individual casting, finishing and painting by hand, with natural floral decorations and subtle finishing touches, assure that no two Dreamsicles are ever exactly alike.

The demand for these collectibles has opened the doors for the Dreamsicles Collectors' Club. Charter members are welcomed with a free cherub figurine, titled "A Star Is Born," a one-time-only piece that will not be available after 1993.

Members will receive a boxed membership kit, which, in addition to the symbol of membership figurine, includes a club binder and printed guides to the Dreamsicles collection. Members also receive a membership card and a subscription to the quarterly *ClubHouse* newsletter, and will have the opportunity to purchase members-only figurines.

Artist
Kristin Haynes

Special Features

This line of sculptures has come on quickly since its debut, showing up in a variety of surveys of best-selling collectibles.

Dreamsicles Collectors' Club

Membership Gifts

Figurine	Years Available	Original Value	Current Value
A Star Is Born	1993	$30	$30

Duncan Royale
Collector's Club

1141 South Acacia Avenue
Fullerton, CA 92631
Director, Kathy Bates
(714) 879-1360
Fax: (714) 879-4611

Featured collectible: Cold-cast, porcelain Santas
Benefits: Porcelain bell, a cloisonne pin, notebook, newsletter, membership certificate, membership card, special offers
Year club founded: 1990
Sponsored by: Duncan Royale, founded in 1983
Club publication: *Royale Courier* newsletter (six-page, full-color)
Annual dues: $30   **Renewals:** $30
Club year ends: December 31
No. of staff devoted to handling club: Three
Membership kits received: Two weeks after application submitted, some available in select stores
How to join: Applications at authorized dealers
How to redeem certificates: At redemption centers

"Winter Santa," members-only figurine

Rich colors and intricate detail distinguish Duncan Royale's figurine series. From literary personalities to mythological characters, these unique depictions reveal just how little we understand about subjects we thought we knew so well. Each piece comes with a mini book detailing a brief history about the figurine.

Duncan Royale is perhaps best known for instigating the "historical Santa craze." President Max Duncan researched the topic of Santas from around the world, then created three series of twelve beautifully crafted Santas, each one with a different personality and history. This became the well-known "History of Santa Claus" collection. As an interesting offshoot, Duncan Royale plans to offer its club members a cruise to "the lands behind the Santas" sometime in the future.

As part of their membership kit, each new member receives clear plastic holders for storing the official registration certificates offered with each figurine.

As a special incentive, new members also receive special gift certificates worth $30 toward the purchase of any Duncan Royale 12-inch figurine.

The Duncan Royale Collector's Club works to familiarize its members with founder Max Duncan. As the driving force behind "the stories that never end," Max is known for his innovation and creativity and an unbridled enthusiasm that is displayed in every unique piece.

In addition to keeping members in contact with Max, the club's newsletter, *The Royale Courier*, carries informative articles on upcoming offerings, letters from collectors, and the Royale Exchange section. Available only to club members, the Royale Exchange offers space to advertise Duncan Royale items to buy, sell, and trade. Buyers and sellers can contact each other by phone and handle the transaction entirely on their own. But members also have the option of using Duncan Royale as an intermediary for a fee of 10 percent of the actual selling price.

Another special service available to club mem-

Founder Max Duncan

Special Features

The Royale Exchange section in The Royale Courier offers free ad space for members looking to buy, sell, or trade Duncan Royale figurines.

Royale Repair Dept. offers repair and replacement services to members.

bers is the Royale Repair Department. Duncan Royale will receive any piece and inspect it for defects, breakage, and authenticity. Any necessary repairs or replacement of boxes are made and charged back to the seller. Duncan Royale also will transfer the registration to the new owner and issue a new registration certificate.

Through the Duncan Royale Collector's Club, members enjoy a guided tour through the historical and artistic world of Duncan Royale figurines.

Members may register their collections free of charge.

Duncan Royale Collector's Club

Membership Gifts

Figurines	Years Available	Original Value	Current Value
Nast Bell	1990	$25	$25
Medieval Santa Bell	1992	$25	$25

Members-Only Pieces

Figurines	Issued	Issue Price	Current Value
Nast and Music, windup musical	1990	$79.95	$80-$85
Today's Nast, ed. 5,000	1991	$80.00	$80-$95
Santa Time (watch)	1991	$39.95	$40
Nast & Sleigh, ed. 5,000	1992	$500.00	$500
Winter Santa	1993	$125.00	$125

"Today's Nast" (left) and "Nast & Sleigh" (right)

My Personal Inventory

Club Name

Description	Number	Size	Issue Value	Current Valuation 1994	1995	1996	1997

E
to
G

In Brief...

Enchantica Collector's Club
P.O. Box 200
Waterville, OH 43566
*Founded in 1990 — features fantasy art by Andrew
Bill, offers a club newsletter, free figurine, members-
only figurines for purchase, annual dues $25*

The Fenton Art Glass
Collectors of America, Inc.
P.O. Box 384
Williamstown, WV 26187
(304) 375-6196
Founded in 1977 — offers a newsletter entitled
Butterfly Net, *annual convention with special sales
and auction of unusual glass exclusives, annual
dues $15*

Franklin Heirloom Doll Club
The Franklin Mint
Franklin Center, PA 19091
(215) 459-6553
Membership free to purchasers of Mint dolls

Gorham Collector's Guild
P.O. Box 6150
Providence, RI 02940
Director, Emily Graham

Gutmann Collector's Club
1353 Elm Avenue
Lancaster, PA 17604-4743
*Founded in 1986 — for collectors of artwork by
Bessie Pease Gutmann, offers members-only
figurine, newsletter, club pin and special offers,
annual dues $25 ($17.50 renewals)*

Enchanted Kingdoms Collector's Club

347 W. Sierra Madre Blvd.
Sierra Madre, CA 91024
Director, Victoria Rangel
(818) 355-1813
Fax: (818) 355-1982

Featured collectible: Hydrostone castle figurines
Benefits: Second-year plaque of the medieval horsemen, two redemption certificates to purchase the Arabian Nights castle in fantasy and natural colors, newsletter and spiral-bound collectors book
Year club founded: 1992
Sponsored by: Hopkins Shop, founded in 1973
Membership size: 750 U.S.
Club publication: *The Enchanted Times* (four-page, newspaper style)
Factory tours: Tours are available by appointment
Annual dues: $20   **Renewals:** $20
Club year ends: December 31
No. of staff devoted to handling club: Three
Membership kits received: One to two weeks after application submitted
How to join: Applications at authorized Enchanted Kingdoms dealers
How to redeem certificates: At an authorized Enchanted Kingdoms dealer

Enchanted Kingdoms Collector's Club

Membership Gifts

Member Gifts	Years Available	Original Value	Current Value
Charter member shield	1992	$20	$20
Second-year Medieval Horsemen shield	1993	$20	$20

Members-Only Pieces

Castles	Issued	Issue Price	Current Value
Ferdinand & Isabella	1992	$50	$50
Arabian Nights	1993	$50	$50

Enesco
Memories of Yesterday
Collectors' Society

P.O. Box 245
Elk Grove Village, IL 60009-0245
Director, Diana Derbas
(708) 228-3738
Fax: (708) 640-8356

Featured collectible: Porcelain bisque figurines from The Memories of Yesterday Collection
Benefits: Free yearly Symbol of Membership porcelain bisque figurine, one year-subscription to *Sharing Memories* newsletter, personalized membership card (charter members receive gold-colored card each year), gift registry with line illustration of all items in the collection, postcard with "Time for Bed" reproduction, opportunity to purchase members-only offerings
Year club founded: 1991
Sponsored by: Enesco Corporation, founded in 1958
Membership size: 30,000; 1,000 combined in Australia, England, Germany, Japan, Netherlands, and Italy
Local chapters available: 20, sponsored by the society, which provides information start-up package, promotion posters, ad slicks, public service announcements, and local chapter bookmarks to a sponsoring retailer
Club publication: *Sharing Memories* (four-color, 12 pages, quarterly)
Annual dues: $20   **Renewals:** $18.75
Club year ends: December 31
Membership kits received: Forty-five days after application submitted, or available immediately from authorized dealers
How to join: Applications at authorized dealers or through Instant Gratification program at select dealers
How to redeem certificates: At an authorized Memories of Yesterday dealer

The touching beauty of artist Mabel Lucie Attwell's children is captured in the porcelain figurines of Enesco's Memories of Yesterday Collection.

Known as a bold artist who spoke plainly and honestly about the problems and joys of English life in the 1900s, her straightforward approach is enjoyed by people from all walks of life. Mabel clearly depicts her fondness for children in her work. She had an incredible talent for capturing the innocence of youth through the curious, winsome expressions used in her illustrations.

Artist Mabel Lucie Attwell

Mabel herself described the realism found in much of her work in explaining the tears found on the cheeks of many of the children in her drawings. She said, "Childhood is not always the happy time that adults make it out to be." In this, Mabel reveals a bit of her gift for capturing both the happy and sad sides of life as a child.

Attwell's popularity was so great that most British children from the 1920s through the 1950s probably owned something designed by her.

Today, collectors can relive their own favorite memories through the porcelain characters in this collection. Every figurine is derived from an original illustration created by the British artist from the 1920s to the '40s. She frequently used her daughter Peggy as a subject.

Enesco marks each figurine with an annual understamp, verifying its inclusion in the MOY collection. The stamp varies from year to year. Understamps include a hat (1993), a Roman numeral five (1992), a flower (1991), a bow (1990) and a heart (1989). Figurines from the first year (1988) had no mark.

Each Society member receives quarterly editions of *Sharing Memories*, the club's official newsletter. New introductions in the collection, event listings, members-only offerings, biographical information on the artist, and collectors' submissions appear in each issue.

Through the sponsored local chapters, the club keeps in close contact with its members, advising about local events, sending mailings regarding spe-

Special Features

Instant Gratification Kits available in many stores allow members to receive their membership gift without waiting, or provides a take-home gift for someone else.

cial artisan tours, and announcing local lectures by historians.

In 1991 and 1992, members were offered tours to England.

Photo contests get members involved in sharing memories.

Enesco Memories of Yesterday Collectors' Society

Membership Gifts

Porcelain Figurines	Years Available	Original Value	Current Value
We Belong Together	1991	$30.00	$54-$96
Waiting for the Sunshine	1992	$30.00	$40-$57
I'm the Girl for You	1993	$30.00	$30-$50

Members-Only Pieces

Porcelain Figurines	Issued	Issue Price	Current Value
Welcome to Your New Home	1991	$30.00	$60-$84
I Love My Friends	1992	$32.50	$48-$57
With Luck and a Friend, I'se in Heaven (ornament)	1992	$16.00	$20-$28
Now I'm the Fairest of Them All	1993	$35.00	$30.00

Membership benefits and "I'm The Girl For You," 1993 Symbol of Membership figurine

"Now I'm the Fairest of Them All"

"I'm the Girl for You"

"With Luck and a Friend, I'se in Heaven"

"Waiting for the Sunshine"

"We Belong Together"

"Welcome to Your New Home"

Enesco Musical Society

1 Enesco Plaza
Elk Grove Village, IL 60007
Director, Kimberly A. Romero
(708) 640-3956

Featured collectible: Small World of Music Collection of musical figurines
Benefits: Pocket folder to hold materials from the society, opportunity to purchase 1993 Members Only Musical, 1993-94 Collectors' Guide calendar featuring new musicals from the Small World collection, *Musical Notes* newsletter, membership certificate, periodic special announcements regarding new introductions and special events
Year club founded: 1991
Sponsored by: Enesco Corporation, founded in 1958
Membership size: 15,000 U.S.; 1,000 combined in U.K., Taiwan, The Netherlands, Brazil, Italy, Germany, Australia
Club publication: *Musical Notes* (four pages, full-color)
Annual dues: $15   **Renewals:** $12.50
Club year ends: December 31
No. of staff devoted to handling club: Two
Also sponsors: Five additional clubs including the Precious Moments Collectors' Club
Membership kits received: One to two months after application submitted in U.S.; two to three months after submission in Canada; available immediately from authorized dealer
How to join: At an authorized Enesco Small World of Music dealer
How to redeem certificates: At an authorized Enesco Small World of Music dealer

Member newsletters (left) and Collectors' Calendar for Musical Society members

A love for music attracts collectors to the Enesco Musical Society. Each piece in the Small World of Music Collection captures attention with its elaborate design and intricately crafted, movable parts. And each collectible tells a story through that animation and musical movement.

There are no limits to what can be incorporated into an Enesco deluxe action musical. Each is the result of creativity, innovation, and technical wizardry — along with a healthy dose of imagination.

The unique qualities and innovative technology of this collection have earned national and international awards, as well as inclusion in the personal collections of numerous musical notables. The Majestic Ferris Wheel, for example, received the 1990 *Collector Editions Magazine* Award of Excellence in the musical category.

The Deluxe Toy Chest was part of the permanent opening of the CBS-TV *Smothers Brothers Comedy Hour* specials, was chosen by *Good Housekeeping Magazine* as one of the top 15 musical gifts, has found its way onto *The Home Show*, and was winner of the Premier Giftware Association Award for best imported item in the United Kingdom. And these are just two of the many pieces included in the Small World of Music Collection.

The Enesco Musical Society continues to grow by leaps and bounds. Not only have the collectibles earned international acclaim and awards, but the society is capturing international prominence as well. Two new countries have been added to the membership roster. More than 150 members from The Netherlands and Belgium combined signed up in 1993. Members from Canada, Germany, Italy, England, Spain, Brazil, Taiwan, and Australia also enjoy the craftsmanship of the small World of Music collectibles.

Members of the society enjoy a four-page, full-color newsletter titled *Musical Notes*. The quarterly issue provides background on artists and musicals, historical information, membership benefits, new introductions to the collection, and related

Enesco President and CEO, Eugene Freedman

Special Feature

Musical Warranty Program offers free repair or replacement for an action musical under warranty that malfunctions.

musical articles. A special column by Eugene Freedman, president and CEO of Enesco Corporation, is included in every issue to keep members up to date on the exciting developments within the Enesco company, specifically those affecting the Enesco Musical Society.

In describing the appeal of the society and its collectibles, Freedman says, "Each individual Small World piece combines drama, romance, and engineering to perfect an action musical of unparalleled quality and beauty."

> "Music has the wonderful ability to soothe, delight, brighten and comfort each of us in a very special way."
> — Eugene Freedman

Enesco Musical Society

Membership Gifts

Musicals	Years Available	Original Value	Current Value
Memories from *Cats*	1991	free	$15
Graceful Gallop	1992	free	$15

Members-Only Pieces

Musicals	Issued	Issue Price	Current Value
Treasures to Share	1991	$30	$30
Cherished Dreams	1992	$85	$85
Do-Re-Mi	1993	$125	$125

"Treasures to Share"

"Cherished Dreams"

"Graceful Gallop"

Enesco Precious Moments Birthday Club

P.O. Box 1529
Elk Grove Village, IL 60009-1529
Director, Julia Kirkwood
(708) 364-3045
Fax: (708) 640-8356

Featured collectible: Precious Moments birthday train made of porcelain bisque
Benefits: New members receive a Symbol of Membership figurine, welcome letter, Certificate of Membership in easel stand/holder. Charter members receive charter figurine each year when they renew their membership
Year club founded: 1986
Sponsored by: Enesco Corporation, founded in 1959
Membership size: 140,000, U.S.; 3,000 in 35 countries
Club publication: *Good News Parade* (12 pages, three times a year)
Annual dues: $16   **Renewals:** $15
Club year ends: June 30
No. of staff devoted to handling club: Five
Membership kits received: 45 days after application submitted
How to join: Applications at authorized Precious Moments dealers
How to redeem certificates: At an authorized Precious Moments dealer

© 1992 Precious Moments Inc.

1992 "Every Man's Home Is His Castle"

Our lives are filled with precious moments, and perhaps none are more precious in children's memories than their birthdays. What better way to remember those special days than by starting a collection to honor those days.

The Enesco Precious Moments Birthday Club allows children of all ages to start their own Precious Moments collection with the Precious Moments Birthday Train. Children love to add a new piece to their train on each birthday, and watch it grow just as they grow.

The 12-page *Good News Parade* newsletter, published three times a year, is designed with children in mind, so it's packed with games and puzzles for them to enjoy.

But it's the figurines that the children will enjoy the most. The animals and pastel colors used in painting the figurines are sure to dazzle their eyes. And, of course, they'll be delighted by the teardrop-eyed children made famous in the Enesco Precious Moments Collection. With these figurines' message of loving, caring, and sharing, they're a perfect addition to any birthday celebration.

"Casey the Clown" art

The Enesco Precious Moments Birthday Club allows children of all ages to start their own Precious Moments collection with the Precious Moments Birthday Train.

©1993 Precious Moments Inc.

"Happiness Is Belonging" 1993-94 gift

Enesco Precious Moments Birthday Club

Membership Gifts

Figurines	Years Available	Original Value	Current Value
Our Club Can't Be Beat (B0001)	1986	$15	$75-$95
A Smile's the Cymbal of Joy (B0002)	1987	$15	$50-$65
The Sweetest Club Around (B0003)	1988	$15	$35-$65
Have a Beary Special Birthday (B0004)	1989	$15	$35-$55
Our Club Is a Tough Act to Follow (B0005)	1990	$15	$25-$45
Jest to Let You Know You're Tops (B0006)	1991	$15	$45
All Aboard for Birthday Club Fun (B0007)	1992	$15	$25

Charter Member Renewal Gifts

Figurines	Issued	Issue Price	Current Value
A Smile's the Cymbal of Joy (B0102)	1987	$15	$60-$70
The Sweetest Club Around (B0103)	1988	$15	$35-$65
Have a Beary Special Birthday (B0104)	1989	$15	$30-$55
Our Club Is a Tough Act to Follow (B0105)	1990	$15	$25-$40
Jest to Let You Know You're Tops (B0106)	1991	$15	$25-$40
All Aboard for Birthday Club Fun (B0007)	1992	$15	$25

Members-Only Pieces

Figurines	Issued	Issue Price	Current Value
Fishing for Friends (BC861)	1986	$10.00	$120-$140
Hi Sugar (BC 871)	1987	$11.00	$85-$100
Somebunny Cares (BC881)	1988	$13.50	$50-$85
Can't Bee Hive Myself Without You (BC 891)	1989	$13.50	$35-$75
Collecting Makes Good Scents (BC901)	1990	$15.00	$35-$40
I'm Nuts over My Collection (BC902)	1990	$15.00	$35-$40
Love Pacifies (BC911)	1991	$15.00	$15
True Blue Friends (BC912)	1991	$15.00	$15
Every Man's House Is His Castle	1992	$16.50	$17
I Got You under My Skin (BC922)	1992	$16.00	$16
Put a Little Punch in Your Birthday (BC 931)	1993	$15.00	$15

Enesco Precious Moments Collectors' Club

P.O. Box 1466
Elk Grove Village, IL 90009-1466
Director, Julia Kirkwood
(708) 640-5228
Fax: (708) 640-8356

Featured collectible: Precious Moments porcelain bisque figurines
Benefits: New members receive Symbol of Membership figurine, large, three-ring binder for holding printed material, small two-ring binder with 300 pages of line-art drawings of all figurines in the collection, welcome letter, and free gift of luggage tag (1993). Charter members receive charter figurine each year when they renew their membership
Year club founded: 1981
Sponsored by: Enesco Corporation, founded in 1959
Membership size: 340,000, U.S.; 7,000 in 45 countries
Local chapters available: 300
Club publication: *Goodnewsletter* (20 pages, quarterly)
Factory tours: Members can visit the facility on Tour of Orient arranged through club headquarters on an annual basis
Annual dues: $25   **Renewals:** $22.50
Extras: Binders, $5
Club year ends: December 31
No. of staff devoted to handling club: Nine
Membership kits received: 45 days after application submitted
How to join: Applications at authorized Precious Moments dealers
How to redeem certificates: At an authorized Precious Moments dealer

1992 gift, "The Club That's Out of This World"

In those moments when we love, care, and share, these are the moments we will recall as precious. And it is in these moments, when people want to express their loving, caring, and sharing with those they love that they have chosen the Precious Moments line of cards and figurines to help share their feelings.

Originally, artist/creator Sam Butcher intended his drawings of teardrop-eyed children simply to encourage and comfort family and friends. With every Precious Moments illustration, he would include an inspirational message of love, caring, and sharing.

Those images soon found their way onto a small line of greeting cards. But in 1978, those cards caught the eye of Enesco president and CEO Eugene Freedman, who took the drawings to Japan to his longtime associate and friend, the master sculptor Yasuhei Fujioka.

Fujioka transformed the illustrations into three-dimensional figurines, and millions of collectors and gift-givers across the globe quickly took these sweet pieces with their inspirational messages to heart.

For the past 15 years, Sam has continued to create hundreds of illustrations that reflect his faith, love, compassion, and personal situations in his life. But the images that lovingly drip from the

Artist
Sam Butcher

Special Features

• Through the Forever Friends program, members received a patch when they enrolled one new member in 1993.

• Through the Sharing Season program, members receive an ornament when they enroll two new members from October through December.

Benefits package for members

end of his pen are just the beginning. From Sam's drawing board, the illustrations are sent to the Precious Moments design studio in Nagoya, Japan, where a team of highly skilled artisans painstakingly translate the flat art into a finely sculpted clay model.

Once the model is deemed worthy of wearing the Precious Moments label, a plaster mold is made. In some cases, several molds are required to create a single figurine. Then, using the finest porcelain bisque materials, these molds are meticulously cast, hand assembled, fired, hand painted, fired again, and given finishing touches.

Extraordinary quality control measures are adhered to at every step in the process to assure that the collectibles meet the highest standard of excellence. It actually requires five to seven days to produce a single Precious Moments figurine.

The quality of these products is so important to its creators, in fact, that each artisan is trained extensively, including the painter, who takes three years to master the famous teardrop eyes — considered the most important and difficult element of the figurine.

This incredible attention to detail obviously has paid off, as millions continue their sweet love affair with these charming collectibles. Nowhere is it more apparent than in the Enesco Precious Moments Collectors' Club. With 340,000 members in the United States alone, and an additional 7,000 members in 45 countries, the support for this club is hard to beat.

To further solidify the club's status in the hobby, the National Association of Limited Edition Dealers (NALED) named it the Collector's Club of the Year for the third consecutive year at the 1993 NALED Achievement Awards. And, by the way, that award has only been presented for the last three years.

"We're very proud of our club and how it began," says Shonnie D. Bilin, executive director of the club. "Almost from the very first moment that Precious Moments porcelain bisque figurines were introduced, people have wanted to know more

Special Features

In the first introduction of its kind, members of the Enesco Precious Moments Collectors' Club may acquire a series of three commemorative cloisonne PM medallions. The scenes on the medallions of a little girl hugging, helping, and tending to her teddy bear will be recreated in upcoming members-only figurines.

about these enchanting collectibles and their talented creator, Sam Butcher.

"Enesco president Eugene Freedman . . . pledged to found and support a Precious Moments Collectors' Club that would be the 'very best club of its kind' — and so it is!"

By joining the club, members receive a special Symbol of Membership porcelain bisque figurine designed, of course, by Sam Butcher. They also receive a subscription to the quarterly, full-color newsletter, *Goodnewsletter*, which includes information on Precious Moments introductions, suspensions, and retirements, along with other topics of interest to collectors.

Members also receive an official binder for storage of important club member materials; a copy of the full-color *Pocket Guide to the Enesco Precious Moments Collection*; *The Official Gift Registry*, featuring more than 300 pages of illustrations identifying every subject in the Precious Moments porcelain bisque collection; and an official membership card.

And, of course, there are the figurines with their simple message that started it all. You see, Sam Butcher believes his talent is God-given, and he honors that belief by spreading his ministry through these little messengers of loving, caring, and sharing. Apparently, people are getting the message.

> "Enesco president Eugene Freedman . . . pledged to found and support a Precious Moments Collectors' Club that would be the 'very best club of its kind' — and so it is!"
>
> — Shonnie D. Bilin, executive director

"His Little Treasure"

1981 members-only pieces
introduced collectors to the
club

1993 PM cruise gave members
a special treat

1991 "Sharing the Good News
Together"

1993 Club Appreciation
Ornament

Enesco Precious Moments Collectors' Club

Membership Gifts

Figurines	Years Available	Original Value	Current Value
But Love Goes on Forever (plaque E0202)	1982	$15	$95-$120
Let Us Call the Club to Order (E0303)	1983	$25	$60-$65
Join in on the Blessings (E0404)	1984	$25	$75-$100
Seek and Ye Shall Find (E0005)	1985	$25	$45-$50
Birds of a Feather Collect Together (E0006)	1986	$25	$45-$50
Sharing Is Universal (E0007)	1987	$25	$45-$55
A Growing Love (E0008)	1988	$25	$40-$50
Always Room for One More (C0009)	1989	$35	$40-$45
My Happiness (C0010)	1990	$35	$35-$40
Sharing the Good News Together (C0011)	1991	$40	$35-$40
The Club That's Out of This World (C0012)	1992	$40	$40-$45
Loving, Caring, and Sharing Along the Way (C0013)	1993	$40	$40

Charter Member Renewal Gifts

Figurines	Years Available	Original Value	Current Value
But Love Goes on Forever (E0001)	1981	$15	$175-$200
But Love Goes on Forever (plaque E0102)	1982	$15	$90-$110
Let Us Call the Club to Order (E0103)	1983	$25	$65-$70
Join in on the Blessings (E0104)	1984	$25	$65-$70
Seek and Ye Shall Find (E0105)	1985	$25	$45-$55
Birds of a Feather Collect Together (E0106)	1986	$25	$45-$55
Sharing Is Universal (E0107)	1987	$25	$45-$55
A Growing Love (E0108)	1988	$25	$45-$50
Always Room for One More (C0109)	1989	$35	$40-$50
My Happiness (C0110)	1990	$35	$40-$45
Sharing the Good News Together (C0111)	1991	$40	$45-$55
The Club That's Out of This World (C0012)	1992	$40	$40
Loving, Caring, and Sharing Along the Way (C0013)	1993	$40	$40

Enesco Precious Moments Collectors' Club

Members-Only Pieces

Figurines	Issued	Issue Price	Current Value
Hello, Lord, it's Me Again (PM811)	1981	$25.00	$400-$450
Smile, God Loves You (PM8210	1982	$25.00	$260
Put on a Happy Face (PM822)	1983	$25.00	$200-$225
Dawn's Early Light (PM831)	1983	$27.50	$100
God's Ray of Mercy (PM841)	1984	$25.00	$65-$90
Trust in the Lord to the Finish (PM842)	1984	$25.00	$65-$90
The Lord Is My Shepherd (PM851)	1985	$25.00	$65-$80
I Love to Tell the Story (PM852)	1985	$27.50	$60-$70
Grandma's Prayer (PM861)	1986	$25.00	$75-$95
I'm Following Jesus (PM862)	1986	$25.00	$75-$80
Feed My Sheep (PM871)	1987	$25.00	$55-$60
In His Time (PM872)	1987	$25.00	$50-$60
Loving You Dear Valentine (PM873)	1987	$25.00	$45-$50
Loving You Dear Valentine (PM874)	1987	$25.00	$45-$50
God Bless You for Touching My Life (PM881)	1988	$27.50	$50-$70
You Just Can't Chuck a Good Friendship (PM882)	1988	$27.50	$40-$45
You Will Always Be My Choice (PM891)	1989	$27.50	$40-$50
Mow Power to Ya (PM892)	1989	$27.50	$50-$55
Ten Years and Still Going Strong (PM901)	1990	$30.00	$45-$50
You Are a Blessing to Me (PM902)	1990	$27.50	$45-$50
One Step at a Time (PM911)	1991	$33.00	$40-$45
Lord, Keep Me in TeePee Top Shape (PM912)	1991	$27.50	$40-$45
Only Love Can Make a Home (PM921)	1992	$30.00	$30-$40
Sowing the Seeds of Love	1992	$30.00	$30-$40
This Land Is Our Land (527386)	1992	$350.00	$400
His Little Treasure (PM931)	1993	$30.00	$30
Loving, Caring, and Sharing Along the Way (ornament-PM040)	1993	$12.50	$12.50

Commemorative Members-Only Pieces

Figurines	Issued	Issue Price	Current Value
God Bless Our Years Together	1985	$175	$250-$290
This Land Is Our Land	1992	$350	$385-$400

Enesco Treasury of Christmas Ornaments Collectors' Club

P.O. Box 245
Elk Grove Village, IL 60009-0245
Director, Gretchen Hagle
(708) 640-5200
Fax: (708) 640-6151

Featured collectible: Treasury of Christmas Ornaments made of Artplas
Benefits: Charter year symbol of membership ornament, quarterly newsletter, membership card, catalog, opportunity to order two members-only ornaments
Year club founded: 1993
Sponsored by: Enesco Corporation, founded in 1958
Membership size: Estimated 20,000-plus U.S.
Local chapters available: None
Club publication: *Treasury Trimmings* (8-1/2 by 11, six pages)
Annual dues: $17.50
Club year ends: June 30
No. of staff devoted to handling club: Two
Also sponsors: Precious Moments Collector's Club, Precious Moments Birthday Club, Memories of Yesterday Society, Maud Humphrey Bogart Collector's Club, Sports Impressions Collector's Club, Musical Society
Membership kits received: Forty-five days after application submitted
How to join: Applications at authorized Enesco dealers
How to redeem certificates: At an authorized Enesco dealer

Left, symbol of member-ship, "The Treasury Card," and right, "Together We Can Shoot for the Stars"

It's beginning to look a lot like Christmas. Whether it's December or the middle of July, collecting Christmas ornaments has become a year-round activity for many collectors. And many of their favorite ornaments come from the Enesco Treasury of Christmas Ornaments Collection, which has delighted collectors for more than 10 years with both original creations by well-known licensed artists and designs by Enesco staff artists.

To help collectors in their pursuit of Enesco ornaments and to educate them on the hobby and the skill of making ornaments, the Enesco Treasury of Christmas Ornaments Collectors' Club kicked off its charter year in July 1993.

"We have been inundated with requests to launch a national ornament collectors club for several years," says Shonnie B. Bilin, Enesco's vice president of collectibles. "Ornament collecting is the fastest growing — and most popular — form of collecting anywhere. The enthusiasm and year-round appeal of ornament collecting has removed ornament sales from being a seasonal business. As a result, most collectibles retailers keep their ornament displays throughout the year, and producers like Enesco now keep new designs coming all year long."

Charter members will receive a free exclusive symbol of membership ornament, a charter year membership card, the official club newsletter, a Collectors' Guide to the Treasury Collection, a list of dealers in the member's area, and the opportunity to purchase members-only ornaments.

Although plans for this new club are still being developed, Bilin promises, "This will be a fun club to join. Ornament collecting is associated with happy, family activities, and we plan to make the club one that every member of the family will participate in and enjoy. We've been diligent in our consumer-collector research, and we plan to give our collectors what they want: a club that is as exciting and unique as the Treasury ornaments they collect."

Shonnie D. Bilin

"Ornament collecting is associated with happy, family activities, and we plan to make the club one that every member of the family will participate in and enjoy."
— Shonnie D. Bilin, vice president of collectibles

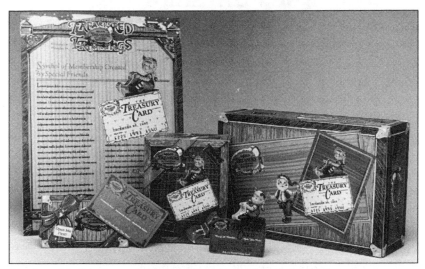

Membership kit for new Enesco Treasury of Christmas Ornaments Collectors' Club

Enesco Treasury of Christmas Ornaments Collectors' Club

Membership Gifts

Ornaments	Years Available	Original Value	Current Value
The Treasury Card (charter year Symbol of Membership ornament)	1993	$20	$20

Members-Only Pieces

Ornaments	Issued	Issue Price	Current Value
Together We Can Shoot for the Stars	1993	$17.50	$18
Can't Weight for the Holidays	1993	$18.50	$19

"Can't Weight For The Holidays," members-only ornament

The Fontanini Collectors' Club

555 Lawrence Ave.
Roselle, IL 60172-1599
Director, Maria Lucca
(708) 529-3000
Fax: (708) 529-1121

Featured collectible: Fontanini Heirloom nativities made of specially formulated polymer

Benefits: New members receive a Fontanini Collectors' Club welcome kit, which includes a complimentary symbol-of-membership figurine ("I Found Him!"), a subscription to the quarterly newsletter, an elegant symbol-of-membership pin, Story Card, Fontanini Heirloom brochure to track purchases, and reservation forms for current members-only figures; first-year members are eligible to acquire "The Pilgrimage" figurine; all members are eligible for each year's members-only offering

Year club founded: 1990

Sponsored by: Roman Inc., founded in 1963

Club publication: *The Fontanini Collector* (four-page, two-color quarterly)

Factory tours: Collectors planning a trip to Italy may visit the Fontanini facilities in Bagni di Lucca, Italy, but must phone The House of Fontanini at least 72 hours in advance to schedule a visit. Call The Fontanini Collectors' Club at 708-529-3000, ext. 345, for more information

Annual dues: $19.50   **Renewals:** $15

Club year ends: July 1

No. of staff devoted to handling club: Five

Membership kits received: Four to six weeks after application submitted

How to join: Applications at authorized Fontanini dealers, or on the back of Fontanini Story Cards enclosed with gift-boxed figurines. Membership kits can be picked up at participating Fontanini Dealers' Guild stores

How to redeem certificates: At an authorized Fontanini dealer

Another Christmas comes along, and it's time to bring down the boxes of decorations from the attic after a long summer's nap. But a chip or crack on a favorite decoration can make you want to deck the halls with a lot more than boughs of holly. The Fontanini family has kept that in mind through the years with the creation of its Heirloom nativity figures.

Each beautifully sculpted figure is crafted of a durable material that is resilient to chipping and breaking, while still capturing the finest details of sculptor Elio Simonetti's exquisite craftsmanship. With these sturdy figurines, children can handle them without fear of breakage, and as the name says, the figures can be handed down from generation to generation as family heirlooms.

"Christmas Symphony," members-only figurine

Collectors are drawn to the Fontanini Heirlooms because the varied sizes of the figures can make for creative displays. They also enjoy the complimentary Story Card that comes with each sculpture. The narratives are set in well-researched Biblical times and can be read aloud each year as families gather to set up their nativity scenes.

Since 1908, three generations of the Fontanini family have crafted figures and decorations of heirloom quality. Today, the Heirloom sculptures begin in the hands of Simonetti, master sculptor for The House of Fontanini. A meticulous molding process follows under the vigilant supervision of the Fontanini family. Then, each figure is painstakingly painted by hand by artisans utilizing skills passed from generation to generation.

Moviegoers got an eyeful of a Fontanini nativity in the hit movie *Home Alone*, which featured a life-size nativity; but through the Fontanini Collectors' Club, they can see even more. The Club provides a forum for Fontanini enthusiasts to share their common interest and learn about Fontanini developments ahead of the general public. They also receive a quarterly newsletter covering such topics as personal experiences from other collectors, decorating ideas, new product and retirement information, and features on American locales where collectors can see breathtaking life-size nativities.

Special Features

A research department is devoted to handling collectors' questions and concerns.

Members also are notified of appearances by Emanuele Fontanini, great grandson of The House of Fontanini founder. Emanuele attends collectibles expositions at South Bend, Ind., and 15 to 20 open houses on the Fontanini Family Personal Tour each year.

The Club offers members the opportunity to win free figures through trivia contests, and the "Day With Fontanini" contest gives a lucky member the chance to spend a day with Emanuele. Past contests included a drawing for an all-expenses-paid trip for two to Italy to visit the Fontanini crafting facility in Bagni di Lucca.

Now, that seems to be the kind of break most collectors are looking for — not the kind that can put a damper on the holidays with a chip or a crack on a favorite ornament.

Each beautifully sculpted figure is crafted of a durable material that is resilient to chipping and breaking, while still capturing the finest details of sculptor Elio Simonetti's exquisite craftsmanship.

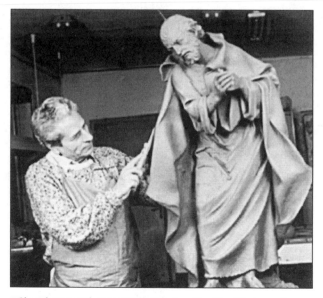

Elio Simonetti, Master Sculptor for the House of Fontanini, sculpting at his Bagni di Lucca studio

The Fontanini Collectors' Club

Membership Gifts

Figurine	Years Available	Original Value	Current Value
I Found Him!	1990-present	$20	$20
He Comforts Me	1993	$15	$15

Members-Only Pieces

Figurines	Issued	Issue Price	Current Value
The Pilgrimage	1990-present	$24.95	$24.95
She Rescued Me!	1992	$23.50	$23.50
Christmas Symphony	1993	$13.50	$13.50

*Emanule Fontanini,
great-grandson of
the House of
Fontanini founder*

*"The Pilgrimage," a
members-only issue*

Forever Friends Collectors' Club

126-1/2 West Broad Street
Chesaning, MI 48616
Director, Cindy Brooks
(517) 845-3990
1-800-4 FRIEND (437-4363)

Featured collectible: Pecan resin figurines
Benefits: Complimentary figurine, quarterly newsletters, subscription to bi-annual magazine (*From the Heart*), redemption certificates for members-only figurines ("Lifetime Friends" and "Sharing Dreams"), membership cards, colored flyers, storage folder, and invitation to the Forever Friends Gathering of Hearts Picnic. Charter members received Forever Friends T-shirt
Year club founded: 1991
Sponsored by: Sarah's Attic Inc., founded in 1983
Membership size: 10,000 U.S.; 2 Australia; 88 Canada; 4 England; 1 Hong Kong; 1 Switzerland
Local chapters available: One, independently organized. Forever Friends assists them with free gifts and literature
Club publication: *Forever Friends Club Newsletter*, published quarterly in black and white; *From the Heart*, 48-page, glossy magazine published twice a year
Factory tours: Tours of Sarah's Attic factory arranged for members by appointment
Annual dues: $25   **Renewals:** $25
Club year ends: May 31
No. of staff devoted to handling club: Ten
Membership kits received: About four weeks after application submitted. Stores that hold special Sarah's Attic promotions with their sales representative stock membership kits
How to join: Applications at authorized Sarah's Attic dealers, or by phone
How to redeem certificates: At an authorized Sarah's Attic dealer

"Ruby" and "Diamond," charter year figurines

Love, respect, and dignity.

They may be three little words, but they're the big-hearted message on which the Sarah's Attic collectibles line was founded. What began as a little sideline job for Sarah Schultz in the back of her husband's pharmacy 10 years ago has exploded into a big collectibles business employing 100 workers at the Sarah's Attic factory and 45 sales representatives across the United States.

Throughout the phenomenal boom in her business, Sarah has maintained the integrity of those three little words in each pecan resin figurine. In fact, each handpainted, highly detailed figurine is adorned with a signature heart to promote her message. And it is Sarah's resolve to love all people, to respect all people, and to give all people the dignity they deserve without regard to race, social class or appearance that has set the Forever Friends Collectors' Club into motion.

Members will know they've stumbled onto something special when they see the "Love Starts with Children" figurine, complimentary to all new members. It depicts two interracial friends discovering hidden treasure in an old trunk in a dusty attic.

In addition, members receive a monthly newsletter and a bi-annual magazine, called *From the Heart*. The *Forever Friends Club Newsletter* features line drawings of new releases and retiring items, plus important club information. The 48-page, slick magazine includes new releases, letters from other collectors, collector show dates, information on and ads from dealers who carry the Sarah's Attic line, and secondary market information. For instance, did you know that while the line retails from $7.50 to $50, items such as the Santas of the Month series see a secondary market increase of 300 percent?

And while you're flipping through the magazine, you won't believe who you'll find milling around in Sarah's Attic. Collectors of the line include former child star Jane Withers, probably best known for her more recent work as Josephine the Plumber in television commercials, and Buffalo Bills right

Artist
Sarah Schultz

Special Features

One full-time employee is devoted exclusively to retired figurines, keeping track of which items have been retired and helping collectors locate specific retired items.

tackle Howard Ballard. Members also can place classified ads in *From the Heart* if they're trying to buy or sell a particular figurine.

In keeping with the fellowship theme of Sarah's Attic's philosophy, the club sponsors the Forever Friends Gathering of Hearts Picnic, which features a Collector Swap-N-Sell booth, signings by Sarah, a Forever Friends Celebration Dinner, entertainment, and door prizes.

Sarah, who was awarded 1992 Wholesale/Retail Entrepreneur of the Year for the state of Michigan, also makes appearances at the South Bend and Long Beach International Collectible Expos, and various open houses and signings throughout the year. She also holds seminars at major collectors' conventions. Wherever she appears, Sarah makes a point to visit with each collector, showing each one a little love, respect and dignity.

> "No matter what kind of being you are, everyone has the same color heart. God put all of us on the Earth to make it a better place to live."
>
> —Sarah Schultz

Forever Friends Collectors' Club

Membership Gifts

Figurines	Years Available	Original Value	Current Value
Forever Frolicking Friends (limit 4,567)	1991-92	$40	$100
Love Starts with Children (limit 7,400)	1992-93	$70	$70

Members-Only Pieces

Figurines	Issued	Issue Price	Current Value
Ruby[1]	1991-92	$36	$36-$42
Diamond[1]	1991-92	$42	$42-$45
Ruby/Diamond, pair	1991-92	$75	$125-$275
Lifetime Friends[2]	1992-93	$75	$75-$83
Sharing Dreams[2]	1992-93	$75	$75-$83

[1]*certificate term 7/31/92;* [2]*certificate term 7/31/93*

1992-93 club pieces

Franklin Mint
Collectors Society

Franklin Center, PA 19091-0001
Director, William Stat
(215) 459-6000

Featured collectible: Dolls, precision models, jewelry, sculpture, coins, stamps, collector games, books, and many other items
Benefits: Subscription to the lavish, four-color publication *The Franklin Mint Almanac*, special offerings and opportunity to purchase annual Collectors Society medallions, eligibility to travel on Franklin Mint-sponsored collector's cruises
Year club founded: 1970
Sponsored by: The Franklin Mint, founded in 1965
Membership size: 1.2 million worldwide
Club publication: *The Franklin Mint Almanac*, 36 pages, bi-monthly
Annual dues: None, membership with purchase of Franklin Mint item
Tours: The Franklin Mint Museum is open Monday-Saturday from 9:30 to 4:30, Sunday from 1 to 4:30, closed for major holidays. Free admission. For information, call (215) 415-6168

Key benefit for Society members, The Franklin Mint Almanac

One of the earliest clubs formed for collectors, the Franklin Mint Collectors Society has been reshaped since its inception in 1970. Today, the Society is possibly the world's largest for collectors. Membership is free.

Originally, a fee was charged to members, who received a bi-monthly issue of the excellent magazine, *The Franklin Mint Almanac*, as well as medallic membership cards, annual gifts and special club issues.

The membership cards, containing sterling silver medals, were issued to regular dues-paying members while gold-on-sterling medals were given to charter members. Since the Society achieved international status and eliminated the membership fees, the medallic cards have been discontinued as free gifts for new members, but the cards are still available to members who wish to continue their collections of the yearly issues.

Gifts to members have ranged from mini coins and jewelry to large pieces of art such as a print of Norman Rockwell's "The Collector."

Given in 1973, the canvas print depicts a white-haired gentleman examining his silver dollar coin collection with a magnifying glass while a younger man looks over his shoulder. A Benjamin Franklin bust (representing the Mint) rests on a pedestal in one corner and the family dog rests his head on the man's desk near a cup of coffee, completing the

Award-winning "Rose Princess" doll

Special Feature

Antique Auto Festival is held on the grounds of the Mint each fall.

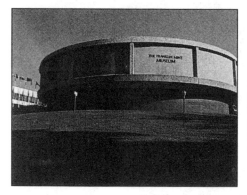

Open year-round, the FM Museum was renovated recently

An example of Franklin Mint collections, "The Heralding Angels" Christmas ornaments came one per month for a year

Collectors who buy Franklin Mint items receive honorary membership in the Society.

cozy scene in the library. (The print seldom comes on the market but has been sold at $100.)

A bronze medal featuring Benjamin Franklin with his kite and key was a gift to members in 1980. The design was a replica of the key produced in a pewter paperweight that was given in 1978.

In 1981, members received a 14-karat gold-plated bust of Franklin offered to ladies in the form of a stick pin and as cuff links for men. More than a dozen medals commemorating the group's annual trips — including excursions to England, Spain, North Africa, Alaska, Hawaii, the Bahamas, and the Riviera — have been issued.

The Society also offered collectibles insurance to members and a Collectors Society room for visitors to the Mint.

Today, members may attend an annual Antique Auto Festival on the grounds of the Mint, held each September. In addition, six shows a year rotate through the Franklin Mint Museum, located just outside Philadelphia and open to all. Among recent additions to the Museum, a Franklin Heirloom Doll room and Star Trek room attest to the popularity of these collectibles.

The Mint's artists have received numerous awards over the years for their innovative designs, including many Doll of the Year Awards. The Mint offers periodic tours and expects to sponsor a collector's group to the Pacific Northwest in 1994. Artists appear occasionally at Gallery Stores, locat-

Bronze medals featuring Benjamin Franklin were the gift to Franklin Mint Collectors Society members in 1980

ed in Boca Raton and Palm Beach Gardens, Florida; Dearborn, Michigan; Glen Burnie, Owings Mills, and Kensington, Maryland; and McLean and Tysons Corner, Virginia.

The Mint has international offices in Australia, Austria, Belgium, Canada, Denmark, England, Finland, France, Germany, Hong Kong, Japan, Malaysia, The Netherlands, New Zealand, Norway, Spain, Sweden, Switzerland, Taiwan, and Thailand.

Collectors will enjoy the focus and design of the *Almanac*, one of the most beautiful and interesting magazines available today. A typical issue features news on Mint artists; collectibles available from the Mint such as the Collector's Treasury of Clocks and The Rose Princess Doll; and presentations of Mint Awards and sculptures to dignitaries ranging from Henry Kissinger to H.S.H. Prince Albert of Monaco.

Art features that relate to Mint collections — perhaps a world-class collector of chess sets, the history of weathervanes, or a review of early luxury cars — give a glimpse of collections that few can ever achieve, except through less expensive replicas such as Franklin Mint offers. Through all their copy, the Mint presents collectors as people with definite panache and an appreciation for the beauty in life.

The Mint inspires collecting in many areas — dolls, porcelains, chess sets, pewter and crystal.

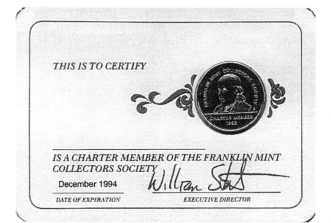

A Franklin Mint Collectors Society membership card with medal is available to charter members for purchase

The "Benjamin Franklin - Printer" plate was a special issue for members in 1978

Gibson Girl bride doll was one of Franklin Heirloom Dolls' most popular editions

Franklin Mint Collectors Society

"Path to Glory" by James Ponter, Franklin Mint offering

Diane Graebner
Collector's Club

P.O. Box 13493
Fairlawn, OH 44334
Director, William Swain
(216) 867-7942

Featured collectible: Limited edition, paper prints depicting the Amish lifestyle
Benefits: Notebook, periodic newsletters, birthday card from artist, members-only purchase opportunities, members-only print, small print upon joining
Year club founded: 1992
Collector sponsored
Membership size: 500 U.S.; 3 Canada; 1 U.S. Armed Forces, Europe
Club publication: *Diane Graebner Collector's Club* (two to four pages, flier format)
Factory tours: Contact participating local gallery to make arrangements to visit Diane's studio
Annual dues: $20
Club year ends: April 30
No. of staff devoted to handling club: Two
Membership kits received: One month after application submitted
How to join: Applications at authorized dealers, and can be dropped off at nearest participating gallery

Diane Graebner Collector's Club

Membership Gifts

	Years Available	Original Value	Current Value
Original painting, remarque	1992-93	$35	$65
With Love, mini print	1992-93	$15	$15
More Love, mini print	1993-94	$15	$15

Members-Only Pieces

	Issued	Issue Price	Current Value
Thank You print	1992-93	$30	$30

The Diane Graebner Collector's Club takes an unusual approach to the collectors' society, offering its members the beauty of print collectibles plus the opportunity to contribute to the health and well-being of society's children. Club president Bill Swain became so enthralled by the simplicity, sweetness, and beauty of Diane's paintings that he personally organized the small collectors' circle that now has grown to more than 500 members.

"Sharing"

All proceeds collected through the society and through contributions of prints and time by Diane herself are given to children's charities. To date, $1,800,000 has been raised for the Ronald McDonald House, Lodi Hospital Auxiliary, the Cancer Society of Medina County, and food programs for several churches.

This achievement suggests that Diane is on her way to realizing one of her ultimate goals: to further the awareness and importance of home and family as portrayed through her Amish images. The simple way of life is depicted in her uncomplicated strokes. She does not paint the faces of her figures out of respect for the Amish way of life, and she strives to portray their strength of religion and family life through her art.

Diane makes sixteen to twenty personal appearances per year at galleries and seven to eight appearances at gallery trade shows. These and other appearances are announced through the club's newsletter, which also includes personal notes from the artists, charities receiving donations from the club, new products, and input from galleries and collectors.

As an added incentive to collectors, all back issues of the newsletter are received upon membership into the club.

Collectors are encouraged to begin local chapters of the club in their area, and they are encouraged to inform the club of additional charities that could benefit from donations through Diane's time and efforts.

Special Features

Proceeds collected through the club, including personal appearances by the artist, are donated to local and nationwide charity groups.

Great American Collector's Guild

Drawer 249
Southern Pines, NC 28388
Director, Viola Janz
(800) 222-3309

Featured collectible: Wood carving reproductions of Old World Santas, teddy bears, and houses; made of resin
Benefits: Newsletter, coupon good for $10 off purchases of set of five Old World Santas, color catalog, new members-only piece to be issued every other year
Year club founded: 1990
Sponsored by: Great American Taylor Collectibles Corp., founded in 1980
Membership size: Under 1,000
Club publication: *Big Bear Tracks*, three times a year, four-page format
Annual dues: Free with purchase of $35 wood carving reproduction, "William," Guild first edition through December 31, 1993, after that $17
Renewals: $17
Club year ends: December 31
No. of staff devoted to handling club: Two
How to join: At an authorized Great American Taylor Collectibles retailer, or by contacting the club directly if no dealers in the area
How to redeem certificates: At an authorized Great American Taylor Collectibles retailer

Great American Collector's Guild

Members-Only Items

Items	Issued	Issue Price	Current Value
William, 9-½"	1993-94	$35	$35

My Personal Inventory

Club Name

Description	Number	Size	Issue Value	1994	1995	1996	1997

Current Valuation

My Personal Inventory

Club Name

Description	Number	Size	Issue Value	1994	1995	1996	1997

Current Valuation

H to K

In Brief...

Kathy Hippensteel Collector's Club
P.O. Box 686
Glenview, IL 60025
*Founded in 1991 — offers a newsletter, club pin,
opportunity to purchase annual, limited edition doll,
annual dues $10*

Jan Hagara Collectors' Club

40114 Industrial Park North
Georgetown, TX 78626
Administrator, Doris Priess
(512) 863-9499
Fax: (512) 869-2093

Featured collectible: Figurines, prints, plates, and other collectibles by Jan Hagara
Benefits: Opportunity to purchase members-only pieces, quarterly newsletter, membership cloisonne pin, three-ring binder, membership card, catalog, Jan Hagara Collection data sheet, invitations to attend national meetings
Year club founded: 1987
Sponsored by: Royal Orleans/Jan Hagara Collectables, founded in 1983
Local chapters available: 13, sponsored
Club publication: *The Official Jan Hagara Collectors' Club Newsletter* (12-page quarterly)
Factory tours: Partial tours of the B&J Company conducted only during the national club meeting in March
Annual dues: $22.50 (outside U.S., $29) **Renewals:** $17.50 (outside U.S., $22.50); $3 more for first-class mailing of newsletters, available in U.S. only
Club year ends: June 30
Membership kits received: Three to six weeks after application submitted
How to join: Applications at authorized dealers
How to redeem certificates: At an authorized Jan Hagara dealer

"Brandon"
by Jan
Hagara,
subject of
various club
issues

For more than a decade now, Jan Hagara has reigned as one of America's most collectible painters of children in nostalgic, turn-of-the-century attire. Whether in the form of figurines, or as prints, plates, or other collectibles, these children draw collectors into an earlier day of innocence.

Artist
Jan Hagara

Each figurine, and other Jan Hagara collectibles, begins as a painting by Jan. Following the completion of a planned pencil sketch, and using pictures of the many models that Jan and her husband and business partner, Bill, have photographed, a painting is carefully created in watercolors on 100 percent rag watercolor paper that has been delicately tinted with a soft ivory color. For the figurines, a drawing must be made to show the rest of the dress, shoes and accessories.

"I paint children with sweet pensive faces dressed in old-fashioned looking clothes with soft fabrics trimmed with laces and ribbons," Jan says. "Flowers are added and old teddy bears are included as accessories for most of the children. . . . It is so exciting to see the children become three-dimensional in the figurines and dolls."

Obviously, that excitement has spilled over to collectors. After all, it's at collectors' requests that the Jan Hagara Collectors' Club was founded in July 1987. Its goal is to make collecting more enjoyable and to expand members' knowledge of the value of Jan Hagara collectibles through the newsletter, national meetings, personal appearances, and local chapters.

People have responded with enthusiasm and membership has grown dramatically. More and more products have been offered to members of the club. Since the general public is not allowed to buy club offerings, these items have become very desirable and some are worth much more than their issue price.

Members receive the quarterly newsletter, which informs them of what's new, what's sold out, and what's getting low. Each newsletter also provides a large "Classified" section devoted entirely to the buying and selling of Jan Hagara items. The

Special Features

At the Club's collectors conventions, the Jan Hagara Collectors' Club sometimes gives a figurine from the regular line to collectors who join or renew their membership during the convention.

"Mailbag" section publishes letters of interest for the benefit of other club members, while the "Travelogue" section lists Jan's upcoming personal appearances, including the International Collectible Expositions and about 30 open houses and special appearances each year.

Members also enjoy participating in numerous contests the club sponsors, such as a 1993 Look-A-Like contest with the winner being the person who most closely resembles "Jenny," the subject of Jan's first figurine, produced in 1983.

An essay contest on "Why I Collect Jan Hagara" drew a flood of responses, published in an ongoing series in various Club newsletters.

Both fun and informative, the Jan Hagara Collectors' Club not only celebrates the children of Jan's creations, but it also celebrates the child within every member.

"It is so exciting to see the children become three-dimensional in the figurines and dolls."

— Jan Hagara

"Mattie" mini figurine, offered from 1991-93

Jan Hagara Collectors' Club

Membership Gifts

Items	Years Available	Original Value	Current Value
Jan at Age 4/plaque	1987-88	$20	$125
Jan at Age 4/cloisonne pin	1987-88	n/a	$25
Mattie/bookmark	1988-89	n/a	$3
Cloud/pin	1988-89	n/a	$25
Bonnie/bookmark	1989-90	n/a	$3
Bonnie/pin	1989-90	n/a	$25
Brandon/pin	1990-91	n/a	$25
Brandon/bookmark	1990-91	n/a	$3
Peggy Sue's Bluebonnet/print[1]	1991	n/a	$55
Cherished/mini bear figurine	1991-92	n/a	$22
Tiffany/pin	1991-92	n/a	$25
Peggy Sue/bookmark[1]	1992	n/a	$3
Enya/print[1]	1992	n/a	$55
Peggy Sue/pin[2]	1991-92	n/a	$25
Larka/pin	1992-93	n/a	$25
Audrey/print[1]	1993	n/a	$35

Members-Only Pieces

Items	Issued	Issue Price	Current Value
Mattie/print	1987-88	$55.00	$180-$275.00
Mattie/notecards	1988-89	$6.00/pk.	$6-$12.00/pk.
Bonnie/print	1988-89	$45.00	$80-$100.00
Mattie/figurine	1988-89	$47.50	$100-$135.00
Mattie/doll	1989-90	$550.00	$594-$750.00
Cloud/figurine	1989-90	$30.00	$30-$65.00
Jan at Age 4/mini figurine	1989-90	$22.00	$30-$42.00
Brandon/print	1989-90	$45.00	$45.00
Bonnie/figurine	1990-91	$40.00	$78-$110.00
Cloud/mini figurine	1990-91	$20.00	$25-$40.00
Bonnie/notecards	1990-91	$6.50/pk.	$6.50
Tiffany/print	1990-91	$55.00	$55.00
Brandon/figurine	1991-92	$40.00	$44-$58.00
Bonnie/doll	1991-92	$395.00	$395-$430.00
Mattie/mini figurine	1991-93	$22.50	$30-$45.00
Brandon/notecards	1991-92	$6.50/pk.	$6.50
Larka/print	1991-92	$75.00	$75-$100.00
Tiffany/notecards	1992-93	$6.50/pk.	$6.50
Tiffany/figurine	1992-93	$50.00	$50-$75.00
Peggy Sue/cross stitch	1992-93	$7.50/leaflet	$7.50
Peggy Sue/figurine[2]	1992-93	$27.50	$27.50

[1] — Gift at National Meeting; [2] — Charter Members Only

Alex Haley Remembers Collector's Society™

THE FIRST GREAT COLLECTION OF THE 21st CENTURY

No longer active. In existence for one year, shipped less than 100 club pieces. Alex Haley signed approximately 40 pieces before his death.

Featured collectible: African-American figurines inspired by the late author Alex Haley's writings
Benefits offered: Members-only figurine offerings, Alex Haley Remembers Collection logo sign, subscription to *Collections* magazine, invitations to society meetings and other events attended by Haley and Collection artists
Years club active: 1991
Sponsored by: Cumberland G.A.P. (Tazewell, TN)
Club publication: *Collections* magazine, four-color
Annual dues: $25
Club year ended: December 31

Alex Haley Remembers Collector's Society™
Membership Gifts

Item	Years Available	Original Value	Current Value
Alex Haley Remembers plaque, signed, dated	1991	$25	$50-$100

Members-Only Item

Figurine	Issued	Issue Price	Current Value
Extra![1]	1991	$25	$100-$350

[1]*Signed and dated pieces were available and have the highest values*

Hallmark Keepsake Ornament Collector's Club

P.O. Box 412734
Kansas City, MO 64141-2734
Manager, Rachel Perkal
((816) 274-4000
Fax: (816) 274-5061

Featured collectible: Ornaments made of wood, acrylic, bone china, porcelain, and handcrafted styles
Benefits: Keepsake of membership ornament, subscription to quarterly newsletters, personalized membership card, Keepsake Ornament Treasury binder, limited edition members-only offerings, preview issue of the Dream Book of the year's new issues, ornament list of each design since 1973, advance notice of special events, and annual conventions
Year club founded: 1987
Sponsored by: Hallmark Cards, Inc., founded in 1910
Membership size: More than 100,000
Club publication: *Collector's Courier*, full-color newsletter, quarterly
Factory tours: During annual conventions
Annual dues: $20 (two years, $38; three years, $56)
Club year ends: December 31
Local chapters: Yes
Membership kits received: four to six weeks after joining
How to join: By picking up membership forms at an authorized Hallmark Keepsake Ornament retailer
How to redeem certificates: At an authorized Hallmark Keepsake Ornament retailer

1987 "Wreath of Memories" was the club's first gift

With all the memories that Christmas evokes, it's not surprising that a club devoted to creating those memories should be one of the world's largest collector's clubs.

Designed to help collectors learn more about collecting ornaments and about the artists who design them, Hallmark's Keepsake Ornament Collector's Club offers solid benefits to members. Firmly established in the top five largest international collectors' clubs, Hallmark generates so much enthusiasm among members that it was forced to host two collector conventions in 1993 to accommodate demand.

Hallmark reports that approximately 12 percent of the U.S. population buy at least one quality designed ornament each year. More than half of those consumers consider themselves collectors — a sizeable potential audience for this club. Hallmark Keepsake Ornament artists and Collector's Club representatives make special appearances at selected Hallmark stores nationwide and at major collector conventions.

At the club's own conventions in Kansas City, members enjoyed previewing the 20th anniversary collection of Keepsake Ornaments, attended workshops, met artists who design the ornaments, and got an inside look at Hallmark headquarters.

Workshop topics included how Keepsake Ornaments artists get their ideas, protecting an ornament collection, and decorating with Keepsake Ornaments. In addition, collectors attended a special banquet and costume party, where collectors came dressed as their favorite Keepsake Ornament. (Winner of the 1991 costume contest was the subject of an ornament designed for 1993.)

Another highlight was viewing three designer-decorated trees created with ornaments from author Clara Johnson Scroggins' collection, as well as touring specially decorated homes.

Manager
Rachel Perkal

Special Feature

Invitations to ornament preview events at local retailers let club members begin enjoying Christmas long before the season begins.

1988 "Angelic Minstrel," limited to 49,900

1988 "Our Clubhouse" gift

1989 Personalized "Visit from Santa" gift ornament

Convention-goers also received an ornament designed exclusively for the convention.

"The conventions provide a natural opportunity not only to bring collectors together, but also a wonderful way of letting our members know we appreciate their loyalty," says Rachel Perkal, club manager.

Club members receive invitations to attend preview events held early enough for collectors to plan their year's ornament purchases. Little extra gifts from the club such as a canvas tote bag and Keepsake Miniature "Crown Prince" ornament given in 1990 add to the fun of being a member.

If you've always wished you could make Christmas last longer, now you can with this club.

"It's incredible that Keepsake Ornament collecting has grown so rapidly in only 20 years," says Rachel Perkal. "What started as a few simple ornaments issued in 1973 has turned into a full-scale collecting phenomenon."

Hallmark Keepsake Ornament Collector's Club

Membership Gifts

Ornaments	Years Available	Original Value	Current Value
Wreath of Memories, ed. 81,000	1987	free	$50-$78
Our Clubhouse	1988	free	$45-$50
Hold On Tight, mini.	1988	free	$65-$75
Visit from Santa	1989	free	$35-$50
Sliding Party, mini.	1989	free	$35-$50
Club Hollow, ed. 110,000	1990	free	$30-$45
Crown Prince, mini., ed. 110,000	1990	free	$35-$45
Hidden Treasure, mini.	1991	free	$30-$40
Five Years Together (charter members)	1991	free	$60
Rodney Takes Flight, stringer	1992	free	$35-$45
Chipmunk Parcel Service, mini.	1992	free	$25
It's in the Mail, ed. 100,000	1993	free	n/a
Forty Winks, ed. 100,000	1993	free	n/a

Second Holiday Heirloom ornament bell

1988 "Christmas Is Sharing"

Members-Only Pieces

Ornaments	Issued	Issue Price	Current Value
Carousel Reindeer	1987	$8.00	$55-$80
Sleighful of Dreams	1988	$8.00	$50-$75
Angelic Minstrel, ed. 49,900	1988	$29.50	$35-$40
Holiday Heirloom, ed. 34,600	1988	$25.00	$35-$60
Christmas Is Sharing, ed. 49,900	1988	$17.50	$25-$40
Holiday Heirloom, ed. 34,600	1989	$25.00	$35-$45
Christmas Is Peaceful, ed. 49,900	1989	$18.50	$35-$45
Noelle, ed. 49,900	1989	$19.75	$35-$40
Armful of Joy	1990	$9.75	$35-$50
Dove of Peace, ed. 25,400	1990	$24.75	$45-$70
Sugar Plum Fairy, ed. 25,400	1990	$27.75	$45-$60
Christmas Limited, ed. 38,700	1990	$19.75	$60-$80
Beary Artistic, lighted	1991	$10.00	$32-$45
Galloping into Christmas, ed. 28,400	1991	$19.75	$55-$70
Secrets for Santa, ed. 28,700	1991	$23.75	$50-$60
Santa's Club List, lighted	1992	$15.00	$45
Christmas Treasures, ed. 15,500	1992	$22.00	$55-$60
Victorian Skater, ed. 14,700	1992	$25.00	$35-$55
Trimmed w/ Memories (20th Anniv. edition)	1993	$12.00	$12
Gentle Tidings, ed. 17,500	1993	$25.00	$25
Sharing Christmas, ed. 16,500	1993	$20.00	$20

Left, 1993 "It's in the Mail" and right, members-only anniversary edition "Trimmed with Memories" ornament

Hallmark Keepsake Ornament Collector's Club

"Rodney Takes Flight," stringer ornament, a 1992 gift

Hand & Hammer
Collector's Club

2610 Morse Lane
Woodbridge, VA 22192
Director, Danny Corgi
1-800-SILVERY
Fax: (703) 491-2031

Featured collectible: Handcrafted sterling silver ornaments and jewelry
Benefits: Quarterly newsletter, annual full-color catalog, postcard announcements of new products, list of Hand & Hammer dealers
Year club founded: 1989
Sponsred by: Hand & Hammer, founded in 1977
Membership size: 5,000
Club publication: *Silver Tidings*, 32-page tabloid newspaper
Factory tours: Members can arrange tours by contacting the Hand & Hammer Club
Annual dues: Free
No. of staff devoted to handling club: One
How to join: Call or write to the address above

1991 Carousel Horse, silver ornament or brooch

From lavish Christmas ornaments to delicate jewelry, Hand & Hammer features the finest handcrafted silver items. Each piece is delicate in nature and rich in detail, each possessing its own separate flair and personality.

The Hand and Hammer Collector's Club works to keep collectors in touch with the organization and to alert them to new items and sources for purchasing Hand & Hammer collectibles. To describe his beginnings, his work, and his art, Chip deMatteo says, "Phil [Thorp] and I were both taught the art of silversmithing by my father [William]. Phil began his apprenticeship when he was in college, and I can't remember when I started, I was so young. We are both lucky to have such wonderful material to work with. Silver is the whitest and most reflective element known to man. It is incredibly malleable and ductile. Its ability to be formed and molded by the craftsman is unmatched and so its potential for artistic expression is limitless.

"Everyone here at Hand & Hammer feels that the care and attention the artisans of the past lavished on their creations should continue today. We are a small group of craft people working in our shop in Virginia. We have a good time together and make every piece the very best it can be."

The craftsmanship exhibited by Hand & Hammer has been recognized among the collecting community as a whole. In 1991, the Peter Rabbit silver ornament was awarded "Collectible of the Show" at the International Collectible Exposition in California.

The Club does provide a newsletter to its members, detailing new products, new outlets, information and comments from the artists, and price listings for collectors. Back issues, if available, are given to collectors free of charge.

Since the Club is free, giveaways have been inconsistent. DeMatteo reports that the Club has given away a few pieces to a few hundred of their best collectors.

Chip deMatteo, silversmith

Special Features

Personal touch of handcrafted art carries through in this club's approach to serving collectors.

Edna Hibel Society

P.O. Box 9721
Coral Springs, FL 33075
President, Ralph Burg
(305) 731-6699

Featured collectible: Porcelain and painting reproductions by Edna Hibel, also dolls and sculptures
Benefits: Free annual Hibel art poster, annual members-only collectibles, personalized membership card, membership as Friend of Hibel Museum, worldwide art tours with artist, invitations to receptions and Hibel exhibitions nationwide, subscription to quarterly newsletter
Year club founded: 1976
Membership size: 10,000 U.S.; 2,000 overseas
Club publication: *Hibeletter* (quarterly, 20-28 pages)
Hibel Museum tours: Available daily, except Monday, located in Palm Beach, Florida
Annual dues: $20 ($35 for two years)   **Renewals:** $20
Club year ends: One year after joining
No. of staff devoted to handling club: Three
Membership kits received: Four weeks after application submitted
How to join: Applications at authorized dealers
How to redeem certificates: At an authorized Hibel dealer or by mail

"Fields of Switzerland" poster and members-only pieces

Who was the first woman artist awarded the Medal of Honor and Citation by a Pope?

Who is the first foreign artist to have two solo art exhibitions in the Soviet Union, and the first foreign woman to produce a television program in that country?

And who was the recipient of Cordon Bleu's Blue Ribbon Award for her artwork, and was bestowed the title of the Honorable Lady Edna?

It could only be one person: Edna Hibel.

More than 10,000 people worldwide have taken Lady Edna to heart, as members of the Edna Hibel Society, the oldest artist fellowship in existence. But the beloved artist's legion of fans is hard to number. Whether it's her incredible artwork or her infectious smile, people flock to Lady Edna. They simply love her.

In fact, in the quarterly newsletter, *Hibeletter*, sent to all Society members, the section designated for letters to Edna is appropriately called "Love Letters." Need some evidence? Just take it from one of her "Love Letters": "You are a great artist and woman, and no snob, and that makes highest regard," writes one admirer. "You have a lot of work, but you have an open ear for anybody. Your art, especially paintings, are done with love, and that's the reason you can express freedom and liberty all over and for the world." Another fan simply stated, "Your art to me is the most beautiful in the world."

That is how personally Edna's work affects those who see it. And that is why the Society founded in her name continues to grow today as more and more people add their names to Edna's long list of friends.

Another reason people flock to her is her lyrical philosophy, which can't help but find itself in her work.

"No matter where I go, I am struck by the beauty of humanity and nature," Edna says. "I am of the school that believes that beauty and harmony are necessary and important ingredients in art as well as life.

"In my paintings, I try to capture how I feel

Artist
Edna Hibel

Special Features

• Annual Hibel Art Tours have been organized since 1979.

• Receptions are held at the Hibel Museum of Art, Palm Beach, Florida.

about my subjects. And since art begins with an appreciation of life, things are important to me in proportion to how they contribute to life.

"One of the most important aspects of beauty is the nobility and dignity with which people bear their burdens," she continues. "I find this especially among people from rural villages all over the world.

"To become a human being in today's world is a proud achievement. I see this pride in people's eyes and in their expressions and postures. I hope I capture this pride in my paintings."

There's no doubt she's done just that in the 60-some years she's been painting. Born in Boston, Mass., in 1917, Edna developed her love for art at an early age. Her talent was encouraged and first developed under the direction of noted portraitist Gregory Michaels. She later studied with the renowned German and Russian masters, Karl Zerbe and Alexandr Yakovlev, at the Boston Museum School of Fine Arts.

She completed her training there in 1939, leaving with a fellowship for a year of study and painting in Mexico. A year later, the Boston Museum of Fine Arts purchased one of her paintings for its permanent collection, making Edna the youngest artist at the time so honored by a major American museum.

How could she have known that almost 40 years later a museum would be founded in her own name? Founded in 1977 by Clayton and Ethelbelle Craig, two well-known patrons of the arts, the Hibel Museum of Art is the world's only non-profit, public museum dedicated to the art of a living American woman. The museum's permanent collection includes more than 1,000 original paintings, drawings, stone lithographs, and porcelain art by Edna Hibel.

Edna paints in many media, including fresco and oil paint on a wide variety of surfaces, such as canvas, board, silk, Philippine shells, and cameo paper. Her pioneering work in oil glaze and gold leaf is perhaps the best known of her diverse mediums. As for subject matter, her legion of fans know

"No matter where I go, I am struck with the beauty of humanity and nature. I believe that beauty and harmony are necessary and important ingredients in art as well as life."
— Edna Hibel

her best for her sensitive portrayals of mothers and children from all cultures.

She also is known for her work in lithography, sculpture, and porcelain art, and her style has been compared to Italian Renaissance artist Leonardo da Vinci and American Impressionist Mary Cassatt.

It's no wonder then that the Edna Hibel Society has grown so quickly in recent years. Through the Society, collectors are able to share the rich treasures of love, beauty, and humanity of Edna Hibel, along with her philosophies.

The information-packed *Hibeletter* provides members with a first-hand look at the history and present of Edna, her work and her friends, complete with pages of photos from Society gatherings and club-sponsored excursions, the most recent of which was a Switzerland art tour and Mediterranean Cruise.

Edna Hibel has packed much life into her 76 years — so much, in fact, that she's been sharing it for most of her life. Members of the Edna Hibel Society have been able to pick up the beauty and harmony that has made Edna Hibel a Lady and so much more.

Hibel Society members have toured all over the world with Edna.

Edna Hibel Society

Membership Gifts

Posters	Years Available	Original Value	Current Value
Three Nudes[1]	1977	$25	$75-$100
Thai Dancers[1]	1978	$25	$75-$100
Hibel in Ghent[1]	1982	$25	$75-$100
Mother Earth[1]	1983	$25	$75-$100
Homage to All Children[1]	1984	$25	$75-$100
Celebration of Life[1]	1985	$25	$75-$100
The World I Love[1]	1986	$25	$75-$100
A Golden Bridge[1]	1987	$25	$75-$100
Diana, Peace Through Wisdom[1]	1988	$25	$75-$100
William, Winnie Cheng's Grandmother[1]	1989	$25	$75-$100
Edna's Grandmother[1]	1990	$25	$75-$100
Darya[1]	1991	$25	$75-$100
Fields of Switzerland[1]	1992	$25	$75-$100
Idyllic Days [1]	1993	$25	$75-$100

[1]*Signed posters command highest values indicated*

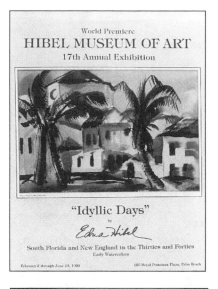

World Premiere
HIBEL MUSEUM OF ART
17th Annual Exhibition

"Idyllic Days"
by
Edna Hibel

South Florida and New England in the Thirties and Forties
Early Watercolors

February 2 through June 18, 1993   150 Royal Poinciana Plaza, Palm Beach

Clockwise from top: 1993 Hibel Society gift poster; 1991 "Blue Trellis" plate and temple jar; and Hibel Society '91 poster, "Darya" with the 1992 "Magdalene et Yves" box and plate, and Hibeletters

Members-Only Pieces

Items	Issued	Original Value	Current Value
Blue Trellis plate, ed. 2,500[1]	1991	$65	$100-$180
Blue Trellis temple jar, ed. 2,500[1]	1991	$95	$150-$300
Magdelene et Yves plate, ed. 2,500	1992	$65	$90-$125
Magdelene et Yves Limoges box, ed. 2,500	1992	$85	$110-$175
Harmony, framed art print, ed. 2,500	1993	$150	$150
Melody, framed art print, ed. 2,500	1993	$150	$150

[1]*Signed pieces and matching numbers available*

Lizzie High®
Society

220 N. Main St.
Sellersville, PA 18960
Director, Alene Yarnall
(215) 453-8200

"Audrey High"

Featured collectible: Wooden folk art dolls by husband and wife Peter Wisber and Barbara Kafka Wisber

Benefits: Collector's catalog and leather binder picturing all dolls, gives first and last name with doll's story, whether retired, space for inventorying and wish list, subscription to *Lizzie High Notebook* newsletter, personalized membership card, pewter pin of Lizzie and Lily, redemption certificates for members-only pieces

Year club founded: 1992-93

Sponsored by: Ladie and Friends™, Inc., founded in 1985

Membership size: 6,330 charter members

Club publication: *Lizzie High Notebook* newsletter, bi-annual, six to ten pages, designed like a school notebook with sections on "Reading," "Art" (decorating photos), and "Arithmetic" (new issues, retirements, and classifieds). Back issues available for $1 each

Annual dues: $15 ($20 outside U.S.) **Renewals:** $10 ($12.50 outside U.S.)

Club year ends: August 31

Membership kits received: Within 45 days of receipt of application

How to join: By picking up an application form at an authorized Lizzie High retailer, or by contacting the club directly

How to redeem certificates: At an authorized Lizzie High retailer

Lizzie High Society

Membership Gifts

Items	Years Available	Original Value	Current Value
Lizzie High pewter pin	ongoing	free	n/a
Signature print	1992-93	free	n/a

Members-Only Items

Dolls	Issued	Issue Price	Current Value
Audrey High	1993	$59	$59

Annette Himstedt
Collector Club

333 Continental Blvd., M1-0114
El Segundo, CA 90245

Featured collectible: Original artist dolls by Annette Himstedt
Benefits: Exclusive European 1993 Images of Childhood Catalog, set of 12 postcards featuring dolls from 1987 to 1993, opportunities to purchase special doll accessories and dresses, quarterly letters from the president of the club, advance notice of U.S. tours, membership card, artist biography, and preview of new dolls
Year club founded: 1993 (Charter Year ends May 31, 1994)
Sponsored by: Timeless Creations/Mattel
Annual dues: $30
Club year ends: May 31
Membership kits received: Four to six weeks after joining
How to join: By picking up membership forms at an authorized Annette Himstedt retailer
How to redeem certificates: At an authorized Annette Himstedt retailer

Mark Hopkins
Sculpture Guild

[signature: Mark Hopkins]

21 Shorter Industrial Blvd.
Rome, GA 30165-1838
Director, L. Susan Fife
(706) 235-8773
Fax: (706) 235-2814

Featured collectible: Bronze sculptures by Mark Hopkins
Year club founded: 1993
Sponsored by: Mark Hopkins Sculpture, Inc., founded in 1988
Membership size: 3,000 U.S.
Club publication: *Bronzeworks* newsletter (four to eight page quarterly, began Spring 1993)
Factory tours: Call for appointment
Annual dues: Free
No. of staff devoted to handling club: Two
Membership kits received: One week after application submitted
How to join: Automatic membership for anyone who purchases or receives a Mark Hopkins Sculpture and registers their ownership using the registration card which comes with each piece
How to redeem certificates: At an authorized dealer

Still in its formation stage, Mark Hopkins Sculpture Guild is designed to enhance the collector's enjoyment of their Mark Hopkins bronze collectibles. These solid bronze pieces are sculpted exclusively in the United States using the lost wax method. The Guild will offer an item locator service, an aftermarket value service, and a listing of dealers working on aftermarket products. The quarterly *Bronzeworks* newsletter will introduce new pieces, inform collectors about the artist and his company, and notify them of pieces that have sold out or been retired.

Mark Hopkins says, "My style is to show a noble subject in a noble metal in its essence, to leave enough for the imagination. I call it Noblessence."

M.I. Hummel Club®

M.I. Hummel Club

Goebel Plaza, P.O. Box 11
Pennington, NJ 08534-0011
President, Kenneth G. Le Fevre
(609) 737-8777; (800) 666-CLUB
Fax: (609) 737-1545

Featured collectible: M.I. Hummel products made of earthenware
Benefits: Free "I Brought You a Gift" figurine; opportunity to
purchase members-only figurines; use of the Research Department
and Collectors' Market to match buyers and sellers of Hummel collectibles; membership card; binder filled with a collector's log, price
list, and facts about M.I. Hummel history and production; club travel
opportunities with members-only tour of the Goebel factory in
Germany, where the figurines are hand crafted. Charter members
received a special membership card identifying charter status, and
in 1991-92 received a special pin for their 15 years of membership
Year club founded: 1977 (as the Goebel Collectors' Club, renamed
in 1989)
Sponsored by: W. Goebel Porzellanfabrik, founded in 1871
Membership size: 165,000
Local chapters available: 115, independently organized
Club publication: *Insights* (quarterly, four-color, 16 pages)
Factory tours: Members can visit W. Goebel Porzellanfabrik, the fac-
tory where the figurines are created, on their own or through a
scheduled club trip. Only club trips offer behind-the-scenes tours
Annual dues: $40   **Renewals:** $32.50
Extras: Binders, $12; M.I. Hummel Care Kit,
$19.95; *M.I. Hummel Guide for Collectors*, $10;
stationery, $12; Christmas cards, $10.95; and gift
wrap, $3.95
Club year ends: May 31
Membership kits received: 6-8 weeks after application submitted
How to join: Applications at authorized M.I.
Hummel dealers, by direct mail, at promotions
and shows, or through Member-Get-A-Member
programs (member receives a gift for signing up a
new member)
How to redeem certificates: At an authorized
M.I. Hummel dealer

*"Gift from a
Friend"*

Sister Maria Innocentia Hummel saw the world through a special pair of eyes.

Wherever the young artist would go, few details of her surroundings would escape her. And more often than not, those details would find themselves re-created in a sketch or on a canvas. Although Sister M.I. Hummel was a member of a Catholic order, her early years were spent pursuing her talent for art. In fact, she was an honors graduate of the prestigious Munich Academy of Applied Art. It has been said that when she announced her intention to enter a religious order, her professors were "profoundly disappointed." They had hoped she would continue her studies and in time join the faculty.

While at the Convent of Siessen in Germany, she did continue her studies and even helped raise money for the convent by exhibiting some of her work. Sister Hummel often used children in her charming artwork as a way of satirizing the manners of adults. She found humor in the amusing self-importance children displayed when playing "grown up."

By 1934, Franz Goebel, a fourth-generation owner of a porcelain factory in Bavaria, discovered the young Sister's work on religious art cards. In her art, he saw the end of his search for a new line of figurines. He would breathe three-dimensional life into her two-dimensional creations.

Though she hesitated at first, afraid that the work would no longer be hers since she was not a sculptor, Sister Hummel agreed once Goebel promised she would have final approval of every piece. To mark her approval, each figurine was incised with her signature.

After Sister Hummel's death in 1946, an artistic board at the Convent of Siessen assumed the role of approving each piece. As stated in *Insights*, the official magazine of the M.I. Hummel Club®, "The board guards her legacy and keeps her truths alive in the translations done in three dimensions by the only company ever authorized to do so, W. Goebel Porzellanfabrik."

Today, a marketing executive and a sculptor

Sister Maria Innocentia Hummel

Special Features

• Collectors' Market matches buyers and sellers of M.I. Hummel collectibles.

• Research Department available to answer members' questions.

• Anniversary Pins — Special pins mark members' fifth, tenth and fifteenth anniversaries in the club.

travel to the convent with clay models of proposed figurines. The board studies the piece and compares it to Sister Hummel's original art. Only then can production begin. Each figurine is hand crafted and hand painted by highly skilled artisans who have been trained by Goebel, beginning with a three-year apprentice program.

The creation of each figurine is a long, detailed process. Production time is determined by the size and complexity of each individual figurine. A six-inch figurine may require as many as 700 hand operations and take several weeks to complete.

It's that kind of care that has reaped many awards for M.I. Hummel figurines, including: Figurine of the Year for the "Crossroads" limited edition, Award of Excellence for "Let's Tell the World," Miniature of the Year for "Stitch in Time," and 1991 South Bend and Long Beach Collectible Show Award for "We Wish You the Best."

Demand and appreciation for the Hummel figurines was so great that in 1977 Goebel founded the Goebel Collectors' Club to create a network for all those who enjoyed the M.I. Hummel figurines, plates and bells. This club helped create the standard for others to meet. It was renamed the M.I. Hummel Club in 1989.

Members of the M.I. Hummel Club are afforded a full range of services, from a research department which provides answers to their questions, to club-sponsored tours to the factory where the figurines are made, W. Goebel Porzellanfabrik in Roedental, Germany. Members who decide to visit the factory on their own may view a film, see a demonstration by a Goebel sculptor and painter, shop in the factory store, and enjoy a free lunch. But for the full-blown behind-the-scenes tour, members must participate in the club tours.

For members who find it hard to get away to far-off lands, about four to six artists tour North America every year to bring Hummel to the people. While visiting the States, they attend collectibles shows and club conventions, and they set up demonstrations at select retail stores. Members are notified of artists' visits through a promotion

Sister M.I. Hummel often used children in her charming artwork as a way of satirizing the manners of adults. She found humor in the amusing self-importance children displayed when playing "grown up."

1992 "Light Up the Night" ornament went to members who gave three gift memberships

calendar in *Insights* and through postcard mailings for in-store promotions.

Insights, a four-color quarterly magazine, also informs members of new releases, the latest M.I. Hummel news; historical looks at Sister Hummel, Goebel, and the world they lived in; general interest articles such as how the figurines are created; and information on in-store events and local chapters.

M.I. Hummel figurines, in fact, have a far-reaching appeal, which has spawned the creation of 115 local chapters throughout North America. The founding club assists local chapters with subscriptions to the quarterly local chapter newsletter, *Chapter & Verse*, a local chapter patch and a sticker for membership cards, invitations to regional conferences hosted by other local chapters, a local chapter program guide, recruitment programs to help chapters add members, and giveaways for conferences.

From Tampa Bay, Fla., to Vancouver, British Columbia, and around the world, collectors are drawn together by the ongoing vision of Sister M.I. Hummel, and they're looking at life a little differently through her special pair of eyes.

"The [convent] board guards Sister Hummel's legacy and keeps her truths alive in the translations done in three dimensions by the only company ever authorized to do so, W. Goebel Porzellanfabrik."

For members only: Preview Edition "Cheeky Fellow" (left) and member exclusive, "My Wish Is Small"

M.I. Hummel Club®

Membership Gifts

Gifts	Years Available	Original Value	Current Value
M.I. Hummel Print	1978-79	free	n/a
MIH Print	1979-80	free	n/a
MIH Print	1980-81	free	n/a
MIH Print	1981-82	free	n/a
Address Book	1982-83	free	n/a
Stationery	1983-84	free	n/a
Note Cards	1984-85	free	n/a
Register Book	1985-86	free	n/a
Memory Book	1986-87	free	n/a
Tote Bag	1987-88	free	n/a
Stationery	1988-89	free	n/a
I Brought You a Gift (figurine)	1989-90	$50-75	$55-$100
Merry Wanderer (sterling silver necklace)	1990-91	$50	$50
Two Hands, One Treat (figurine)	1991-92	$65	$65-$80
Lucky Fellow (figurine, renewal)	1992-93	$75	$75
A Sweet Offering (figurine, renewal)	1993-94	$80	$80

Members-Only Pieces

Figurines	Issued	Issue Price	Current Value
Valentine Gift, HUM 387	1977-78	$45	$490-$900
Smiling Through (plaque), HUM 690	1978-79	$50	$150-$225
Hummel Bust, HUM 3	1979-80	$75	$210-$324
Valentine Joy, HUM 399	1980-81	$95	$200-$300
Daisies Don't Tell, HUM 380	1981-82	$80	$250-$300
It's Cold, HUM 421	1982-83	$80	$250-$300
What Now?, HUM 422	1983-84	$90	$200-$300
Valentine Gift (pendant)	1983-84	$85	$225-$300
Coffee Break, HUM 409	1984-85	$90	$174-$250
Smiling Through, HUM 408	1985-86	$125	$275-$325
Birthday Candle, HUM 440	1986-87	$95	$200-$300
What Now? (pendant)	1986-87	$125	$180-$200
Morning Concert, HUM 447	1987-88	$98	$190-$250
The Surprise, HUM 431	1988-89	$125	$225-$275
Hello World, HUM 429	1989-90	$130	$150-$175
I Wonder, HUM 486	1990-91	$140	$160-$185
Gift From a Friend, HUM 485	1991-92	$160	$160
My Wish Is Small, HUM 463/0	1992-93	$170	$170
I Didn't Do It, HUM 626	1993-94	$175	$175

Redemption Forms are valid for two years. Dates from beginning of club year.
(Anniversary Figurines — "Flower Girl" for 5 years, "The Little Pair" for 10 years, and "Honey Lover" for 15 years — do not have expiration dates. They are ongoing offers for members who reach their fifth, 10th and 15th year of membership. Current values are $125-$150, $185-$250, and $225-$300, respectively.)

1993-94 "I Didn't Do It"

"I Brought You A Gift" and other club benefits

"A Sweet Offering," 1993-94 renewal gift

International Bossons Collectors Society

Collectors Society

21-C John Maddox Drive
Rome, GA 30165
Director, Dr. Robert E. Davis
(706) 232-1266
Fax: (706) 290-0379

Featured collectible: Plaster character wall masks, figurines, and wall plaques
Benefits: Membership certificate, quarterly newsletter, members-only Winston Churchill wall mask, swap and shop opportunities, and contacts for discontinued pieces
Year club founded: 1982
Sponsored by: W.H. Bossons Company of Congleton
Membership size: 1,300 U.S.; 30 U.K.; 50 Canada; 15 combined in several additional countries
Local chapters available: One, independently organized
Club publication: *Bossons Briefs* (four-color, 10-12 pages, issued quarterly)
Factory tours: Given on an individual basis by calling or writing in advance; factory located at Brook Mills in Congleton, Cheshire, England
Annual dues: $35 **Renewals:** $35
Extras: Autographed copy of book *The Imagical World of Bossons*, by Dr. R.E. Davis ($47.50), IBCS embossed notecards, hip packs and sweatshirts ($7)
Club year ends: December 31
No. of staff devoted to handling club: Three
Membership kits received: Three to four weeks after application submitted
How to join: Membership brochure and application form are inserted into boxes of Bossons artware at factory. Application must be mailed to IBCS headquarters

Gift to members, Churchill mask

Lifelike expressions and intricate detail make Bossons wall masks come alive with character and realism. It is this realism that first attracted Dr. R.E. Davis, the Society's founder, to the Bossons artwork. Having bought his first piece in 1967, Davis couldn't have known that this collectors' circle today would boast hundreds of members in more than 15 countries. Or that a makeshift office in the back of his dental office would soon need more than one room to handle the flood of interest in the society.

Understanding the challenge involved in obtaining an "entire" collection of these art pieces, Davis created the society to provide information about hard-to-find Bossons products and facilitate correspondence between collectors. The tasks of the club have increased in number and now include educating members about all aspects of Bossons artware and collecting, providing a central source for information on the company and products and further appreciation for Bossons artware.

For example, in June 1993, the "Mountie" was nominated for "Best Figurine over $75 Retail," in Canada in recognition of its fine craftsmanship and realistic detail.

Intrigued with the faces and masks of his collection, Dr. Davis saw a need for a comprehensive catalog of Bossons artware, and published *The Imagical World of Bossons* in 1982 to assist other collectors assembling their own collections.

The society distributes information through its quarterly newsletter, *Bossons Briefs*, which features color pictures of new models, new discoveries and variations, meeting announcements, answers to members' questions, auction prices, and an advertising section.

One interesting aspect of the *Bossons Briefs* is a section introducing and exploring the life of the models for some of the wall masks. In essence, this gives collectors the chance to meet and understand a bit about the faces behind the masks.

Dr. Robert E. Davis

Special Features

• **Research provided for members' questions**

• **Swap and shop section in newsletter**

• **Appraisals on Bossons artware**

Bossons
heads cap-
ture charac-
ter faces in
a dramatic
form.

"Bargee"   *"Fisherman"*   *"Smuggler"*

International Bossons Collectors Society

Membership Gifts

Wall Masks	Years Available	Original Value	Current Value
Winston Churchill	1989 - present	$35	$35

Members-Only Pieces

Wall Masks	Issued	Issue Price	Current Value
Pierre	1989	$60	$60
Paddy	1990	$75	$75
Bargee	1991	$100	$100
Smuggler	1992	$100	$100
Fisherman	1993	$100	$100

Iris Arc Crystal
Collectors Society

114 East Haley Street
Santa Barbara, CA 93101
Contact: Chris Berry
(805) 963-3661
Fax: (805) 965-2458

Featured collectible: Full-lead crystal figurines
Benefits: Free crystal membership gift, membership card, quarterly newsletter, color brochures and entry into Grand Prize Drawings for a trip to Iris Arc's studios in Santa Barbara, California
Year club founded: 1992
Sponsored by: Iris Arc Crystal, founded in 1976
Membership size: 5,000 U.S.
Club publication: *Illuminations* (four to six pages, black-and-white, photos)
Factory tours: Contact the Collectors Society administrator to arrange for tour
Annual dues: $25   **Renewals:** $25
Club year ends: June 30
No. of staff devoted to handling club: Four
Membership kits received: Two to four weeks after application submitted, and available from stores for immediate take-home
How to join: Visit an authorized Iris Arc Crystal dealer or contact the society directly for membership forms and information
How to redeem certificates: At an authorized Iris Arc Crystal dealer

Charter year "Gramophone" figurine

The name for the Iris Arc Crystal Collectors Society comes from the Greek myth of Iris, the goddess of the rainbow who was sent by Zeus to Earth on a rainbow to give a message to mortals. When Jonathan Wygant and Francesca Patruno founded Iris Arc Crystal in 1976, they could not have anticipated where their venture would lead. As they evolved from a marketer of prisms into the first American manufacturer of faceted crystal figurines, they helped build interest in crystal as a medium for collectors.

"Light is the essence of what crystal is all about. Consequently, every single piece we have in our collection is a prism — cut and faceted so the light plays through it, breaking up into rainbows of color," Wygant says.

Using imported 32 percent full-lead crystal, each figurine is hand crafted in Santa Barbara, Calif. Each piece depicts a particular theme, including romance, architecture, Americana, floral, fantasy, sports, child's world, Christmas and miniatures. Each theme is designed to delight the eye with sparkling color.

In 1991, Iris Arc received a number of honors including Awards of Excellence from *Collector Editions* magazine, Best Crystal Design at the Long Beach International Collectible Exposition and New Design Award from the Corning Museum of Glass. Iris Arc Crystal also has been presented as awards to honor the exceptional achievement of such world personalities as Lech Walesa, Mother Theresa, and Stevie Wonder.

A distinct emotional appeal, the high quality, fine detail, and innovative sculpting techniques rendered by skilled artists attract collectors to this new society. Club members enjoy the beauty of crystal as a medium, the intriguing history of Iris Arc, and the story behind the designs.

In the effort to keep members enthusiastic and involved in the workings of the society, the quarterly newsletter *Illuminations* covers issues of company history, design history, secondary market information, artists' backgrounds, and collectors'

Special Features

Iris Arc creates colored crystal under the copyrighted name of Rainbow Crystal.

backgrounds. In addition, new members wishing to obtain back issues can do so from the club, free of charge.

Members also receive first notice of new figurine releases, design retirements, artists' appearances, and other special events. Emphasizing its American manufacturing, Iris Arc plans to focus on classic Americana themes for its subjects.

Iris Arc Crystal Collectors Society

Membership Gifts

Crystal Figurines	Years Available	Original Value	Current Value
Heart paperweight	1992-93	$30	$30
Snowflake ornament	1993-94	$30	$30

Members-Only Pieces

Crystal Figurines	Issued	Issue Price	Current Value
Annual Edition Gramophone	1992-93	$100	$100
Annual Edition Classic Telephone	1992-93	$150	$150

"Classic Telephone"

"Heart" paperweight

Jerri Collector's Society

651 Anderson Street
Charlotte, NC 28205
(704) 333-3211 or
(800) 248-2188
Fax: (704) 333-7706

Featured collectible: Porcelain dolls
Benefits: Periodic newsletters, opportunity to attend annual conventions, pin, membership card, color brochures and mailings, opportunity to purchase members-only dolls
Year club founded: 1987
Sponsored by: Dolls by Jerri, founded in 1975
Membership size: 4,000
Club publication: *Jerri Collector's Society* (6-8 pages)
Factory tours: Call in advance
Annual dues: $10   **Renewals:** $10
Extras: Binders, pins, T-shirts
Club year ends: One year after joining
No. of staff devoted to handling club: Five
Membership kits received: Four to six weeks after application submitted
How to join: Applications at authorized dealers
How to redeem certificates: At an authorized Dolls by Jerri dealer

1993 "Daniella"

1989 "Goose Girl"

Porcelain dolls are one of the most popular collectibles in the hobby. With their delicate features and dewy-eyed expressions, these lifelike dolls can capture the heart almost as quickly as a newborn baby.

When many collectors think dolls these days, they're thinking about Dolls by Jerri, which has been in the business of winning hearts since 1975.

The enthusiasm with which people collect Jerri's dolls is evident in the success of the Jerri Collector's Society. The idea started in 1987 when a small group of collectors approached founders Jerri and Jim McCloud and asked their permission to establish a club and newsletter to provide an information source for collectors. The first newsletter was produced in the fall of 1987 with Jerri and Jim providing their support. The first members-only doll, "The Goose Girl," was produced in the fall of 1988, with a new piece added to the members-only collection each year since.

Then came the first Society convention in April 1991. "The collectors who came to the convention were the most congenial, warm, and wonderful group of people we have ever met," Jerri remembers. "There were no strangers, only friends bonded together by a mutual love of dolls."

Now in its sixth year, the Jerri Collector's Society has grown in membership to 4,000. Each year, more collectors gather at the annual convention than the year before. But while things keep moving forward, that "mutual love of dolls" has stayed the same.

Doll maker Jerri McCloud

Special Features

The Jerri Collector's Society offers a toll-free telephone number to provide members with up-to-date information about the club and Dolls by Jerri collectibles.

Jerri Collector's Society

Members-Only Pieces

Dolls	Issued	Issue Price	Current Value
Goose Girl	1989	$300	$300-$450
Milk Maiden	1990	$325	$325-$455
Abbie	1991	$350	$350-$455
Enchanted Princess	1992	$425	$422-$510
Daniella	1993	$425	$425

Emmett Kelly Jr.
Collectors' Society

P.O. Box 93507
Atlanta, GA 30377-0507
Director, Mary Lee Graham
(404) 352-1381
Fax: (404) 352-2150

Featured collectible: Bisque porcelain, clown theme figurines
Benefits: EKJ Collector's Plaque, *EK Journal* quarterly subscription, EKJ Binder, EKJ lapel pin, annual full-color catalog, free registration of pieces, and annual registry list with secondary market information
Year club founded: 1983
Sponsored by: Flambro Imports Inc., founded in 1965
Club publication: *EK Journal* (three to four pages, issued quarterly)
Annual dues: $25   **Renewals:** $15, optional four-year $50 renewal
No. of staff devoted to handling club: Three
Also sponsors: Pleasantville 1893 Historical Preservation Society, with plans to start other clubs
Membership kits received: Three to four weeks after application submitted, also available at participating dealers
How to join: Applications at authorized Flambro dealers
How to redeem certificates: At an authorized Flambro dealer

1993 "The Ringmaster"

The charming and often melancholy world of clowns is captured in the bisque porcelain figurines collected by members of the Emmett Kelly Jr. Collectors' Society. An attraction to clowns and the Kelly story — the family history of clowning — draws collectors into this organization.

Emmett Kelly Jr.

The Society strives to promote and strengthen interest in Emmett Kelly Jr. collectibles, as well as provide service and support to collectors. Part of the service includes a new, special registration program that provides members with an annual listing of their "Emmetts" along with a listing of each figurine's current value. The Society also offers a Products Merchandise department that takes questions and suggestions from all members on a collectors' product line.

Special membership incentives offered to members include the Christmas Gift Program, which gives each new member an EKJ musical figurine.

Other incentives and membership offerings are announced in *EK Journal*, the Society's official quarterly newsletter. Features include articles on new products; members-only figurines; announcements regarding tours and contests; a buy, sell, trade classified section; collector's stories; and secondary market information.

Emmett Kelly Jr.'s travel schedule and appearances also are announced in the newsletter. Kelly makes appearances at authorized collector centers throughout the year, and he appears at gift shows twice a year to talk with collectors, sign collectibles, and be photographed with members.

Special Features

• Free EKJ musical figurine upon joining the Society

• Special registration program gives collectors an annual listing of their figurines and each piece's secondary market value.

Emmett Kelly Jr. Collectors' Society

Members-Only Pieces

Porcelain Figurines	Issued	Issue Price	Current Value
Merry Go Round	1990	$125	$240-$400
10 Years of Collecting	1991	$100	$160-$200
All Aboard	1992	$75	$75
The Ringmaster	1993	$125	$125

Thomas Kinkade
Collectors' Society

P.O. Box 90267
San Jose, CA 95109
Director, Ms. Bobbi Kurani
(800) 366-3733
Fax: (408) 287-1169

Featured collectible: Canvas lithographs and luminous archival paper prints
Benefits: A free luminous archival paper print, the opportunity to purchase a members-only canvas lithograph (the chosen print changes every June), and the quarterly newsletter
Year club founded: 1992
Sponsored by: Lightpost Publishing, founded in 1988
Membership size: Not available
Club publication: *Thomas Kinkade Collectors' Society Newsletter* (four-page, 8-1/2 by 11 inch quarterly)
Annual dues: $35   **Renewals:** $35
Club year ends: One year after member joins
No. of staff devoted to handling club: Six
Membership kits received: 2-3 weeks after application received
How to join: Applications at authorized dealers, by phone, gift memberships
How to redeem certificates: At an authorized Thomas Kinkade dealer

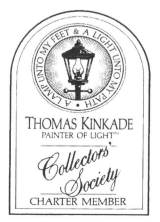

THOMAS KINKADE
PAINTER OF LIGHT™

Collectors'
Society

CHARTER MEMBER

"Morning Lane,"
gift for members

Thomas Kinkade sheds a unique light on every canvas he paints. His trademark is the soft glow of light, be it sunlight, candlelight, or artificial light, and how it illuminates the beautiful and peaceful scenes he painstakingly commits to canvas.

"I try to recreate paintings that are a window for the imagination," he says. "If people look at my work and are reminded of the way things once were or perhaps the way they could be, then I've done my job."

A list of his accolades shows that he certainly has done his job, and done it well. Kinkade received two certificates of merit from the New York Society of Illustrators, two Founder's Awards from the National Parks Academy for the Arts, and was chosen as the official artist for the 1989 National Parks Collector's Print and the 1990 Commemorative Press Collector's Print.

His canvas lithographs, all hand-retouched by skilled artisans under the guidance of Kinkade, are casting a glow on collectors as well. Members of the Thomas Kinkade Collectors' Society can find out more about this "painter of light" through the society's quarterly newsletter, which covers topics ranging from Thomas' family life to his appearance schedule to his new releases.

Artist Thomas Kinkade

"If people look at my work and are reminded of the way things once were or perhaps the way they could be, then I've done my job."

— Thomas Kinkade

Thomas Kinkade Collectors' Society

Membership Gifts

Archival Paper Print	Years Available	Original Value	Current Value
Morning Lane	1992-93	$150	$150

Members-Only Pieces

Canvas Lithograph	Issued	Issue Price	Current Value
Skater's Pond	1992-93	$295	$325-$365

(Certificate term: July 1992-July 1993)

Krystonia Collectors Club

110 E. Ellsworth
Ann Arbor, MI 48108
(313) 677-3510
Fax: (313) 677-3412

Featured collectible: Cold-cast porcelain animal and whimsical figurines
Benefits: Members-only gift, members-only redemption figurine, quarterly newsletter, contests
Year club founded: 1989
Sponsored by: Precious Art, founded in 1980
Membership size: 16,000 U.S.; 4,000 Canada
Club publication: *Phargol Horn* (6 pages on parchment-like paper)
Factory tours: Contact Precious Art for reservations at above address.
Annual dues: $25   **Renewals:** $25
Club year ends: January 31
No. of staff devoted to handling club: Four
Membership kits received: Four to six weeks after application submitted
How to join: Join through mail-in application at dealers or form available in back of merchandise booklets
How to redeem certificates: At an authorized Krystonia dealer

Krystonia creators David Woodard and Pat Chandok

"I am Kephren, the Recorder of tales of the past and deeds of the present." So begins *The Chronicles of Krystonia*, thus launching a collector's passage into the world of these whimsical, magical, and fanciful collectibles.

Krystonia factories are situated in Stoke-on-Trent in England, a region well known for its pottery. Highly skilled painters and sculptors collaborate to bring this tradition of quality to the collector, sometimes accenting pieces with magical crystals.

The Krystonia line has been nominated for Collectible and Figurine of the Year by NALED, and nominated Figurine of the Year by *Collectors Edition*, as well as capturing an award for Best New Product by Gift Creation Concepts.

Hobbyists who enjoy make-believe and fantasy have been drawn to this collectors' club. Each figurine boasts a personality all its own. The Krystonia figurines fit into a make-believe kingdom with every character created to elicit a particular emotion from the hobbyist. An additional draw are the miniature storybooks that accompany the figurines. Each book unfolds a new part of the story of Krystonia and makes each new character come to life.

Also unique to this collectors club is the society's newsletter. *The Phargol Horn* presents news from Krystonia, a club update, information on retired pieces, new additions to the collection, announcements regarding contests and hobby news, and a buy/sell section for club members. The newsletter resembles an Old World scroll with its parchment-type paper and Old English headlines.

The Krystonia Collectors Club informs and entertains collectors; answers questions; provides insurance listings; and transports hobbyists into the whimsical world of Krystonia through the stories, figurines, and fanciful newsletter anecdotes.

"Vaaston,"
members-only
issue

Special Features

Storybooks included with figurines tell a story of each character and how it is included in the kingdom.

"Sneaking A Peek"

Sales of 750,000-plus Krystonia books back up the popularity of Krystonia's collectibles.

"Pultzr"

"Spreading His Wings"

Krystonia Collectors Club

Membership Gifts

Porcelain Figurines	Years Available	Original Value	Current Value
Key to Krystonia	1989-90	$25	$95-$150
Kephren Chest	1990-91	$30	$100-$150
Lantern	1991-92	$30	$50-$75
Sneaking a Peek	1993	$55	$55

Members-Only Pieces

Porcelain Figurines	Issued	Issue Price	Current Value
Pultzr	1989-90	$55	$250-$500
Dragon's Play	1990-91	$65	$150-$230
Vaaston	1991-92	$65	$65-$125
Spreading His Wings	1993	$60	$60

161

Sandra Kuck
Collector's Club

No longer active. Founded in 1990 and closed in 1992.

Featured collectible: Figurines and prints by artist Sandra Kuck
Benefits: Offered members a gift figurine, membership card and certificate, opportunity to purchase two members-only pieces and a bi-annual newsletter
Sponsored by: V.F. Fine Arts and then John Hine Studios Inc.
Club publication: *Artist's Diary*, two-color, four pages
Annual dues: $30 the first two years, then $35

Sandra Kuck Collector's Club

Membership Gifts

Items	Years Available	Original Value	Current Value
Kitten	1991	$30	$85-$100
Retrospective poster[1]	1992	$15	$55-$65
La Belle figurine	1992	$30	$85-$90
Lullaby	1992	gift	$85-$90

Members-Only Items

Figurines	Issued	Issue Price	Current Value
Friends for Keeps figurine[1]	1992	$45	$150-$200
Friends for Keeps lithograph[1]	1992	$75	$250-$300

[1]-*Signed pieces available and command highest values*

Left, "Kitten" was the club's first issue by Kuck (right)

Sandra Kuck
Collectors Club

My Personal Inventory

Club Name

Description	Number	Size	Issue Value	Current Valuation				
				1994	1995	1996	1997	

My Personal Inventory

Club Name

Description	Number	Size	Issue Value	1994	Current Valuation 1995	1996	1997

L
to
Q

In Brief...

Lee's Little Kids Klub
P.O. Box 346
Berne, IN 46711
Established in 1991, members of the Lee's Little Kids Klub receive dolls at a special members-only price, with the same serial number reserved for members' dolls, dues $50 for life of the series

Seymour Mann Collectible Doll Club
P.O. Box 2046
Madison Square Station
New York, NY 10159
Contact: Evelyn Rockwall
Founded in 1989 — offers a periodic newsletter, official membership card, limited edition doll poster, background information on the artist, and opportunity to buy members-only dolls, annual dues $5

The Moe Head Club
John Hine Studios
8130 La Mesa Boulevard, 338
La Mesa, CA 91941
Founded in 1993 — features the art of Maurice (Moe) Wideman, announcements of new releases and personal appearances, gift of Moe Head ceramic badge to wear at promotions and functions (members promise to bake Moe a cake the next time he comes to their town and to wear red shoes to after-promotion parties and other special club events)

Phyllis' Collector's Club
Rt. 4, Box 503
Rolla, MO 65401
Founded in 1989 — offers a newsletter about artist Phyllis Parkins dolls, new product information, opportunity to purchase members-only pieces, and attend annual convention, annual dues $20

Lalique
Society of America

400 Veterans Blvd.
Carlstadt, NJ 07072
Director, Susan Stashkevetch
800-CRISTAL
Fax: (201) 939-4492

Featured collectible: Primarily crystal art designed by three generations of the Lalique family, also jewelry, tableware, crystal stemware,
perfume, and textiles
Benefits: Exclusive members-only crystal design each year,
embossed print, magazine portfolio, subscription to the *LALIQUE
Magazine*, advance notice of special events around the country, and
chartered trips to Lalique special events around the globe
Year club founded: 1989
Extras: Back issues of magazine, binders, Lalique notecards, cata-
logs, books at discount, and Lalique lines not generally available in
United States: jewelry, silk scarves and shawls, and perfume
Sponsored by: Lalique, France, operates under the direction of U.S.
subsidiary Jacques Jugeat, Inc.
Membership size: About 5,000
International chapters: In Holland, Singapore, and Canada
Club publication: *LALIQUE Magazine*, full color, quarterly
Factory tours: Only to members and their guests during bi-annual
membership tours to France
Annual dues: $40   **Renewals:** $40 (or $25 with order of members-
only piece)
Club year ends: March 31
No. of staff devoted to handling club: Two
Membership kits received: Four to five weeks after receipt of appli-
cation
How to join: Through applications available at authorized Lalique
retailers or contacting the society
How to redeem certificates: At an authorized Lalique retailer

As an artist, René Lalique (1860-1945) was the quintessential master of the decorative arts during the Art Nouveau and Art Deco periods. A prolific jewelry designer who was constantly searching for new mediums, Lalique experimented by incorporating glass into his designs. His jewelry was favored by members of the European elite, including celebrated actress Sarah Bernhardt.

Art historians describe René's designs as deft application of stylized, natural motifs, a renowned mastery of line, characterized by innovative use of materials, and delicate sense of proportion. By using the cire perdue (lost wax) method traditionally used in metal work for glass design, he created the distinctive frosted and mottled surface associated today with Lalique crystal.

At age 37, Lalique received the Legion d'Honneur for his artistic achievements — the highest civilian award presented by the French government. Lalique also designed perfume bottles for top parfumier François Coty, an art area that the company has moved back into with the recent launch of its own perfume and bottle designed by granddaughter, Marie-Claude Lalique.

Throughout the company's history, Lalique crystal has been commissioned for many innovative projects, including decorative accessories, fountains, furniture, doors, chandeliers, and even automobile hood ornaments. René's legacy continues in the accomplished art of his son, Marc, and granddaughter.

With the introduction of the Society, Lalique collectors have access to a wealth of information about this distinctive and evolving art form. The award-winning members' magazine features lavish color articles about the history of past and present designs, decorating,

Director Susan Stashkevetch

Special Feature

A summer 1993 auction of Lalique art set a record for a Marie-Claude Lalique design, $36,300, for an "Anemones" screen. This type of market for Lalique designs puts Lalique Society issues in rarefied company.

"Lily of the Valley" perfume bottle — 1991

individual collections, and letters from members. A letter from Marie-Claude in each issue gives her thoughts about Lalique activities. Details on annual Lalique auctions, museum events, and annual tours round out the coverage.

As members of the Lalique Society, collectors share the excitement of creation as this distinguished company continues to build upon its rich heritage.

> The next annual Lalique Society tour to France will be in 1994.

Lalique Society of America

Membership Gifts

Items	Years Available	Original Value	Current Value
En homage à mon grand père, embossed print (new members)	1989-now	$30-$40	$40
Lalique Note Cards (renewals)	1991-now	$10	$10
La Parfum Lalique	1992-now	n/a	n/a

Members-Only Items

Items	Issued	Issue Price	Current Value
Degas, box[1]	1989	$295	$650
Hestia, medallion[2]	1990	$295	$450
Lily of the Valley, perfume bottle[3]	1991	$275	$375
La Patineuse, medallion on base[4]	1992	$325	$360
Enchantment, lovebirds figurine[5]	1993	$395	$395

Certificates expired: [1]*April 30, 1990;* [2]*April 30, 1991;* [3]*May 1, 1992;* [4]*April 30, 1993;* [5]*June 1, 1994*

Left, "La Patineuse" crystal medallion on base, 1992; right, "Enchantment," 1993

Lawton
Collectors Guild

P.O. Box 969
Turlock, CA 95381
Secretary, Linda Smith
(209) 632-3655
Fax: (209) 632-6788

Featured collectible: Original artist dolls by artist Wendy Lawton
Benefits: Annual set of postcards (78 issued since 1986), redemption card to purchase members-only doll, quarterly newsletter, advance notice of special offers and artist appearances, membership card, exclusive members-only contests, annual conventions
Year club founded: 1989
Sponsored by: Lawton Doll Company
Membership size: About 2,000
Club publication: *Lawton Collectors Guild*, four-page, two-color, with "Wants and Wishes" column, "Reflections" from the artist, letters from readers, new doll photos
Factory tours: During annual conventions
Annual dues: $15   **Renewals:** $7.50
Club year ends: Dec. 31
Membership kits received: Four to six weeks after joining
How to join: By picking up membership forms at an authorized Lawton Doll Company retailer, or by contacting the Guild directly
How to redeem certificates: At an authorized Lawton Doll Company retailer

"Little Boy Blue" appears on a Lawton postcard

"I've loved dolls since before I could talk," says Wendy Lawton, artist and founder of the Lawton Doll Company. "Perhaps because a doll is a reflection of our human form, it has a powerful appeal."

That appeal has reached collectors across the country. Nowhere is that more apparent than in the eight award nominations Lawton Doll Company received for its 1993 line alone. Four of the company's dolls were nominated for *Doll Reader*'s Doll of the Year award. An additional four nominations were received in *Dolls* magazine's Award of Excellence program. With seven dolls nominated, the 1993 line was Lawton's most acclaimed collection to date.

But acceptance doesn't come in accolades alone. The Lawton Collectors Guild, aimed at fans of Lawton dolls, has grown to about 2,000 members. These collectors not only enjoy collecting dolls but also postcards of the dolls, which have become an integral part of their collections. Lawton has issued 78 different postcards since 1986.

Members also enjoy participating in club-sponsored contests, such as 1993's "My Favorite Doll" contest, in which members were asked to describe their favorite doll. For members wishing to buy or sell Lawton dolls, the quarterly newsletter, called *Lawton Collectors Guild*, runs such want ads twice a year.

In the last year, Wendy has made numerous appearances — all announced in advance in the newsletter — at such events as the Dolly Dears Show in Birmingham, Ala.; Toy Village's annual Garden Party in Lansing, Mich.; and the Collectors United Annual Gathering in Atlanta, which drew more than 800 collectors.

The Lawton Doll Company uses dolls to illustrate the human experience, from beloved literature to customs and celebrations the world over.

Lawton Collectors Guild

Members-Only Pieces

Dolls	Years Available	Original Value	Current Value
Baa Baa Black Sheep, ed. 1,003	1989	$395	$700-$1,200
Lavender Blue, ed. 781	1990	$395	$495-$590
To Market, to Market, ed. 683	1991	$495	$495-$575
Little Boy Blue, ed. 510	1992	$395	$395-$440
The Lawton Logo Doll	1993	$350	$350

Ron Lee's Greatest Clown Collector's Club

2180 Agate Court
Simi Valley, CA 93065
Director, Sheila Cohen
(805) 520-8474
Fax: (805) 520-8472

Featured collectible: Fine white metal or pewter figurines with 24-karat gold plating and hand painting (hand-cut onyx bases with gold beading)

Benefits: Clown sculpture gift ($65 value), coupons for members-only purchases, updates on personal appearance schedule, club certificate signed by Ron Lee, advance notice of new releases in color, club membership card, special novelty items, subscription to newsletter (approximately quarterly)

Year club founded: 1987

Sponsored by: Ron Lee's World of Clowns, founded in 1976

Membership size: 30,000 U.S.; 3,000 Japan; 500 Canada; 300-plus Europe

Local chapters available: One

Club publication: *Collectible News From Ron Lee* (single-page letter from the artist with original art)

Factory tours: Free guided tours by appointment only; reservations requested for all sizes, all groups. Ron Lee Gallery and Collector's Club on premises; 20,000 sq. ft. facility

Annual dues: $28.50   **Renewals:** $28.50

Club year ends: Annual anniversary

No. of staff devoted to handling club: Three

Membership kits received: Four to six weeks after application submitted

How to join: Every collectible sold includes an application that should be mailed to the address above

Membership gifts and members-only pieces

Hand cast, hand finished, hand painted, and individually hand wrapped. Ron Lee's clown creations receive devoted care and attention to detail from the beginning of production to the end of the process. And that attention is what attracts collectors to this club.

Ron Lee was the first to capture a two-dimensional image from an animation cel and translate it into a three-dimensional sculpture. His work, commissioned from such well-known names as The Walt Disney Company, Warner Bros. and Hanna-Barbera Productions Inc., brings to life figures and images like never before.

Using 120 talented artisans. Lee creates one of the few lines of "Made in America" collectibles, insisting on high quality while creating his whimsical and fanciful characters completely by hand, not mechanically.

Working to keep Ron Lee collectors informed of the artist's activities, new sculpture introductions and collector information, the club was established to aid the collector and enhance enjoyment of Ron Lee's limited editions and specially crafted collectibles.

The quarterly newsletter, *Collectible News from Ron Lee*, offers information about Ron, his techniques, new sculptures, awards, and personal thoughts from the artist. As flamboyant as the characters he depicts, Ron travels more than 50 times a year to keep in close contact with his collectors. Members have the first available information on his travels.

Though not involved with research on the secondary market, the club will locate resources and information for club members, assisting them in any way possible.

Collectors who are drawn by the imagination of clowns, the adventures of the circus, and the humor of cartoon characters will find a place in this club.

"Hasn't humor and fun been the guideline for my whole life?" asks Ron Lee. " When have I not gone for the punch line, to make someone laugh,

Artist Ron Lee

"I wanted to recreate these wonderful characters so I could share them with my children, fans . . . and my collectors," says Ron Lee.

to see a happy smile, to entertain, and who do you know more dedicated to that concept than the high-spirited energetic clown?

"As we sit in the audience, captivated, haven't we all wondered about what's behind the garish make-up and the bright-colored costumes? Haven't we wondered what clowns feel? I guess there's no better reflection of myself: the entertainer, the clown, the sculptor," says Lee.

Special Features

Materials and guidelines are available for forming local chapters.

Ron Lee's Greatest Clown Collector's Club

Membership Gifts

Figurines	Years Available	Original Value	Current Value
Hooping it Up	1987-88	$65	$65
Pudge	1988-present	$65	$65
Pals	1989	$65	$65
Potsie	1990	$65	$65
Hi! Ya!	1991	$65	$65
Bashful Beau	1992-93	$65	$65
Little Mate	1993-94	$65	$65

Members-Only Pieces

Figurines	Issued	Issue Price	Current Value
Doggin' Along	1987	$65.00	$90-$140
Midsummer's Dream	1988	$65.00	$120-$175
Pub Mirror	1988	$42.50	$43
Peek-a-Boo Charlie	1989	$65.00	$75-$110
Get the Message	1989	$65.00	$75-$100
Puppy Love Snowdome	1989	$25.00	$25
Let it Snow Snowdome	1989	$52.50	$53
Anywhere Snowdome	1989	$26.50	$27
Me Too! Snowdome	1989	$26.50	$27
I'm So Pretty	1990	$65.00	$65-$90
Christmas Ornament	1990	$49.50	$50
It's for You	1991	$65.00	$65-$90
Apron	1991	$65.00	$65
Doll (Hobo Joe Flowers)	1991	$32.50	$33
Doll (Hobo Joe Hiking)	1991	$32.50	$33
It's Time for Ron Lee	1992	$67.50	$68

Leroy's World Collector Society

690 N.E. 13th Street
Ft. Lauderdale, FL 33304-1110
Director, Pat Owen
(800) 327-2297
Fax: (305) 462-2317

Featured collectible: Black art figurines of cold cast stoneware
Benefits: Members receive all catalogs and price lists as they become available, periodic newsletters, members-only prices on pieces
Year club founded: 1991
Sponsored by: Viking Import House Inc., founded in 1948
Club publication: *Leroy's World Newsletter* (various formats)
Factory tours: The Naturecraft Ltd. factory, located in Congleton, Cheshire, England, is open daily from 9 a.m. to 5 p.m.
Annual dues: $10   **Renewals:** $10
Club year ends: One year after joining
No. of staff devoted to handling club: One
Also sponsors: Memory Lane Collector's Society
Membership kits received: Two weeks after application submitted
How to join: Applications available at authorized Leroy's World dealers, or by calling club headquarters
How to redeem certificates: At an authorized dealer

Leroy's World figurines show children in humorous situations

Charter member plaque

Collectors in 22 countries have been keeping an eye out for Leroy for 18 years now — and for good reason. Originated by Peter Tomlins, Leroy is a mischievous little black boy who just can't seem to behave himself.

The humorous figurines, made of cold cast stoneware, capture Leroy in the middle of a variety of pranks, and no one is safe — not Mom, not Dad, not the family pet, not even Santa Claus.

Tomlins says the images were drawn partly from his own childhood and partly from the best-remembered pranks of his friends. "You can't imagine how much fun it is to translate all these antics into that rascal Leroy," he says with a mischievous twinkle of his own in his eye.

Promoting the growing line of Leroy figurines and encouraging fellowship among club members, the Leroy's World Collectors Society distributes a periodic newsletter that keeps up with the free-for-all spirit of Leroy. Sometimes a slick black-and-white newsletter, sometimes simply a letter accompanied by various brochures, *Leroy's World Newsletter* informs members of new releases and retirements and provides them with a question and answer forum to get to know the pieces and their creator a little better.

Mandy Thomas, the chief painter from Naturecraft, where the figurines are produced in England, has appeared at two recent collectibles shows, and Tomlins is expected to make appearances at future collectibles shows.

The club also will announce soon the first piece that is being created exclusively for club members.

In the meantime, drop by the factory in merry ole England. "We are delighted to receive anybody in our factory showroom," Tomlins says. "Everyone is given a warm welcome."

> Since childhood mischief is universal, Tomlins has a backlog of inspirations he calls up for his Leroy figurines.

Leroy's World Collector Society

Membership Gifts

	Years Available	Original Value	Current Value
Leroy Plaque	1991-92	$10	$10

Lilliput Lane Collectors' Club

9052 Old Annapolis Road
Columbia, MD 21045
Director, Dawn Wylie
(410) 964-2043
Fax: (410) 964-5673

Featured collectible: Miniature cottages made of amorphite
Benefits: Free cottage (different each year), opportunity to buy members-only editions, membership card, quarterly club magazine, accessories catalog, full collection catalog, invitations to special events, entry to Lilliput Lane Visitor Centre, exclusive member offers, entry in club competitions
Year club founded: 1986, in England
Sponsored by: Lilliput Inc. (formerly Gift Link Inc.)
Membership size: 60,000 worldwide
Local chapters available: Local chapters are in the process of being formed
Club publication: *Gulliver's World* (lavish full-color quarterly magazine with 24 pages)
Factory tours: Arrangements to visit the studio in Penrith, England, can be made by contacting the Collectors' Club in Maryland
Annual dues: $30; 2 years: $50   **Renewals:** $30
Extras: *Gulliver's World* binder, $15.95; *Cottages of Lilliput Lane* book, $39.95 standard, $79 limited edition; prints (four), $35; polo shirt, $24.95; table mats $29.95 (six); coasters (six), $14.95
Club year ends: April 30
No. of staff devoted to handling club: Three
Membership kits received: Four to six weeks after application submitted
How to join: Applications at authorized dealers, gift memberships, and brochures in every product box
How to redeem certificates: At an authorized Lilliput Lane dealer

Want to feel big? Take a look at the lovely cottages of Lilliput Lane. Each miniature figure is cloaked in exquisite detail and is hand painted based on an actual cottage, giving you a giant's view of a Lilliputian world.

Now, want to feel small? The Lilliput Lane Collectors' Club serves 60,000 members worldwide. Either way you look at it, the Lilliput Lane Collectors' Club offers members Gulliver-sized opportunities.

From free cottages to club-sponsored trips to merry old England, where you can find the Lilliput studios, this club offers the best of all worlds.

Lilliput Lane Limited was founded in September 1982 by David J. Tate with six other family members and friends. From the company's modest beginnings in an old, run-down barn, Lilliput Lane has evolved into a leader in the cottage collectibles market.

As the founder and technical director, Tate established high standards and new manufacturing techniques essential for the vernacular reproductions of extremely detailed sculptures. David has spent years researching the architecture of England and has a collection of reference books and thousands of photographs that he utilizes for his designs. He and his team of skilled artists and technicians work on new pieces for months at a time to ensure that all the historical features are accurately portrayed in the finest detail.

In recognition of his accomplishments, David was invested as an M.B.E. (Member of the Order of the British Empire) by Her Majesty Queen Elizabeth II of England in the 1988 New Years Honors List, an award for which he gives credit to everyone in the company.

Collectors have been delighted with the Lilliput Lane Collection's selection of English, Scottish, Irish, German, Dutch, and French cottages, as well as the Blaise Hamlet Village Collection and the American Landmarks Series.

Members of the Lilliput Lane Collectors' Club receive the quarterly magazine, *Gulliver's World*, a

Founder
David Tate

Special Features

Informal referral of retailers available to club members searching for a particular piece.

high-quality, full-color publication filled with information about new cottages, special events, competitions, special offers and more. Detailed articles reveal the fascinating history behind the original buildings that inspired the Lilliput Lane cottages.

Members also receive invitations to special events and member evenings, held throughout the year. The largest and most important event is the two-day Lilliput Lane Collectors Fair, held annually at a different stately home in Britain. The event attracted 12,000 members and fellow enthusiasts in 1992.

The Lilliput Lane Visitor Centre in Penrith, open exclusively to members, their families and friends, offers a behind-the-scenes tour, where you can meet the staff and witness the intricate processes involved in creating these cottages. Rose Cottage, also at the Visitor Centre, houses a museum of Lilliput Lane sculptures and a shop selling the entire current range of cottages.

It's a world even Gulliver couldn't have dreamed up.

Each miniature figure is cloaked in exquisite detail and is hand painted based on an actual cottage, giving you a giant's view of a Lilliputian world.

Members-only cottage, "Forget-Me-Not" 1992-93

Lilliput Lane Collectors' Club

Membership Gifts

Cottages	Years Available	Original Value	Current Value
Pack Horse Bridge	1986-87	free	$575-$1,000
Little Lost Dog	1987-88	free	$300-$525
Wishing Well	1988-89	free	$145-$195
Dovecot	1989-90	free	$125-$200
Cosy Corner	1990-91	free	$100-$150
Puddlebrook	1991-92	free	$85-$125
Pussy Willow	1992-93	free	$30
The Spinney	1993-94	free	$30
Petticoat Cottage	1994-95	free	n/a

Members-Only Pieces

Cottages	Issued	Issue Price	Current Value
Crendon Manor, ed. 1,500	1986-87	$285.00	$875-$1,000
Yew Tree Farm	1988-89	$160.00	$250-$500
Wenlock Rise	1989-90	$175.00	$200-$400
Lavender Cottage	1990-91	$50.00	$165-$200
Bridle Way	1990-91	$100.00	$150-$270
Gardeners Cottage	1991-92	$120.00	$150-$200
Wren Cottage	1991	$13.95	$150-$200
Forget-Me-Not	1992-93	$130.00	$130
Heaven Lea Cottage	1993-94	$165.00	$165
Curlew Cottage (w/gift membership)	1993	$18.95	$40.00
Woodman's Retreat	1994-95	n/a	n/a

"Pussy Willow" membership gift

Members may purchase "Curlew Cottage" after getting a friend to join

Little Cheesers Collectors' Club

908 Niagara Falls Blvd.
North Tonawanda, NY 14120-2060
Director, Patrick Wong
(800) 724-2950
Fax: (416) 851-6669

Featured collectible: Figurines and musical pieces featuring cold cast resin mice
Benefits: Yearly free membership piece, minimum of two newsletters per year, club binder, item checklist, button
Year club founded: 1993
Sponsored by: Ganz, founded in 1950
Club publication: *The Cheeserville Gazette* (four-color, eight-page bi-annual newsletter)
Annual dues: $25   **Renewals:** $25
Club year ends: One year from joining
No. of staff devoted to handling club: Three
Also sponsors: Plans to start Pigsville, Cowtown in 1994-95 (tentative)
Membership kits received: Six to eight weeks after application submitted
How to join: Applications at authorized Little Cheesers dealers, at trade shows, or by phone
How to redeem certificates: At preferred Little Cheesers dealers

Little Cheesers Collectors' Club
Membership Gifts

Figurines	Available	Original Value	Current Value
Charter Member	1993	$25	$25

Say "cheese"!

The Little Cheesers, those lovable little mice with their oversized ears, pudgy hands and softly rounded snouts that give way to a grin, are bringing smiles to collectors' faces.

And now the Little Cheesers Collectors' Club should make collectors of these pieces even happier.

Designed to enhance the collectibility of Little Cheesers figurines and musical pieces, the Club provides members with history and little-known facts about the pieces; introduces new items and announces retired ones; and works to develop a solid and close relationship between collectors, dealers, and the producer of the pieces.

Little Cheesers figurines are available in four themes: Christmas, picnic, wedding, and the new Springtime line. Pieces include ornaments, picture frames, music and trinket boxes, and miniature accessories.

These affordable collectibles are the creation of Christine Thammavongsa, who was inspired by the global concern for the ecology.

"I wanted to make something that could relate to a lot of things," she says. "A place that would parallel human worlds, but with not as harsh a reality — more imaginary and dreamlike. A pleasant, warm, heartfelt way to express concerns for the environment, the closeness of family, and the way the group bands together."

As Little Cheesers opens the doors to its charter members, that closeness of banding together will now extend to collectors, too.

Artist Christine Thammavongsa

Special Features

• A toll-free number is available to members seeking answers to their questions about Little Cheesers pieces.

•Club members are given advance notice of special signings and appearances by the artist.

Only Charter Year members will receive Little Cheesers' first gift

Lladró
Collectors Society

43 W. 57th Street
New York, NY 10019-3498
Director, Hugh R. Robinson
(201) 807-0018
Fax: (201) 807-1168

Featured collectible: Lladró figurines made of porcelain
Benefits: Subscription to quarterly magazine and *Lladró Antique News*; a bas-relief porcelain plaque featuring the image of Don Quixote and bearing the signatures of the Lladró brothers; opportunity to purchase members-only figurines; complimentary gifts such as the Winter Bell (1994 gift to new and renewing members), part of the Four Seasons Bell series, and a binder for the magazines
Year club founded: 1985
Sponsored by: Lladró USA
Membership size: 105,000
Local chapters available: At press time, the local chapter program was being reorganized
Club publication: *Expressions* (32-page, four-color quarterly magazine)
Factory tours: Tours of the factory in Valencia, Spain, can be arranged by contacting the Lladró Collectors Society
Annual dues: $35   **Renewals:** $27.50
Extras: Binder for storing issues of *Expressions*; "Clay, Colour & Fire" video, $19.50 VHS; LCS Address Book, $20; Collectibles Register, $25; "Magic World of Porcelain" book, $55
Club year ends: December 31
No. of staff devoted to handling club: Fifteen
Membership kits received: Six weeks after application submitted
How to join: Applications available at authorized dealers. Special programs and incentives are run on a periodic basis
How to redeem certificates: At an authorized Lladró dealer

Lladró benefits

Long regarded as the finest examples of porcelain artistry throughout the world, Lladró figurines are a tradition for collectors everywhere. These beautifully crafted creations have been given as gifts to heads of states and are in numerous museums and private collections across the globe. Their exquisite detailing has created a universal appeal of unmatched proportions.

Director Hugh R. Robinson

Each figurine is crafted by hand under the direction of the three Lladró brothers, Juan, Jose, and Vincente, in Valencia, Spain. The care put into creating each piece continues once the piece finds a home, often handed down as a family heirloom for the next generation to enjoy.

The Lladró Collectors Society was formed in 1985 to offer increased enjoyment of Lladró porcelains by providing valuable insights into the creation of figurines and to give Society members the means of sharing their enthusiasm for these exceptional works.

"The most important benefit of the Lladró Collectors Society for most members is the special figurine that is issued each year," says Society Director Hugh Robinson. "Since these are not available to the public and since they tend to appreciate rapidly in value, one can readily see why they are so coveted. Only enough of each special figurine is created to supply those members who redeem their certificates."

Society members are the first to see each new creation and the first to know which figurines will be retired, never to be made by Lladró again. They also are given exclusive opportunities to acquire figurines which are never offered to the general public.

Members-only tours of Spain are sponsored each year by the Society, and of course the highlight of each trip is the guided tour of the Lladró factory in Valencia, which includes a farewell dinner with a member of the Lladró family. However, the Lladró brothers also schedule personal appearance tours of the United States, in which they meet and greet many enthusiastic fans.

Special Features

• Collectors Information Exchange is a buy/sell service that puts members in contact with each other, but is not involved in the sale.

• Collectors Lounge available for members who visit the facility on 57th Street in New York.

"One senses their excitement at being able to add signed porcelains to their personal collections whether their intention is its future value on the secondary market or its very special value as a family heirloom," Robinson says.

One of the benefits of joining the LCS is the subscription to the club's exclusive *Expressions* magazine, which is now published in three languages and reaches members in North America, Europe, and Asia. Each issue details the fascinating process that goes into creating a particular piece, complete with informative photos showing the work in progress. In addition to New Figurine and Special Events sections, each issue includes a Museum department, which keeps members abreast of upcoming activities and special exhibits at the Lladró Museum and Galleries in New York City.

Periodic newsletters, which also are sent to all LCS members, point out interesting opportunities for collectors. For instance, the 1993 piece, "Jester's Serenade," was limited to just 3,000 figurines worldwide at a suggested retail price of $1,995. Members were given the opportunity to reserve the entire edition by a given date, thereby ensuring that the figurine would never be available to the general public. Through its publications, the Society also regularly reports on secondary market activity, including current prices.

Collectors' love for this art is apparent in a 1991 survey of Lladró Collectors Society members. According to its findings, most members own up to twenty figurines, while many members own more than forty pieces. All of those surveyed said they collected Lladró figurines because of their beauty, and most of the members said they were collectors before they joined the Society.

Obviously, the love the Lladró brothers put into their work has found its way into the Collectors Society. As Mercedes Manrique said in the local chapter newsletter, *Expressly Yours*, "Lladró is love expressed through figurines, through collecting, and by becoming friends."

"Collectors truly appreciate the Lladró brothers for their aesthetic sensitivity and artistic vision. They recognize that it is this vision and insight that is translated so beautifully into the figurines they treasure and collect. No wonder these wonderful porcelains are recognized and admired all over the world as Lladró art."

— Society Director Hugh R. Robinson

"Little Traveler" 1986

**Top valued
*"Little Pals" 1985***

"My Buddy" 1989

Lladró Members-Only Sculptures

"Summer Stroll" 1991

Lladró Collectors Society

Membership Gifts

Renewal Gift Item	Years Available	Original Value	Current Value
Lladró Collectors Register	1986	$10	$25.00
Lladró Address Book	1987	$10	$20.00
All Occasion Greeting Cards	1988	$10	$10.50
LCS Tote Bag	1989	$10	$12.50
LCS Umbrella	1990	$15	$15.00
Spring Bell (1st in 4 bell series)	1991	$35	$45.00-$75.00
Summer Bell (2nd in 4 bell series)	1992	$35	$40.00-$60.00
Autumn Bell (3rd in 4 bell series)	1993	$35	$35.00-$50.00
Winter Bell (4th in 4 bell series)	1994	$35	$35.00

(Note: Upon joining, new members receive a New Member Kit that contains the LCS membership plaque and an Expressions binder. In addition, one bell from the Four Seasons Bell series was included in the kits for the years indicated.)

Members-Only Pieces

Figurine	Issued	Issue Price	Current Value
Little Pals[1]	1985	$95	$3,500-$4,100
Little Traveller[2]	1986	$95	$1,200-$1,700
Spring Bouquets[3]	1987	$125	$700-$1,200
School Days[4]	1988	$125	$425-$800
Flower Song[5] (special museum commemorative)	1988	$175	$600-$750
My Buddy[6]	1989	$145	$300-$600
Can I Play?[7]	1990	$150	$300-$565
Summer Stroll[8]	1991	$195	$300-$500
Picture Perfect[9] (special 5-year anniversary)	1991	$350	$440-$750
All Aboard[10]	1992	$165	$315-$400
Best Friend[11]	1993	$195	$195

Dates of Eligibility (date of retirement): [1]Jan. 1, 1985 - Dec. 31, 1985 (April 30, 1986); [2]Jan. 1, 1986 - Dec. 31, 1986 (April 30, 1987); [3]Jan 1, 1987 - Dec. 31, 1987 (April 30, 1988); [4]Jan 1, 1988 - Dec. 31, 1988 (April 30, 1989); [5]Jan. 1, 1988 - June 30, 1989 (Sept. 30, 1989); [6]Jan. 1, 1989 - Dec. 31, 1989 (April 30, 1990); [7]Jan. 1, 1990 - Dec. 31, 1990 (April 30, 1991); [8]Jan. 1, 1991 - Dec. 31, 1991 (June 30, 1992); [9]Jan. 1, 1990 - Dec. 31, 1990 (Dec. 31, 1991); [10]Jan. 1, 1992 - Dec. 31, 1992 (June 30, 1993); [11]Jan. 1, 1993 - Dec. 31, 1993 (June 30, 1994)

"Picture Perfect" 1991

Lladró Members-Only Sculptures, 1991-1993

"All Aboard" 1992

"Best Friend" 1993

Madame Alexander Doll Club

P.O. Box 330
Mundelein, IL 60060-0330
President, Tanya McWhorter
(512) 241-3105

Featured collectible: Original artist dolls by Madame Alexander
Benefits: Membership card, exclusive members-only offerings of limited edition Madame Alexander dolls, quarterly newsletters, club pin, and an annual convention
Year club founded: 1961 (named Madame Alexander Fan Club until December 1985)
Sponsored by: No sponsor; collector run, a not-for-profit group assisted by the Alexander Doll Company
Membership size: 14,000
Club publication: *The Review*, full color quarterly newsletter, and six *Shoppers* (listings for dolls wanted and for sale by members)
Annual dues: $10 ($20 outside the U.S.)   **Renewals:** $20
Extras: Annual Madame Alexander Doll catalog, $7.50
Club year ends: One year after joining
Membership kits received: Six to eight weeks after joining
How to join: By mailing in the membership form boxed with each Madame Alexander doll
How to receive members-only dolls: Return information letter order form to club headquarters

Left, 1985 "Mary, Mary" convention doll, and right, 1987 "Cowboy" convention doll

Played with by little girls since the 1920s, Madame Alexander dolls continue to delight collectors of all ages today. Before her death in 1990 at the age of 95, the beloved Madame Alexander created hundreds of doll subjects. Much honored around the world for her generosity and charm, she was treated like a queen by her fans.

During her 47 years with the Manhattan-based Alexander Doll Company, Madame Alexander donated collections to the Brooklyn Children's Museum, the Museum of the City of New York, the Smithsonian Institute, and many others throughout the United States and in India.

The club that bears her name began modestly in November 1961 as a correspondence group with about 24 members. Today, the Madame Alexander Doll Club boasts 14,000 dedicated members.

The group originally circulated a typed letter with information about Madame Alexander dolls and individual collectors. In the early years, no dues were charged and membership was restricted to a pre-set amount, closing for the year when that number was reached.

In 1976, the club gave an unusual formula for pricing a doll to be sold on the secondary market: "Take the actual retail price, rounded off (example, $40), add the number of years from the time of purchase (1980 to 1991 = 11 years), $40 + 11 = $51. This would be the price to charge for an ordinary doll. If the doll were exceptionally mint or rare, double the price ($50 x 2 = $100)."

Dues were $6 in 1980, then jumped to $15 in 1982 to cover professional printing of the newsletter and addition of a separate monthly Shopper for member ads.

The group's first convention occurred in 1983 in Merrillville, Ind., with 239 members present, including actress-collector Jane Withers, who made a surprise appearance. The club began a service award at the first convention and has continued it since then to honor outstanding members. A club pin was introduced mid-year.

To members' delight, Madame Alexander attend-

Madame Alexander holds the "Tanya" doll (photo courtesy Tanya Inc.)

Special Feature

Started as a correspondence club, the Madame Alexander Doll Club embodies the essence of today's clubs with its emphasis on sharing information and fun.

ed her first club convention in 1985. Another special event occurred when a Fan Club Lunch was held at Walt Disney World in November with Madame as guest of honor. The club became a not-for-profit organization in December 1985 and replaced the "Fan" with "Doll" in its name. Membership stood at 1,715.

Madame Alexander sold the Alexander Doll

Madame Alexander Doll Club
Membership Gifts

Convention Souvenir Dolls	Years Available	Original Value	Current Value
Fairy Godmother outfit (no doll), ed. 239	1983	n/a	$250
Pink Ballerina w/ banner, 8", ed. 350	1984	$28	$250
Mary, Mary, ed. 450	1985	$30	$250
Scarlett, 8", w/ red satin sash	1986	$32	$275
Davey Crockett outfit (no doll)	1987	$35	$150
Flapper (Portrette), 10" in black costume, ed. 550	1988	$40	$200
Briar Rose, 8", (Sleeping Beauty w/ Portrctte head)	1989	$40	$300
Scarlett, Premiere, 8", ed. 291	1990	$42	$200
Riverboat Queen Lena, 8", ed. 825	1990	$42	$350
Queen Charlotte, 10"	1991	$55	$350
Springtime, Premiere, 8", ed. 1,600	1991	$44	$150
Prom Queen, 8"	1992	$48	$250
Wintertime, Premiere, 8"	1992	$44	$150
Diamond Lil, 10"	1993	$65	$350
Homecoming, Premiere, 8"	1993	$46	$125

(*Given as gifts at annual member conventions, Premiere events, and Snowflake Premiere Symposiums, the early dolls were factory originals with club revisions, then later were supplied by the factory with alterations made exclusively for the club.*)

Members-Only Items

Dolls	Issued	Issue Price	Current Value
Cowboy, 8"	1987	$35	$450
Wendy, 8"	1989	$50	$295
Polly Pigtails, 8"	1990	$60	$250
Miss Liberty, 10"	1991	$75	$100
Miss Godey, 8"	1992	$95	$250

Company in early 1988, a few months before her 93rd birthday. The club hosted a gala celebration for her in San Antonio, complete with children's events. Madame enjoyed the children's presence, emphatically saying that her dolls were meant to be played with, not to gather dust on shelves.

In 1989, the new owners agreed to assist the club financially; dues were dropped to $10 and membership forms put in each doll box shipped from the factory. Following this additional exposure, membership quickly climbed to its present high, and continues to grow.

Club events are held throughout the year around the country, with Premieres from February to April, and the national convention in July. For the $150 registration, members take home souvenirs and gifts worth at least three times as much.

With an American icon as its inspiration, the Madame Alexander Doll Club continues to provide its membership the most important ingredients of a successful club: enthusiasm, information, and fun.

Members receive souvenirs and gifts worth about $500 at national conventions.

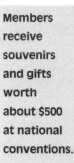

1992 "Miss Godey" members-only doll

1989 "Wendy" members-only doll

1993 "Homecoming" Premier doll

Melody In Motion
Collectors Society

One North Corporate Drive
Riverdale, NJ 07457
Director, Barbara McLaughlin
(201) 616-1660
Fax: (201) 616-1631

Featured collectible: Animated and musical porcelain bisque figurines
Benefits: Free porcelain figurine, subscription to newsletter, membership card and certificate, redemption certificate, members savings coupon, Melody In Motion catalog, personal purchasing record, retired edition summary, Melody In Motion collectors centers list
Year club founded: 1992
Sponsored by: WACO Products Corporation, founded in 1978
Membership size: 6,000-plus U.S.; just beginning in Europe
Club publication: *Melody Notes* quarterly newsletter (two-color, four pages)
Factory tours: Showroom open by appointment only
Annual dues: $27.50 **Renewals:** $27.50
No. of staff devoted to handling club: Twelve
Membership kits received: Three to four weeks after application submitted
How to join: Applications at authorized dealers, via phone, and gift memberships
How to redeem certificates: At an authorized dealer

Assortment of Melody in Motion animated and musical figurines

Billed as "the only porcelain, moving, animated, stereo sound musical collectible," the Melody In Motion figurines have set collectors' hearts to singing. Each figurine is a faithful reproduction of an original sculpture by Seiji Nakane of Japan, who first began working in clay at age 18. Now, more than 35 years later, his unique work has been made even more special with the addition of music and motion.

Sculptor Seiji Nakane

Merging art and technology, each meticulously hand-painted figurine is painstakingly hand-assembled, adjusted, and fitted with gears, cams, motor, amplifier, and speaker. The result is a life-like figurine of movement and song that takes up to four weeks to create.

To give collectors the opportunity to learn more about this fascinating process and the artist who inspired it all, the Melody In Motion Collectors Society was established in 1992.

Members receive a figurine, a personal redemption certificate, members' coupons worth $10 on a future purchase, and more.

The *Melody Notes* newsletter, published quarterly, informs members of new issues, gives advance notice of soon-to-be-retired pieces, and previews exclusive and limited edition introductions. It also provides a useful after-market exchange section where members can advertise and trade retired, limited or exclusive pieces.

Seiji Nakane must constantly deal with the limitations of the mechanics that drive Melody In Motion. His philosophy is to constantly merge the beauty of sculpting with technical achievements.

Melody In Motion Collectors Society

Membership Gifts

Figurines	Years Available	Original Value	Current Value
Willie the Conductor	1992	$35	$35
Charmed Bunnies	1993	$45	$45

Members-Only Pieces

Figurines	Issued	Issue Price	Current Value
Amazing Willie the One Man Band	1992-94	$130	$130

Memory Lane
Collector's Society

690 N.E. 13th Street
Ft. Lauderdale, FL 33304-1110
Director, Pat Owen
(800) 327-2297
Fax: (305) 462-2317

Featured collectible: Miniature cottages made of cold cast stoneware
Benefits: Complimentary cottage, periodic newsletters, catalogs and price lists of cottages, opportunity to buy members-only pieces. Charter year members received their membership cards personally signed by Peter Tomlins, originator of the cottages
Year club founded: 1991
Sponsored by: Viking Import House, Inc., founded in 1948
Membership size: N/A
Local chapters available: None
Club publication: *Memory Lane Newsletter* (periodic, various formats)
Factory tours: Peter Tomlins, owner of Naturecraft and the originator of all Memory Lane Cottages, says, "We are delighted to receive anybody in our factory showrooms. They are always open from 9 a.m. to 5 p.m., and everyone is given a warm welcome." The Naturecraft Studios are situated in Congleton, Cheshire, England
Annual dues: $25   **Renewals:** $25
Club year ends: One year from joining
No. of staff devoted to handling club: One
Also sponsors: Leroy's World Collector Society
Membership kits received: Two weeks after application submitted
How to join: Applications at authorized dealers, or by phone
How to redeem certificates: At an authorized dealer

"Kentish Oast," first members-only piece

Take a walk down Memory Lane with Peter Tomlins and the talented artists who recreate the magic of bygone days in a lovely collection of cottages. Many of the buildings that served as models for the pieces still exist, but the lost buildings have been reproduced from history books and black line drawings.

**Artist
Peter Tomlins**

Unlike most cottages on the market today, the Memory Lane Cottages are glazed and fired after being hand painted. This means the pieces may be delicately handwashed, and that the sun will not fade them.

Tomlins, who originated the Memory Lane Cottages, has a simple philosophy — offer nothing less than the best. He feels fortunate to live in the beautiful English countryside of Cheshire, where he is surrounded by the historic Tudor and Elizabethan cottages he loves.

"It's like a dream come true to be able to spend my life exactly where I want to be and have a career in creating the cottages in miniature for the rest of the world to enjoy," Tomlins says.

The Society was founded in late 1991 to help promote knowledge of the Memory Lane Cottages and the fellowship of its club members. It also serves as a source for information and illustrations on the newest releases and retirements.

> Though relatively new in the United States, the Memory Lane Cottages have been sold in Europe for many years.

Memory Lane Collector's Society

Membership Gifts

Cottages	Years Available	Original Value	Current Value
Fool's Nook	1991-92	$75	$75
Primrose End	1993	$50-$75	$50-$75

Members-Only Pieces

Cottages	Issued	Issue Price	Current Value
Kentish Oast	1992	n/a	n/a

Lee Middleton
Collectors Club

Lee Middleton Original Dolls.

1301 Washington Blvd.
Belpre, Ohio 45714
Director, Gerald Urick
(313) 299-4715
Manager, Mark Putinski
(614) 423-1717

Featured collectible: Artist's original dolls of porcelain and vinyl
Benefits: Soon to open general memberships with club pin, certificate, quarterly newsletter
Year club founded: 1991
Sponsored by: Lee Middleton Original Dolls, founded in 1980
Membership size: 500 charter members (including one member in Germany and one in Canada)
Club publication: *Lee's Dolls Today* (16-page, 8-1/2 by 11 slick quarterly)
Factory tours: Tours arranged, 9 a.m.-3 p.m., Monday-Friday, and Saturdays May through August, call 1-800-223-7479
Annual dues: $35 (charter members paid $150)
Club year ends: December 31
No. of staff devoted to handling club: Three
Membership kits received: Thirty days after application submitted
How to join: General membership applications will be available in doll magazines, at authorized Lee Middleton dealers, or by calling the company at 1-800-843-9572
How to redeem certificates: At an authorized Lee Middleton dealer

Lee Middleton Collectors Club
Membership Gifts

Dolls	Years Available	Original Value	Current Value
Christmas Angel	1991	$150	$150

A look into the face of one of Lee Middleton's dolls is like looking through the eyes of a child. That may be because many of the dolls in her collection, with its emphasis on babies, are designed using actual children as models.

Artist
Lee Middleton

It's that realism that has attracted people to her work over the years. And soon, collectors will be able to participate in general membership of the Lee Middleton Collectors Club.

More than 500 charter members got an early jump on the club in 1991, receiving a certificate of membership, club pin, quarterly newsletter, 1991 catalog, and the 1991 Christmas Angel doll for a $150 charter membership fee.

Each newsletter offers a frank and homey view of Lee's personal developments, the company, and its collectibles. Get a look behind the factory doors and pick up some pointers on doll care and storage, sample some of Lee's earlier pieces, and learn about other collectors, dealers, employees, and upcoming and retiring products.

Her dolls have shown up in *Collector's mart*'s annual survey of best-selling items, and have been nominated for *Doll Reader*'s DOTY award and *Dolls Magazine*'s Award of Excellence. Lee includes a tiny Bible with each of her creations, giving, as she says, "credit where the *real* credit is due."

"Echo"

Special Features

The Middleton doll factory resembles a Victorian doll house and offers 20-minute tours of the doll-making process.

Lee Middleton Original Dolls in Belpre, Ohio, attracts thousands of visitors each year

Myth & Magic Collectors Club

1201 Broadway, Suite 309
New York, NY 10001
Director, Susan Miller
(212) 679-7644
Fax: (212) 532-0839

Featured collectible: Fantasy figurines of wizards, dragons, and the Arthurian legend
Benefits: Free gift for joining ($40 value), subscription to club newsletter, complete catalog of the Myth & Magic Collection, opportunity to purchase two members-only pieces through dealer, opportunity to travel to England for Club convention
Year club founded: 1989, in England; 1990, in U.S.
Sponsored by: Fantasy Creations, The Tudor Mint, founded in 1966
Membership size: 3,000, U.S.; 20,000, throughout the world, including U.K. and Canada
Club publication: *The Methtintdour Times* (12-page, full-color, semi-annual newsletter)
Factory tours: Tour arranged in conjunction with annual convention in England
Annual dues: $37.50   **Renewals:** $37.50
Club year ends: June 30
No. of staff devoted to handling club: Two
Membership kits received: Four weeks after application submitted
How to join: Applications at authorized dealers, or in box of each Myth & Magic figurine
How to redeem certificates: At an authorized Myth & Magic dealer

"The Mystical Encounter"

In 1989, the Tudor Mint began its Myth & Magic Collection of fantasy figurines, a delightfully mystical world of wizards, dragons, and anything Arthurian.

After establishing itself in England, the Myth & Magic Collectors Club branched out to the United States in 1990, bringing together people whose common interest is a fascination with the mysterious world of these legends of days gone by.

You may scratch your head at the name of the

Roger Gibbons,
Head Mold
Maker

semi-annual newsletter, the *Methtintdour Times*, but it's simply an anagram for The Tudor Mint. Inside it you'll find Club news, views, illustrations, a serialized fantasy tale, as well as letters, special competitions, and prize drawings.

It's the kind of club that legends are made of.

"The Dragon of
Methtintdour"

Sharon Riley,
Chief Designer

Myth & Magic Collectors Club

Membership Gifts

Figurines	Years Available	Original Value	Current Value
Jovial Wizard, 800 ed.	1990-91	$30.00	$60
Dragon of Destiny, 1,500 ed.	1991-92	$35.00	$50
Dragon of Methtintdour, 3,000 ed.	1993-94	$37.50	$38

Members-Only Pieces

Figurines	Issued	Issue Price	Current Value
Well of Aspirations	1991-92	$95.00	$180
Playmates	1991-92	$40.00	$60
Enchanted Pool	1992-93	$95.00	$120
Friends	1992-93	$45.00	$45
Mystical Encounter	1993-94	$45.00	$45

P. Buckley Moss Society

601 Shenandoah Village Dr.
Waynesboro, VA 22980
Administrator, Mary Ann Guerrieri
(703) 943-5678
Fax: (703) 949-8408

Featured collectible: Pat Buckley Moss' distinctive artwork of Amish and Mennonite subjects, landscapes, and other subjects
Benefits: Pewter geese pin designed by Pat and manufactured by Kirk Stieff Pewter, binder, membership certificate and card, three newsletters per year, opportunity to purchase members-only prints. Renewing members receive a jewelry-quality porcelain pin depicting one of the artist's works. Charter members' first renewal gift was a pewter wreath to accompany the pin
Year club founded: 1987
Membership size: 14,500, U.S.; 40, Canada; and members in Australia, England, Israel, and Japan
Local chapters available: 50, independently organized
Club publication: *Sentinel* (12 pages on recycled paper, three times each year)
Annual dues: $25   **Renewals:** $25
Extras: Members-only print available each year for $45-$50
No. of staff devoted to handling club: Three
Membership kits received: Two to four weeks after application submitted
How to join: Applications at authorized P. Buckley Moss dealers
How to redeem certificates: At an authorized P. Buckley Moss dealer

1992 "Winter's Friend" renewal pin

Having lived in Virginia's Shenandoah Valley for more than 20 years, artist Pat Buckley Moss has been greatly influenced by the Amish and Mennonite life, sharing their respect of family, land and animals.

That quiet and warm way of life is captured in her artwork, which blends realism with the abstract, a style that collectors have taken to their hearts.

But the warmth of Pat Buckley Moss doesn't find its sole release through her eye-catching artwork. No, that warmth also extends to her devotion to charitable endeavors, primarily those benefiting learning disabled children and other at-risk young people.

Dealing with her own dyslexia and having to cope with the frustrations of its ensuing problems throughout her school days, Pat takes a personal stance when it comes to the future of children. That's why she continually donates prints, as well as original art pieces, to specific children's charities, which has helped raise hundreds of thousands of dollars for the health, welfare and education of children.

Now, through the P. Buckley Moss Society, Pat has been able to reach even more collectors, both those attracted to her art and those driven by her causes.

"The Society, its chapters, and its multitude of dedicated members have made it

Artist Pat Buckley Moss

P. Buckley Moss Museum in Waynesboro, Virginia

possible for us to help many children with learning differences and also numerous other public causes," Pat says. "Every day, I am conscious and appreciative of this great support in our efforts to help those in need."

The Moss Portfolio has sponsored nine conventions from 1988 to 1993. Pat also appears at numerous dealer shows annually, including four a year at the P. Buckley Moss Museum and the Barn, her home in Waynesboro, Va.

In addition, the society has sponsored nine trips, which were open to all members. These comprised three to Montreal, three to Europe, a Caribbean cruise, a fall New England cruise, and a bus tour of Virginia.

The *Sentinel*, the newsletter which goes to all members, is published three times a year, informing members of various society activities and Pat's itinerary. It also provides a personal message from the artist and a Collectors' Corner full of ads for those wishing to buy or sell Moss art.

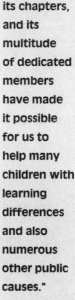

"The Society, its chapters, and its multitude of dedicated members have made it possible for us to help many children with learning differences and also numerous other public causes."

— Pat Buckley Moss

1991 "Timeless Treasures" print

P. Buckley Moss Society

Membership Gifts

Pins	Years Available	Membership Size	Current Value
Wreath surround for pewter pin	1988	3,810	$25
Mary with the Lambs, porcelain	1989	6,000	$125-$200
The Newborn, porcelain	1990	8,000	$100-$150
Chorus Line, porcelain	1991	10,000	$75-$125
Winter's Friend, porcelain	1992	13,000	$75-$125
Friendship, porcelain	1993	14,000	$25

Members-Only Pieces

Prints	Issued	Issue Price	Current Value
Winter's Friend, ed. 2,400	1987	$45	$200
Arm in Arm, ed. 4,100	1988	$45	$100
Family Heritage, ed. 6,000	1989	$45	$100
The Generations, ed. 6,000	1990	$45	$90
Timeless Treasures, ed. 7,000	1991	$45	$100
Cherished Eve, ed. 8,400	1992	$45	$45
Give Thanks	1993	$50	$50

1992 "Cherished Eve" print

1992 membership card

P. Buckley Moss Society

New member pin

Art for 1995 pin, "Golden Winter"

"The Chorus Line" 1991 renewal pin

1993 membership card

Art for 1993 pin "Friendship"

*Art for 1994 pin,
"Country Wedding"*

1991 membership card

1993 "Give Thanks" print

*Art for 1996 pin,
"Christmas Carol"*

Old World Christmas®
Collectors' Club

P.O. Box 8000, Department C
Spokane, WA 99203
Director, Inge Star
(800) 962-7669, ext. 160
Fax: (509) 534-9098

Featured collectible: German holiday collectibles made of wood or glass
Benefits: Exclusive members-only opportunities to purchase collectibles, periodic newsletters, free Collectors' Guide featuring 100 full-color pages of holiday treasures, and a gift of heirloom quality ornaments
Year club founded: 1992
Sponsored by: Old World Christmas®, founded in 1976
Membership size: 5,000 U.S., 500 Canada, 100 in other countries
Club publication: *Old World Christmas® Star Gazette* (full color, four to eight pages, issued quarterly)
Factory tours: Members may contact Old World Christmas® for details on visiting German manufacturers.
Annual dues: $30   **Renewals:** $30
Club year ends: December 31
Membership kits received: Two to four weeks after application submitted
How to join: Applications at authorized dealers, or interested parties may call or write to Old World Christmas®; gift memberships and multiple year membership discounts available
How to redeem certificates: At an authorized Old World Christmas® dealer

Old World orna- ments feature a star- shaped hanger

Christmas comes to life like never before through the Old World Christmas Collection. Glass ornaments produced by the German family workshop of Inge-Glas are blown in authentic antique molds that have been passed down for generations.

The rich traditions of Christmas from the Old World are carried on where craftsmen still produce holiday heirlooms in the same manner as generations past.

Artist
E.M. Merck

All the ornaments in this collection are produced with quality materials and exacting detail. In addition, each nutcracker ornament is burnished with the maker's insignia, KWO, and signed by the artist.

E.M. Merck, the premier designer for the collection, has the philosophy that "when designing high quality collectible pieces, I wish to capture the magical feeling of the holidays and develop creations that I would be proud to have in my home and pass on as family heirlooms."

Star-shaped hangers are attached proudly to each ornament to guarantee collectability and authenticity.

Club members enjoy the quarterly installments of the *Old World Christmas Star Gazette.* The newsletter features a variety of subjects including the history of collectibles, a collectors' exchange and buying and selling services in classified form, introduction of new products and announcements of retired pieces, decorating ideas, and an "In the News" section. For new members, back issues are available at $3 apiece.

The club newsletter also contains letters to Ms. Star. Inge Star, the Old World Christmas Collectors' Club president, attempts to personally answer members' request for specific information, keeping collectors involved and informed about the club's activities.

Old World Christmas attended the International Collectible Exposition in Long Beach, California, in March 1993. All Collectors' Club members within a ten-state radius received a personal invitation to attend the event and meet E.M. Merck. This is only

Special Features

When planning trips to Germany, members can receive information on visiting Old World factories.

"Dresdener Drummer"

one of many such appearances that are planned for shows in the future.

The club emphasizes keeping its members up to date on each new addition and activity within the Old World Christmas Collection.

Old World Christmas® Collectors' Club

Membership Gifts

Ornaments	Years Available	Original Value	Current Value
Mr. & Mrs. Claus (glass)	1992-93	$25.00	$25.00

Members-Only Pieces

	Issued	Issue Price	Current Value
Christmas Maidens (set of four ornaments, glass)	1992-93	$35.00	$35.00
Dresdener Drummer, nutcracker	1992-93	$98.50	$98.50

Gift to members, Mr. & Mrs. Claus ornaments

PJ's Carousel Collectors Club

P.O. Box 610
Newbern, VA 24126
Director, Jim Hennon
(703) 674-4300
Fax: (703) 674-2356

Featured collectible: Miniature, molded wood replica carousel horses
Benefits: Engraved shelf plaque, music tape, annual members-only horse, annual members-only renewal piece, bi-annual newsletter
Year club founded: 1990
Sponsored by: PJ's Carousel Collection, founded in 1983
Membership size: 450 U.S.
Club publication: *PJ's Carousel Collectors Club* (two to six pages, black and white)
Factory tours: Can be arranged in advance by phone, or members are invited to stop by without previous reservations
Annual dues: $40   **Renewals:** $40
Club year ends: One year after joining
No. of staff devoted to handling club: Two
Membership kits received: Four weeks after application submitted
How to join: Applications at authorized dealers, by phone
How to redeem certificates: At an authorized dealer

PJ's Carousel Collectors Club

Membership Gifts

Carousel Horses	Years Available	Original Value	Current Value
Shelf plaque	1990	$20	$25-$35
Chariot side	1991	$20	$20-$35
Plate	1992	$20	$20
Horse Bust	1993	$20	$20

Members-Only Pieces

Carousel Horses	Issued	Issue Price	Current Value
Myrtle Beach Horse	1990	$100	$200-$250
Spokane, WA Horse	1991	$100	$125-$150
Holland, MI Horse	1992	$100	$100

More than 3,000 carousels once flourished in America. Members of PJ's Carousel Collectors Club can capture some of the magic carved by the masters of the 1900s through PJ's Carousel Collection.

Depicting horses and menagerie animals duplicated in miniature, each piece is sculpted by using the best available pictures or prints for reference, turned into a mold and produced in gemwood. The pieces then are hand painted in colors true to the horse or animal it represents in editions as small as 500.

This unique society preserves a piece of Americana by capturing the American carousel in replica pieces, and providing general information about carousel pieces and trivia. Members keep up with the club via a simple four-page newsletter. Each issue offers information about club activities, limited edition pieces, historical references, and retired pieces.

Members are encouraged to visit the PJ Carousel plant in Wytheville, Va. Not only can one observe the actual production of the miniature carousel horses, but free carousel rides on some of the original pieces are available as well.

PJ's is the only company in the world that produces wood product replicas of actual, in-play carousel figures. To collectors, that means this society is the only organization with such a unique collectible line, and the only club offering additional information and enthusiasm.

A six-horse carousel from PJ's

Special Features

A tape of carousel music is one membership benefit.

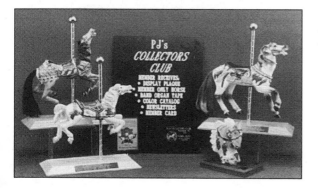

PJ's membership gifts and members-only horses

The Pangaean Society

cp smithshire

The Lance Corporation
321 Central Street
Hudson, MA 01749
Director, Jim Swiezynski
(508) 568-1401
Fax: (508) 568-8741

Featured collectible: The Shirelings of cp smithshire, made of Sheramic, a unique blend of sculptor's materials developed specifically for its ability to capture the detail sculpted into the original

Benefits: Free "Fellowship Inn" charter-year membership figurine, enameled "Merlin" collector pin, opportunity to purchase members-only sculptures, six free names in the Aftermarket Facilitation program, semi-annual newsletter, personalized membership card, cp smithshire catalog

Year club founded: 1993

Sponsored by: The Lance Corporation, founded in 1968

Club publication: *Shirespeak* (semi-annual)

Factory tours: cp smithshire dealer-sponsored tours available

Annual dues: $25   **Renewals:** $25

Club year ends: One year after joining

No. of staff devoted to handling club: One

Also sponsors: Sebastian and Chilmark

Membership kits received: Four to six weeks after application submitted

How to join: Applications at authorized dealers

How to redeem certificates: At an authorized cp smithshire dealer

"Eva" and "Adamo," the first two Shirelings from which all others originate

In the history of Smithshire, Pangaea refers to the single large land mass that would eventually divide over time to become the continents of the world. Such is the purpose of The Pangaean Society, to join all collectors as one, united in the common love of the Shirelings.

The line and individual pieces of the Shireling collection evoke whimsical remembrances for the collector and prompt memories of childhood innocence and curiosity — where all was good, and imagination and creativity were qualities to be cherished.

Each Shireling sculpture is a faithful reproduction of a design by artist Cindy Smith. They are hand-cast in "Sheramic," a unique blend of sculptor's materials developed specifically for its ability to capture every detail of the original.

The sculpture is then painted entirely by hand, with as many as four separate coats applied to replicate the distinctive hues of the original.

While in reality Shirelings attain an age of 300 years, in the cp smithshire collection, their "lifetime" lasts no more than three years. At the end of this time, each Shireling will "Go Home to the Forest," or in other words, is retired.

Collectors enjoy the Shirelings because each piece is part of a story, which is told in "The Allegory of The Shirelings," an introductory tale penned by cp smithshire founder W.H. Mitchell. Members will find themselves caught up in this ongoing tale and will be informed of new pieces and collector events, and will find out which pieces are "Going Home to the Forest" in the semi-annual newsletter, *Shirespeak*.

Get ready for an adventure in discovery!

Sculptor
Cindy Smith

Special Features

Aftermarket Facilitation Procedure helps collectors buy figures no longer available at retail. For a charge of $1.50 per request, registrants are entitled to the first name and telephone number of collectors in their area interested in aftermarket transactions.

The Pangaean Society

Membership Gifts

Items	Years Available	Original Value	Current Value
Fellowship Inn (figurine)	1993-94	$45	$45
Merlin (enameled pin)	1993-94	free	n/a

PenDelfin
Family Circle

1250 Terwillegar Ave.
Oshawa, Ontario L1J 7A5, Canada
Director, Nancy Falkenham
(416) 723-9940
Fax: (416) 723-0514

Featured collectible: Miniature, stoneware, handpainted rabbits
Benefits: Free founder member figurine, redemption card for exclusive
members-only figurine, *The PenDelfin Times* newsletter, PenDelfin
Family Circle membership card, official founder member certificate,
free drawing to win retired models, studio tours
Year club founded: 1992
Sponsored by: PenDelfin Studios Ltd., founded in 1953
Membership size: 5,000 U.S., 15,000 U.K., 5,000 Canada
Club publication: *The PenDelfin Times* (full-color, four to eight pages)
Factory tours: Members can visit the factory by contacting PenDelfin
Studios Ltd., in advance at Cameron Mill, Howsin Street, Burnley,
Lancashire, BB10 1PP, England
Annual dues: $30   **Renewals:** $30
Club year ends: December 31
No. of staff devoted to handling club: Three
Membership kits received: Four to six weeks after application sub-
mitted, or available for immediate take-home at authorized PenDelfin
dealers
How to join: Applications at authorized PenDelfin dealers, by phone
How to redeem certificates: At an authorized PenDelfin dealer

PenDelfin Family Circle
Membership Gifts

Rabbit Figurines	Years Available	Original Value	Current Value
Herald	1992-93	$30	$30

Members-Only Pieces

Rabbit Figurine	Issued	Issue Price	Current Value
Bosun w/ Scrimshaw Parrot	1992-93	$100	$100

The whimsical quality of the rabbits of the PenDelfin family offer a uniqueness and quality that create an individual personality in each character. In fact, two of the figurines, "Sunny" and "Bosun" were nominated for Canadian Collectible of the Year Awards in 1992.

The PenDelfin Family Circle invites collectors to become part of this unique collectors' club, formed to bring together the many people who have been collecting the pieces during the past 40 years.

A barrage of gifts and incentives welcome the new PenDelfin Family Circle member: a chance to win a retired piece; an official, personalized membership scroll; studio tours for members and their families; and a membership card that entitles the collector to purchase exclusive members-only figurines and attend exclusive special events.

Membership also brings with it a subscription to *The PenDelfin Times*, the organization's official newsletter. Each issue presents information regarding special events, insight from the artist, introduction of new pieces, and membership gifts.

Originated by English artists Jean Walmsley Heap and Jeannie Todd as a hobby, PenDelfin production began in 1953 with a plaque of a witch riding her broom. The company has moved beyond its simple beginnings in a potting shed by tapping the talents of others, but still hand crafts each sculpture in the PenDelfin family of bunnies.

Jean Walmsley Heap attends major shows in England, and members receive notification when painters tour retailers in North America.

Model designer Doreen Noel Roberts

Special Feature

Members may win models of retired pieces in special contests.

Left, "Herald," charter year gift and right, "Bosun with Scrimshaw Parrot"

PenniBears
Collectors Club

P.O. Box 1200
Norman, OK 73068
Director, Michael Redwine
Collector Coordinator, Letitia Ingram
(405) 872-3468
Fax: (405) 360-4442

Featured collectible: PenniBears, made of bonded porcelain
Benefits: Yearly redemption certificates allowing purchase of the members-only PenniBears figurine, official membership card, newsletter, opportunity for special purchases
Year club founded: 1990
Sponsored by: United Design Corp., founded in 1973
Membership size: 4,500
Club publication: *PenniBears Post* (six to eight pages, bi-annual)
Factory tours: Tours scheduled Monday-Friday from 10 a.m. to 1 p.m. (except holidays). Tours originate in gift shop at 1600 N. Main in Noble, Oklahoma, phone: (405) 872-7131
Annual dues: $5   **Renewals:** $5
Club year ends: One year from joining
No. of staff devoted to handling club: Two
Also sponsors: Legend of Little People, Legend of Santa Claus, Angels Collection, Easter Bunny Family
Membership kits received: Two to four weeks after application submitted
How to join: Applications at authorized dealers, gift memberships
How to redeem certificates: At an authorized PenniBears dealer

L-r, charter issue "First Collection," 1991 "Collecting Makes Cents," and 1992 "Today's Pleasures, Tomorrow's Treasures"

Penni Jo Jonas "just loved to make miniatures," so that's exactly what this housewife did — in her kitchen, she took baker's clay, a food processor and a toaster oven, and created little bear figurines that captured collectors' hearts and quickly grew into a bustling business.

PenniBears are limited-edition collectible miniatures with an average height of 1½ inches, which are hand-cast in bonded porcelain. Using Penni Jo's sculpted original, delicate molds are made that capture every detail. Cold casting in bonded porcelain allows this detail to remain in each cast piece, which is then carefully painted by hand. A final protective coat of clear resin is applied, and each PenniBear has a trademark copper penny inserted in its base.

Members of the PenniBears Collectors Club have the opportunity to purchase special members-only figurines. They also receive a subscription to the *PenniBears Post*, the official club newsletter, which provides advance information about each season's new designs, lists current PenniBears pieces, and informs members of upcoming events and other items of interest.

Penni Jo enjoys the interaction with PenniBears collectors, as is evident in the *PenniBears Post*, which shows her meeting and greeting numerous fans at major collectibles expositions throughout the country.

It's a long way from the kitchen, but Penni Jo and her fans are having the times of their lives.

**Creator
Penni Jo Jonas**

"The art, no matter what format, has brought us all together. The art has strummed a chord of emotion within us to live. We are charmed, delighted, pleased and often deeply moved within. We share these feelings and they bring us together."

— Penni Jo Jonas

PenniBears Collectors Club

Members-Only Pieces

Item	Issued	Issue Price	Current Value
First Collection, PB-C90	1990	$26	$75-$100
Collecting Makes Cents, PB-C91	1991	$26	$60-$75
Today's Treasures, Tomorrow's Pleasures, PB-C92	1992	$26	$40-$50
Chalking up Another Year, PB-C93	1993	$26	$26

Pleasantville 1893 Historical Preservation Society

P.O. Box 93507
Atlanta, GA 30377-0507
Director, Mary Lee Graham
(404) 352-1381
Fax: (404) 352-2150

Featured collectible: Bisque porcelain village figurines
Benefits: Pleasantville Gazette building, *Pleasantville Gazette* newsletter, full-color catalog, bisque porcelain Christmas ornament, and Pleasantville lapel pin (first pin in annual series)
Year club founded: 1992
Sponsored by: Flambro Imports Inc., founded in 1965
Club publication: *Pleasantville Gazette* (two to four pages, newspaper style)
Annual dues: $30 **Renewals:** $15
No. of staff devoted to handling club: Three
Also sponsors: EKJ Collector's Society
Membership kits received: Four to six weeks after application submitted
How to join: Receive more information through authorized retailers, club newsletter, trade publication ads, or contact the club by phone

Membership benefits for Pleasantville 1893 Society

The village and townspeople of the book *Pleasantville 1893* come alive through the art and words of Joan Berg Victor. A family-oriented collectible treasure, everyone will enjoy the nostalgia and beauty of the lighted village and the imagination and creativity of the book detailing the life and times of the Pleasantville residents.

Victor, the artist and author, wanted to capture a piece of Americana from 1893. To teach about life during this colorful time period, she has created her Pleasantville village with historically authentic details.

The Preservation Society binds together collectors who wish to share in this special collection of history. Members receive a quarterly newsletter, *The Pleasantville Gazette*, informing them of events in Pleasantville, as well as collectible information and letters from Society members.

Joan makes frequent appearances at shows as well as individual stores for autograph/photograph sessions. Members are notified of her planned appearances through the newsletter. And club officials contact members directly, as well.

Through a combination of historical relevance and vivid imagination, the beauty of the Pleasantville collectibles is passed on to members of the Society, and the village of 1893 is captured forever.

Author and creator Joan Berg Victor

Special Features

A group known as the Happy Homesteaders regularly communicates ideas on Pleasantville villages and shares recipes with members.

Pleasantville 1893 Historical Preservation Society

Membership Gifts

Village Pieces	Issued	Issue Price	Current Value
Pleasantville Gazette Building	1993	gift	$40.00
Preservation Society lapel pin	1993	gift	n/a
Christmas at the Tubbs book	1993	gift	n/a

Pocket Dragons
& Friends

41 Regent Road
Hanley, Stoke-on-Trent
England ST1 3BT
Secretary, Liz Wood
0782 212885; fax 0782 212891

Featured collectible: Pocket Dragons figurines made of porcelain resin

Benefits: Free figurine, membership card, quarterly newsletter, member-only exclusives, factory tours, exclusive membership print, invitations to special events, telephone hotline, competitions

Year club founded: 1992 (originally founded as Land of Legend Collectors' Fellowship in 1989)

Sponsored by: Land of Legend, founded in 1988

Membership size: 5,000 worldwide

Club publication: *Pocket Dragon Gazette*, six-page, four-color quarterly newsletter

Factory tours: Cardholding members may tour Collectible World Studios factory in Stoke-on-Trent by appointment; phone club in advance

Annual dues: $29.50   **Renewals:** $29.50

Club year ends: May 30

No. of staff devoted to handling club: Two

Also sponsors: Land of Legend Fellowship

Membership kits received: Six to eight weeks after application submitted

How to join: Membership available by mail, by phone, or through promotions, authorized dealers or gift memberships

How to redeem certificates: At an authorized Pocket Dragons dealer

Who could possibly resist Real Musgrave's whimsical world of Pocket Dragons? Of course, then again, who would want to? The irrepressible dragons, as well as the wizards, gargoyles and other creatures Musgrave sculpts, can bring a smile to even the stodgiest consumer. And then there's the challenge of deciphering the runes, little secret messages often found decorating the borders and trims of Real's pieces.

Sculptor
Real Musgrave

His pieces have "fun" written all over them, so to speak, and that's the aim of the Pocket Dragons & Friends collectors club — to encourage the enjoyment of collecting. Members also will find up-to-date information on new products and assistance in locating pieces they may be having trouble finding.

The colorful, quarterly newsletter, boasting the latest additions to his doe-eyed menagerie, lists retirements, personal appearances by Musgrave, letters from collectors, and messages from Real and his wife Muff, also his full-time creative partner. One recent feature gives a floor-by-floor tour of the Musgraves' four-level home. Members also are encouraged to exercise their own creativity

Special Features

Introduce a friend to the Club and receive "Naptime," "Playing Footsie," or "Oops" as a free gift.

1993-94 gift,
"Want A Bite?"

with contests, such as designing a club magazine cover or stating in 25 words or less why they collect Pocket Dragons.

To create this medieval world, one would expect Musgrave's studio to be cloistered in a castle in some far-off land, but the truth of it is, he works out of his Brae Edenhall homestead in North Texas. All it takes is imagination and a little magic.

"No matter what technique I use," says Musgrave, "I always strive to produce a piece that has a certain enchanted feeling to it. The best fantasy ought to make us believe in magic. It should help us discern more easily the humor and whimsy in the world we inhabit, while instilling wonder about worlds we can only imagine. Magic is simply another way of seeing."

"I always strive to produce a piece that has a certain enchanted feeling to it. The best fantasy ought to make us believe in magic."

— Real Musgrave

"Self Taught"
1990-91

"Pen Pals" 1993-94

Pocket Dragons & Friends

(Founded as Land of Legend Collectors' Fellowship with art by various sculptors, including Tom Raine, Hap Henrikson, Martin Bower, and Real Musgrave. All issues after 1992 are by Musgrave.)

Membership Gifts

Items	Years Available	Original Value	Current Value
Sword in the Stone (figurine, Raine)	1989-90	$25.00	$25
Padlock style key ring	1989-90	free	$5
Take a Chance (figurine, Musgrave)	1990-91	$30.00	$30
Brass wizard's bookmark	1990-91	free	$5
Collecting Butterflies (figurine, Musgrave)	1991-92	$30.00	$30
Key to My Heart (figurine, Musgrave)	1992-93	$29.50	$30
Want a Bite? (figurine, Musgrave)	1993-94	$29.50	$30
Bitsy, bonus pewter pin	1993-94	free	$15

Members-Only Pieces

Items	Issued	Issue Price	Current Value
Hubble Bubble (figurine, Raine)	1989-90	$95.00	$95
Self Taught (figurine, Henriksen)	1990-91	$100.00	$100
The Wizard's House (print, 1,500 ed., Musgrave)	1991-93	$39.95	$40
Won't You Join Us?, A Spot of Tea (fig. set, Musgrave)	1991-92	$75.00	$75
Special Friends (figurine, Henriksen)	1991-92	$55.00	$55
Balador (figurine, Henriksen)	1992-93	$90.00	$110
Albenon the Forest Dragon (figurine, Henriksen)	1992-93	$75.00	$90
Book Nook (figurine, Musgrave)	1992-93	$140.00	$140
Pen Pals (figurine, Musgrave)	1993-94	$90.00	$90

The Polland
Collectors Society

P.O. Box 2468
Prescott, AZ 86302
(800) 553-0671
(602) 778-1900

Featured collectible: Miniature pewter sculptures of scenes and
people from the Old West
Benefits: Free annual membership figurines (a $125 value), redemp-
tion card to purchase members-only figurine, quarterly newsletter,
advance notice of special offers, membership card, exclusive
members-only contests, and an insurance value list
Year club founded: 1987
Sponsored by: Polland Studios, founded in 1970
Membership size: 1,600
Club publication: *Collectors Review,* four to eight page newsletter,
8½ by 11 inches
Annual dues: $35
No. of staff devoted to handling club: Four
How to join: By picking up membership forms at an authorized
Don Polland retailer, or by contacting the Society directly
How to redeem certificates: At an authorized Don Polland retailer

The Polland Collectors Society
Membership Gifts

Sculptures	Years Available	Original Value	Current Value
I Come in Peace	1987	free	$600
The Hunter	1988	free	$545
Crazy Horse	1989	free	$470
Chief Pontiac	1990	free	$420
War Drummer	1991	free	$330
Collector's cabinet sign	1992	free	$125
Mountain Man	1993	$125	$125

Members-Only Items

Sculptures	Issued	Original Value	Current Value
Silent Trail	1987	$300	$1,300
Disputed Trail	1988	$300	$1,055
Apache Birdman	1989	$300	$970
Buffalo Pony	1990	$375	$800
The Signal	1991	$375	$730
Warrior's Farewell	1992	$350	$400
Blue Bonnets & Yellow Ribbon	1993	$350	$350

R

In Brief...

The Christopher Radko Family of Collectors
Starlight
Planetarium Station
P.O. Box 770
New York, NY 10024
Founded in 1992 — offers members-only ornament ("Angels We Have Heard on High," limit 5,000), color quarterly magazine, Starlight, *features Radko's Old World style glass ornaments, membership card, annual dues $20*

Red Mill Collector's Society
One Hunters Ridge
Summersville, WV 26651
Founded in 1990 — features Red Mill's distinctive pecan resin sculptures in the tri-annual newsletter, annual dues $15

Reichardt Collector's Club
P.O. Box 8031
Port Huron, MI 48601-8031
Founded in 1992 — offers free Reichardt limited edition print, club pin, quarterly newsletter, special product coupons, discounts for visits to Sedona, Ariz., opportunity to purchase members-only plate, and chance to win a trip for two to Sedona to visit the artist's home, annual dues $45 U.S. and $50 in Canada

Rockwell Society of America
597 Saw Mill River Road
Ardsley, NY 10502
Founded in 1974 — sponsors various plate series from Knowles China and answers questions about Rockwell and his art, offers newsletters and medals. Contact director Michael J.P. Collins for details

Norman Rockwell Club
(Dave Grossman Designs)

No longer active.
Was formed in 1981,
and ceased in 1985.

Featured collectible: Figurines inspired by the art of Norman Rockwell
Sponsored by: Dave Grossman Designs of St. Louis, Missouri
Club publication: *The Illustrator* newsletter, quarterly, included a column about Rockwell from former child Rockwell model, Scott Ingram, and new product information

Norman Rockwell Club
(Dave Grossman Designs)
Members-Only Items

Figurines	Issued	Issue Price	Current Value
Young Artist, (RCC-1)	1981	$96	$150-$200
Diary, (RCC-2)	1982	$35	$75-$100
Runaway Pants, (RCC-3)	1983	$65	$120-$180
Gone Fishing, (RCC-4)	1984	$30	$75-$100

Royal Doulton International Collectors Club

700 Cottontail Lane
Somerset, NJ 08873
Administrator, Diane Goedkoop
(800) 582-2102
Fax: (908) 356-9467

Featured collectible: Character jugs and figurines made of bone china
Benefits: Four quarterly mailings per year, opportunity to purchase members-only items four times per year, free identification service, free admission to factory tours, special notice of special events, new introductions and discontinuations
Year club founded: 1980
Membership size: 5,000 U.S., 20,000 worldwide
Local chapters available: Eight, independently organized. National club supplies items for raffles three or four times per year and announces local chapter meetings in newsletter
Club publication: *Gallery* (four-color quarterly, 18 pages), and a U.S. newsletter featuring a sell and swap section for U.S. club members
Factory tours: Reservations made through club offices
Annual dues: $25   **Renewals:** $25
Extras: Binders, $10; sweat-shirts, $10; tote bags, $10
Club year ends: Month to month
No. of staff devoted to handling club: One
Membership kits received: Six weeks after application submitted
How to join: Applications at authorized dealers
How to redeem certificates: At an authorized Doulton dealer

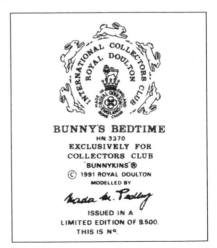

BUNNY'S BEDTIME
HN 3370
EXCLUSIVELY FOR
COLLECTORS CLUB
"BUNNYKINS"®
© 1991 ROYAL DOULTON
MODELLED BY

nada M. Padley

ISSUED IN A
LIMITED EDITION OF 9,500.
THIS IS Nº.

Backstamp for "Bunny's Bedtime"

One hundred years ago in the art studios of Burslem, England, the first Royal Doulton figurines were created. The goal was to introduce them to the world at the World Columbian Exhibition, which was scheduled for Chicago, Ill., that year. The introductions were made, and the public was enchanted.

From that moment on, the collection grew rapidly. And as it grew, so too did its followers. The force behind the initial creations was Charles Noke, a modeller who had served his apprenticeship in Worcester. He took the traditional sculpture forms of the figure and the toby jug and brought them to life by depicting everyday events and everyday people in his creations. Some of the figures were freestanding, but according to *Gallery*, the Royal Doulton International Collectors Club magazine, "others adorned vases, wall pockets, comports, and the then novel electric light fitting."

As time passed, the diversity of Doulton art expanded. From the elegance of shimmering freestanding sculptures to the humor of the ornate character jugs, collectors of every kind have found something that catches their eye in the Royal Doulton Collection.

The Royal Doulton Collectors Club was established in 1980 to bring those collectors of diverse interests together and to educate, inform, and entertain them with the history of these products.

An issue of the club's colorful, quarterly magazine would not be complete without a historical perspective, as well as essays on the various subject matter these pieces depict. One issue may focus on character jugs, while another might delve into the collection's mythological pieces or perhaps pieces that portray animals in human guises (most notably the collections' popular Bunnykins figurines). Beautiful photography distinguishes this magazine.

U.S. members also receive newsletters highlighting pertinent information for the U.S. market, such as special events and regional antiques shows.

In addition to sending representatives to major collectibles shows, the Club hosts conferences on

Club ambassador Michael Doulton

Special Features

A staff of museum curators aids members in the identification of out-of-production pieces.

the east and west coasts to address issues such as: how to care for your antiques, the history of Doulton pieces, charity auctions, and more.

More than 2,000 Doulton pieces have been created in the last 100 years, many have been retired and many more are being introduced. This connection between the past and the future, of antiques and antiques-to-be, no doubt will continue to enchant collectors for hundreds of years to come.

> Doulton represents a figure or thought in clay using traditional methods but today's technology.

Royal Doulton International Collectors Club

Members-Only Pieces

Pieces	Issued	Issue Price	Current Value
John Doulton (jug)	1980	$70.00	$125
Sleepy Darling (figurine)	1981	$100.00	$195
Dog of Fo (Flambe)	1982	$50.00	$50
Prized Possession (figurine)	1982	$125.00	$475
Loving Cup (Beswick)	1983	$75.00	$275
Springtime (figurine)	1983	$125.00	$350
Sir Henry Doulton (jug)	1984	$50.00	$125
Pride & Joy (figurine)	1984	$125.00	$225
Top of the Hill (plate)	1985	$34.95	$75
Wintertime (figurine)	1985	$125.00	$195
Albert Sagger (jug)	1986	$34.95	$70
Auctioneer (figurine)	1986	$150.00	$195
Collector Bunnykins	1987	$40.00	$295
Summertime (figurine)	1987	$140.00	$150
Top of the Hill (mini figurine)	1988	$95.00	$125
Beefeater (jug)	1988	$25.00	$125
Old Salt (teapot)	1988	$135.00	$150
Geisha (Flambe)	1989	$195.00	$195
Flower Sellers (plate)	1989	$65.00	$65
Autumntime (figurine)	1990	$190.00	$190
Jester (mini figurine)	1990	$115.00	$115
Old King Cole (jug)	1990	$35.00	$100
Bunny's Bedtime (figurine), ed. 9,500	1991	$195.00	$250
Charles Dickens (jug)	1991	$100.00	$100
Key Fob (giveaway)	1991	$4.95	$5
Tissot Lady (figurine), ed. 5,000	1991	$295.00	$295
Chris Columbus (jug), ed. 7,500	1991	$95.00	$95
Discovery (figurine)	1992	$160.00	$160
King Edward (jug)	1992	$250.00	$250
Master Potter (Bunnykins)	1992	$50.00	$50
Eliza Farren (figurine), ed. 5,000	1992	$355.00	$355
Barbara (figurine)	1993	$288.00	$288

Clockwise from top left: club exclusives "Bunny's Bedtime," "Christopher Columbus," "Discovery," "Charles Dickens," and "L'Ambitieuse"

My Personal Inventory

Club Name

Description	Number	Size	Issue Value	Current Valuation			
				1994	1995	1996	1997

S to Z

In Brief...

Sandicast Collector's Guild
8480 Miralani Drive
San Diego, CA 92126
*Founded in 1990 — offers annual Collector's Guild
sculpture, semi-annual* Paw Press *newsletters, identification card, announcements of new and limited
releases, access to the Guild's toll-free "help"
number, current product information and brochures,
annual dues $15*

Rotraut Schrott Fan Club
1620 S. Sinclair St.
Anaheim, CA 92806
*Founded in 1987, provides photos of doll artist
Rotraut Schrott, information about her and special
offers for her dolls, free membership. Director is
Fredrica Lam*

Silver Deer's Ark Collector's Club
4824 Sterling Drive
Boulder, CO 80301
*Founded in 1991 — offers members-only figurine,
membership card and certificate, quarterly newsletter and opportunity to purchase redemption pieces,
annual dues $25*

Silver Deer's Crystal Zoo Collector's Club
4824 Sterling Drive
Boulder, CO 80301
*Founded in 1991 — offers opportunity to purchase
redemption pieces, membership card and certificate,
quarterly newsletter, and gift figurine, annual
dues $25*

Spangler's Realm Collector's Club
11733 Lacklan Road
Maryland Heights, MO 63146
*Offers a members-only figurine gift and newsletter,
annual dues $50*

Steinbach/KSA Collectible Nutcracker Club
1107 Broadway
New York, NY 10010
Being formed at press time, will make special offers and offer promotion news

Fred Stone Society Collector's Club
P.O. Box 8005
Lake Bluff, IL 60044
Offers members a Fred Stone poster, membership card, updates on new Fred Stone horse subject art and updated quote sheets — annual dues $35

Summerfield Editions Limited
2019 E. 3300 South
Salt Lake City, UT 84109
Founded in 1992 — offers updates on new releases, free artcards, and listing of current and upcoming shows by artists, annual dues $5

VickiLane Collectors Club
3233 NE Cadet Avenue
Portland, OR 97220
Director: Ron Anderson
(800) 456-4259
Featuring the art of Vicki Anderson, collectible figurines of rabbits, mice, cows, cats, and angels, with charter memberships available during 1994. Annual dues are $25 for a collector's pin, quarterly newsletter, and members-only figurine, "Sweet Secrets"

Zook Kids Club
1519 S. Badour Road
Midland, MI 48640
Founded in 1991 — offers a newsletter, calendar/catalog, inside information on dolls, and opportunity to purchase members-only doll, annual dues $25

The Santa Claus Network

6 Perry Drive
Foxboro, MA 02035
Director, April Bargout
(508) 543-5412
Fax: (508) 543-4255

Featured collectible: Clothtique Santa Claus figurines — made of stiffened cloth, resin, and porcelain — and accessories
Benefits: Membership card, free Santa figurine, quarterly newsletters, dealer listing, Collector Guidebook & Collector Log, reservation card to purchase members-only Clothtique figurines
Year club founded: 1992
Sponsored by: Possible Dreams, founded in 1982
Membership size: 10,000 U.S.
Club publication: *The Santa Claus Network Newsletter* (four-color quarterly, four pages)
Factory tours: Not available
Annual dues: $25   **Renewals:** $25
Club year ends: July 31
No. of staff devoted to handling club: Two-plus
Also sponsors: Plans to start Citizens of Londonshire
Membership kits received: Six weeks after application submitted
How to join: Members enroll through authorized dealers, at collector shows, and directly with the club
How to redeem certificates: At an authorized dealer

"Special Delivery" is SCN's second membership gift

'Twas the night before Christmas, or maybe six months hence. . . .

With the Santa Claus Network, you don't have to wait until December for those visions of sugarplums to start dancing in your head.

Begun in 1992, the Network was founded to acquaint consumers with the Possible Dreams Clothtique Collectibles line of specially designed Santa Claus products.

Artist Judi Vaillancourt

If you've never seen one of these holly-jolly creations, Clothtique is created by combining stiffened cloth, porcelain, and resin. The earliest records of a technique similar to Clothtique can be traced back to southern Europe. But the creative forces at Possible Dreams have made it uniquely their own. Says a Possible Dreams spokesperson, "We named it Clothtique for one very good reason. So that the world would never confuse our Santas with imitations produced by others. For them it's an *impossible* dream."

Each figurine may be decorated with any assortment of holiday cheer — sometimes wreaths or tags, sometimes musical instruments or sacks, sometimes trees or sometimes all of these at once. Many of the Santa Claus figurines are exclusive Possible Dreams designs, while others are based on original artwork by such American artists as Tom Browning, Mark Alvin, Judi Vaillancourt, and Judith Ann Griffith. In the last six years, 40 distinct Santas have come out of the Possible Dreams workshop, each with that unmistakable look of Clothtique.

Members of the Santa Claus Network receive a free 8-inch Clothtique Santa, a membership card, the opportunity to buy members-only, limited edition Santas, a brochure depicting all Clothtique Santas, and a subscription to the quarterly newsletter. They also receive an annual Collector Guidebook.

Still in its charter year, the Santa Claus Network has yet to unwrap everything it has to offer, but with that red nose guiding its sleigh, the Network promises something that's merry and bright.

Special Features

• Buy & Sell Wish List available in quarterly newsletter.

• Network will research any questions members have regarding Possible Dreams products.

A sampling of the benefits Santa Claus Network members receive

"We named it Clothtique for one very good reason. So that the world would never confuse our Santas with imitations produced by others. For them it's an impossible dream."

Santa Claus Network

Membership Gifts

Item	Years Available	Original Value	Current Value
The Gift Giver	1992-93	$40	$40
Special Delivery	1993-94	$40	$40

Members-Only Pieces

Item	Issued	Issue Price	Current Value
Santa's Special Friend	1992-93	$59	$60

Artwork for display to hold membership forms

Sebastian Miniatures Collectors Society

SEBASTIAN MINIATURES
COLLECTORS SOCIETY

321 Central Street
Hudson, MA 01749
Director: Cyndi Gavin McNally
(508) 568-1401
Fax: (508) 568-8741

Featured collectible: Sebastian Porcelain Miniatures (bonded porcelain)

Benefits: Prescott Baston miniature, "Self Portrait," current year copies of the *Sebastian Miniatures Collectors Society News* and *The Sebastian Exchange Newsletter*, a *Sebastian Exchange Value Register Handbook*, and redemption certificates for current members-only miniatures

Year club founded: 1980

Sponsored by: Lance Corporation, founded in 1968 (Sebastian Miniatures began in 1938)

Membership size: 5,000

Club publications: *The Sebastian Miniatures Collector Society News* (three times/year, six to eight pages, black & white) and *The Sebastian Exchange Newsletter* (secondary market update, three times/year, six to eight pages, black & white)

Factory tours: Contact dealer to make arrangement for dealer-sponsored tours

Annual dues: $20   **Renewals:** $20

Club year ends: One year after joining

No. of staff devoted to handling club: One

Also sponsors: The Chilmark Gallery and the Shirelings Collectors Club

Membership kits received: Four to five weeks after application submitted

How to join: Applications at authorized Sebastian Miniatures dealers or contact society by phone

How to redeem certificates: At an authorized Sebastian Miniatures dealer

Between the years of 1938 and 1975, Prescott Baston produced well beyond 400 different Sebastian Miniature designs with very little notion that they would be so ardently collected some forty years later. Following his death in 1984, the creative world of Sebastian Miniatures was handed down to his son, Woody, who carries on the traditions and detailed depiction of a world in miniature.

Prescott (Woody) Baston Jr.

"Two goals have guided my work through the years," Prescott said. "First, to do the most honest portrayals I can. Second, to create scenes so appealing that other people immediately experience a sense of pleasure from them."

As America's longest continuously produced collectible line, Sebastians have been hand painted in New England by cottage industry since 1938, and still are produced there today. This is also one of the oldest, active clubs in the country.

The collectibles exhibit a pure American flavor, depicting themes including historic, literary, advertising, and "ordinary people doing ordinary things." The sense is one of nostalgia and a stirring of memories of things gone by.

Providing collectors with information on new releases, artist appearances, and special collector events guide the goals of this organization. Aftermarket updates, historical information, and restoration also are made available to collectors through a variety of sources including the *Sebastian Miniatures Collectors Society News* newsletter, distributed three times per year. Each newsletter covers news from the artist and offers extensive information in the area of the secondary market.

As a special service, collectors may inquire via mail or phone about detailed information on any Sebastian Miniature including background, edition size, years produced, and current aftermarket values as listed in the *Value Register*. The Society also gladly furnishes information regarding buying and selling on the secondary market.

It's an ongoing and ever-changing collection, and as said by Woody, "This is only the beginning.

Special Features

Members who renew receive special enamel pins based on the year they joined.

Only now are Americans . . . beginning to discover and collect this over 40-year-old expression of a man's life. The future is unpredictable in terms of the extent to which Sebastian Miniatures will become part and parcel of our American heritage."

An annual Sebastian Miniatures Festival encourages collector involvement with seminars, Look-Alike Contests, and auctions. Collectors also may meet Woody at 10-12 events a year.

This is a "uniquely New England collection," says director Cyndi Cavin McNally.

Sebastian Miniatures Collectors Society

Membership Gifts

Plaques	Years Available	Original Value	Current Value
Charter Membership Plaque	1980	$15.00	$50-$75
1981 Membership Plaque	1981	$15.00	$20-$30
1982 Membership Plaque	1982	$15.00	$20-$30
1983 Membership Plaque	1983	$15.00	$20-$30
1984 Membership Plaque	1984	$15.00	$20-$30
Self Portrait	1984-present	$49.50	$50

Members-Only Pieces

Miniatures	Issued	Issue Price	Current Value
Washington Irving Series			
Rip Van Winkle	1980-83	$19.50	$25-$35
Dame Van Winkle	1981-83	$19.50	$25-$35
Ichabod Crane	1981-83	$19.50	$25-$35
Katrina Van Tassel	1982-83	$19.50	$25-$35
Brom Bones	1982-83	$22.50	$35-$35
Diedrich Knickerbocker	1983	$22.50	$25-$35
Shakespearean Series			
Henry VIII	1984	$19.50	$20
Anne Boleyn	1984	$17.50	$18
Falstaff	1985	$19.50	$20
Mistress Ford	1985	$17.50	$18
Romeo	1986	$19.50	$20
Juliet	1986	$17.50	$18
Malvolio	1987	$21.50	$22
Countess Olivia	1987	$19.50	$20
Touchstone	1988	$22.50	$23

Miniatures	Issued	Issue Price	Current Value
Audrey	1988	$22.50	$23
Mark Anthony	1989	$27.00	$27
Cleopatra	1989	$27.00	$27
Shakespeare	1988	$23.50	$24
The Collectors	1990	$39.50	$40
Holiday Memories Series			
Thanksgiving Helper	1990	$39.50	$40
Leprechaun	1991	$27.50	$28
Trick or Treat	1991	$25.50	$26
Father Time	1993	$27.50	$28
Baby New Year	1993	n/a	n/a
Christopher Columbus	1992	$28.50	$29

Woody Baston cuts the ribbon for the re-dedication of the Official Miniatures Museum in Walpole, Mass.

Paul Bunyan enameled pin is given to renewing members who joined in 1991

"Shaker Lady," one of the first pair of miniatures Baston sculpted in 1938

"In The Candy Store," produced since 1947, is still a best seller

"Harry Hood," limited edition private label Sebastian Miniature

Shelia's Collectors Society

1856 Belgrade Ave., Bldg. C
P.O. Box 31028
Charleston, SC 29417
Director, Kathy Pisano
(803) 766-0485
Fax: (803) 556-0040

Featured collectible: Miniature, handpainted houses made of wood
Benefits: Membership card, collectors notebook and checklist, information on Shelia and her company, retired pieces directory, newsletter, color sheets of houses, redemption voucher. Charter members receive a signed and numbered print of the Ann Peacock House and a collectible of the Susan B. Anthony House
Year club founded: 1993
Sponsored by: Shelia's Inc., founded in 1979
Membership size: 1,200
Club publication: *Our House* (black-and-white photos, 8 ½ by 11, four to eight pages)
Factory tours: Arrangements made through the club
Annual dues: $25   **Renewals:** $20
Club year ends: May
No. of staff devoted to handling club: Three
Membership kits received: Six weeks after application submitted
How to join: Applications at authorized dealers and by phone
How to redeem certificates: At an authorized Shelia's Inc. dealer

Above, Ann Peacock House, right, membership kit with print, notebook and Susan B. Anthony house

What began as a project of need to earn money to buy her children Christmas presents has turned into a thriving business for Shelia Thompson. Now, her line of Shelia's Fine Handpainted Collectibles, ironically, have become the perfect gift for Christmas or any occasion.

Shelia Thompson

These handpainted, miniature houses are produced from Shelia's original drawings of historically significant buildings. Each is screen printed and handpainted on wood using custom-mixed paints and inks to match the colors and features of the original buildings. "I think it's our passion for quality and our attention to the smallest details that have made our miniatures popular," Shelia says.

In response to growing collector interest, Shelia's Collectors Society was established to help promote these collectibles by creating a network of dealers and collectors throughout the United States and to offer special products and services to those individuals who collect Shelia's Fine Handpainted Collectibles.

Some collectors enjoy selecting buildings just because they appreciate their look, while others enjoy collecting miniature buildings from specific regions of the country. No matter why they collect them, fans of Shelia's collectibles have finally found a place they can call home in Shelia's Collectors Society.

Special Features

• Retired Pieces Directory helps members locate stores that still have retired pieces in stock.

• Well-designed and thorough materials fill the member binder.

Shelia's Collectors Society

Membership Gifts

Items	Years Available	Original Value	Current Value
Susan B. Anthony Collectible	1993	$20	$20
Ann Peacock Print (Matted)	1993	$30	$30

Members-Only Pieces

Item	Issued	Issue Price	Current Value
Ann Peacock Collectible, ed. 5,000	1993	$16	$16

Harry Smith
Collectors' Club

50 Harden Avenue
Camden, ME 04843
Director, Marsha Smith
(207) 236-8162
Fax: (207) 236-8169

Featured collectible: Miniature sterling silver and wood figurines
Benefits: Newsletter, membership service, notification of special pieces including one-of-a-kinds and very limited editions, and a sterling silver candle snuffer
Year club founded: 1990
Sponsored by: Harry Smith Studio, founded in 1959
Membership size: 1,200 including members in Canada, England, and Africa
Club publication: *Harry Smith Collectors' Club* newsletter (two to four pages, with full color photographs of pieces)
Studio tours: By appointment only. Contact Harry Smith to make arrangements
Annual dues: None. Membership is free with purchase of Harry Smith miniature
Club year ends: December 31
No. of staff devoted to handling club: Onc
How to join: Automatic upon purchase of a Harry Smith miniature

Left to right, Three-Light Candelabrum, Grape Motif Wine Cooler, and Four-Light Candelabrum, miniatures with editions of 75 to 150

A master miniaturist, goldsmith, author, illustrator, and sculptor, Harry Smith initiated the Harry Smith Collectors' Club to help keep members in touch with the beauty, excitement, and fun of collecting miniatures.

Smith has participated in more than fifty one-man shows and exhibitions during the last thirty years, displaying his fantastic, tiny pieces of miniature life. Exquisite attention to detail and delicate craftsmanship have earned him a listing in *Who's Who in American Art* and invited comparisons to the precious works of Carl Faberge.

In attending various lectures and gallery openings nationwide, Smith brings to the public magnificent works that portray a realism and gem-like quality all presented on a one-inch scale. His art can be seen displayed prominently in government and corporate collections around the world, including pieces exhibited by the House of Representatives in the United States.

Berry Tracy, the late director of the American Wing of the Metropolitan Museum of Art in New York City described Harry's miniature furniture for an exhibit catalog as "utter perfection in his carefully selected materials, minutely executed joinery, and expertly carved and painted ornament."

From his studio in Camden, Maine, Harry also has authored and illustrated several books, including *The Art of Making Furniture in Miniature*. Not one to guard precious "secrets," this how-to guide includes complete instructions on recreating eighteen of his original pieces and offers the reader invaluable tips that took Harry years to master.

Working by the motto "Each piece must be better than the last," Smith reproduced one of history's most spectacular interiors in Louis XV's royal study in Versaille, truly showing off his talents for recreating not only the furniture and complicated embellishment of a particular room, but his unique ability to reproduce the feel for the environment and the time period, as well.

When it comes to reproducing in miniature, Harry believes in the magic of what you don't see. By knowing which details must be included, as

Special Features
Members-only opportunity to purchase special and extremely limited miniatures.

well as which can be left out, Smith can bring a one-inch figure to life.

Smith offers free membership to any collector who purchases one of his pieces. Members enjoy an informative newsletter detailing new pieces and offering bits of news from Harry about life in Maine. Opportunities to purchase special and limited edition miniatures are extended to members, giving them the first chance to acquire the newest and rarest of pieces. Members are also invited to make an appointment to visit Harry in his studio and witness the creation of a world in miniature.

> "The secret is in what you don't see, not what you see."
> — Harry Smith

Harry Smith Collectors' Club

Membership Gifts

Silver Miniatures	Years Available	Original Value	Current Value
Candle snuffer	1990	$45	$75

Members-Only Pieces

Silver Miniatures	Issued	Issue Price	Current Value
Dolphin candlestick, ed. 300	1990	$55	$55
Four-light candelabrum (w/center cup), ed. 150	1990	$225	$225
Three-light candelabrum (circular), ed. 150	1990	$175	$175
Three-light candelabrum (in line), ed. 150	1990	$175	$175
Two-light wall sconce, ed. 150	1990	$135	$135
Grape motif wine cooler, ed. 75	1991	$185	$185
Mystical Dragon, real ruby eyes & quartz crystal ball, ed. 75	1991	$175	$175
Cat on pillow, real emerald eyes & grey patina on cat, ed. 150	1991	$145	$145
Tiny bell (w/working clapper), ed. 50	1991	$75	$75
French candlestick, ed. 300	1991	$75	$75
Commemorative vase, ed. 35	1992	$45	$95
Seven-light candelabrum, ed. 12	1992	$485	$900
Shell dessert stand (w/mermen riding dolphin on beaded base), ed. 75	1992	$365	$365
Turtle shell salt cellar (w/spoon), ed. 300	1992	$55	$55
Victorian shell pitcher two mermen holding shells, supported on turtle's back), ed. 150	1992	$235	$235

Some pieces are available in 18K gold.

Snowdome
Collectors' Club

P.O. Box 53262
Washington D.C. 20009
Director, Nancy McMichael
(202) 234-7484
Fax: (202) 234-7484

Featured collectible: Plastic and glass snowdome (waterglobe)
paperweights
Benefits: Club newsletter, annual meeting and swap meet
Year club founded: 1990
Membership size: 13,000 U.S.; 6 U.K.; 20 Canada; 6 Italy; 3 France
Club publication: *Snow Biz* (12 pages, quarterly)
Annual dues: $10   **Renewals:** $10
No. of staff devoted to handling club: One
How to join: Send dues to the address above

"I could never understand why these
charming little 'individual worlds' never got
that much press or attention. I am so thank-
ful someone finally decided to give importance
to this collectible," writes a new member of
Snowdome Collectors.

And from the growing popularity of the
Snowdome Collectors' Club, that sentiment from
one hobbyist is shared by many. This organization
seeks to enhance the knowledge, enjoyment, and
collections of snowdome enthusiasts. Once just
a small collectors' circle, the number of club members is on the rise.

After the club was formed, Nancy McMichael,
editor of the club's newsletter, *Snow Biz*, said, "The
response to *Snow Biz* took me by surprise. Not
only are there far more collectors than I ever imag-
ined, but so many of you are extremely enthusiastic and affectionate about snowdomes."

The club works to increase that enthusiasm,

helping members enlarge their collections by providing sources of domes; manufacturers' and dealers' advertisements; an Exchange column in the newsletter for snowdome buying, selling, and trading; and through annual swap meets.

In fact, *Snow Biz* emphasizes the importance of keeping collectors in contact with one another. This communication not only enhances each hobbyist's enjoyment, but provides collectors the opportunity to gather their favorite items from one another.

"I have learned from personal experience that collectors can help each other in many ways," Nancy says. "We don't all equally enjoy the same domes, we inevitably acquire duplicates, and we receive unwanted gifts. So when we are lucky enough to meet each other, we can trade, as well as share information about where domes are for sale."

In addition to serving as a communication link between members, *Snow Biz* provides tips on cleaning, caring for, and displaying snowdomes. Issues include profiles on individual collectors, historical looks at snowdome scenes, marketplace listings of snowdome retailers, personal anecdotes from collectors nationwide, and "The Snowline," which allows members from the same area to meet and get acquainted.

As one collector writes, "I have received a lot of teasing over my collection, and it's nice to know I'm not alone in my love of snowdomes."

Snow Biz advises: "Storing snowdomes in complete darkness for long periods of time may cause the water to discolor and turn brown. The longer the globe has been kept out of light, the darker the water gets. This is especially important for collectors who pack Christmas globes away in boxes for seasonal storage."

Sports Impressions Collectors' Club

P.O. Box 633
Elk Grove Village, IL 60009-0633
Director, Susan Summers
Collectors: (708) 956-5400
Retailers: (800) 4-ENESCO
Fax: (708) 640-8356

Featured collectible: Sports Impressions collectible sports memorabilia, made of porcelain or resin, depending on the particular edition
Benefits: Annual Symbol of Membership piece, pocket folder, membership card with holder, subscription to Club newsletter, opportunity to purchase members-only editions. Other benefits vary from year to year. Charter members are distinguished by the letter "C" on their membership cards
Year club founded: 1989
Sponsored by: Sports Impressions, founded in 1985
Membership size: 15,000 U.S., 200 Canada
Club publication: *The Lineup* (four-page, full-color quarterly newsletter)
Annual dues: $25   **Renewals:** $25
Extras: Other items occasionally offered for limited periods of time
Club year ends: December 31
No. of staff devoted to handling club: One
Membership kits received: Within 45 days after application submitted
How to join: Applications at authorized Sports Impressions dealers, by phone, gift memberships, friend referral
How to redeem certificates: At an authorized Sports Impressions dealer

1993 members-only plate, "1927 Yankees"

Sports Impressions collectors love sports! Each collectible in this collection accurately depicts a sports favorite on a plate or figurine, and each is fully licensed by the respective leagues and their players.

The Sports Impressions Collectors' Club provides sports collecting enthusiasts with highly exclusive, limited edition, members-only collectibles. For instance, in 1992, a series of hand-signed collectibles was introduced with the autographs of 11 sports legends, including Mickey Mantle and Nolan Ryan, available on both plates and figurines.

The quarterly newsletter, *The Lineup*, informs members of new arrivals such as these, fills them in on edition retirements, artist profiles, dealer information, and important club news. There are also the always entertaining Trivia Challenges and puzzles. All correct answers to the Challenge are entered into a drawing for a collectible signed by either an artist or an athlete.

Sports Impressions also participates in the annual International Collectible Expositions, where you can often find sports celebrities greeting fans in the Sports Impressions booth.

Whether you're dazzled by America's Pastime, or you prefer the hardwoods or the gridiron, this is one club that's sure to make an impression on you.

Joe Timmerman, president

Special Features

Although Club headquarters doesn't operate a formal research department, all members' inquiries are thoroughly researched, and members will receive a response to every request.

1992 benefits package featured "USA Basketball Team" plate

Sports Impressions Collectors' Club

Membership Gifts

Item	Years Available	Original Value	Current Value
The Mick, figurine, #5000-01	1990	$75.00	$75-$85
Mick/7, plate, #5001-02	1991	free	$25-$30
USA Basketball Team, plate, #5008-30	1992	free	$30-$50
Nolan Ryan Collector's Card, #SIC047	1993	free	n/a

Members-Only Pieces

Item	Issued	Issue Price	Current Value
Willie, Mickey & Duke, plate, #5003-04	1991	$39.95	$95-$120
Rickey Henderson, figurine, ed. 2,500, #5001-11	1991	$49.95	$50-$60
Nolan Ryan, figurine, ed. 995, #5002-01	1991	$195.00	$200-$225
Babe Ruth, figurine, #5006-11	1992	$40.00	$65-$89
Walter Payton, figurine, #5015-01	1992	$50.00	$50-$65
1927 Yankees Team Plate, #SIC058	1993	$60.00	$60

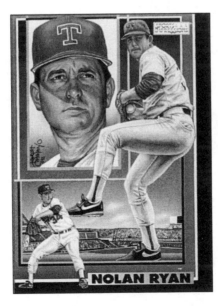

Autographed Nolan Ryan cards were randomly inserted in Sports Impressions' 1993 membership kits.

Steiff Club
USA^{SM}

225 Fifth Avenue, Ste. 1033
New York, NY 10010
Manager, Margret Brocks
(212) 779-CLUB
Fax (212) 779-2594

Featured collectible: Plush teddy bears with trademark "button-in-ear"

Benefits: Free sterling silver teddy bear club pin, membership card, redemption cards for exclusive editions, *Steiff Club USA Magazine*, and club magazine file case

Year club founded: 1993

Sponsored by: Margarete Steiff GmbH, founded in 1880

Membership size: About 4,000 midway through its charter year

Club publication: *Steiff Club USA Magazine*, four-color, quarterly, eight pages

Factory tours: Call the club in advance to arrange tours in Germany

Annual dues: $35

Extras: Limited edition bronze bear sculpture, $1,000

Club year ends: March 31

No. of staff devoted to handling club: Four

Membership kits received: Eight to 12 weeks after joining

How to join: By picking up membership forms at an authorized Steiff retailer

How to redeem certificates: At designated Steiff retailers

"Sam" and "Teddy Clown" are Steiff's Charter Year bears

In 1880, German seamstress Margarete Steiff was running a successful dressmaking shop. It was rare for a woman to own a business at all, but she was even more remarkable because she was handicapped. Confined to a wheelchair because of a bout with polio as a child, Margarete showed great determination in becoming an accomplished seamstress.

Club Manager
Margret Brocks

The story goes that one day Margarete stitched together a few elephant pincushions made of felt and filled with lambswool. She used them as small gifts for family and friends, and before year's end, eight had been sold. Soon after, she began creating other felt creatures and the world's first stuffed toy company was founded.

In 1903, Margarete's nephew registered a design for a jointed bear — eventually known as a "teddy" after President Theodore Roosevelt. The company emphasizes that its toys are built to last decades — and thus many will become heirlooms. Collectors know to look for the "button-in-ear" trademark to distinguish Steiff bears from others. At auction, collectors have bid as much as $86,000 for an original Steiff animal.

Now, with a new club to join, Steiff collectors will be able to keep up with the company's special offerings more easily, while enjoying access to news about Steiff activities — past and present.

Special Features

Members who sport the sterling silver teddy bear pin will be readily identified by other Steiff collectors.

Steiff Club USA℠

Membership Gifts

Items	Years Available	Original Value	Current Value
Sterling silver teddy bear pin	1993	$35	$35

Members-Only Items

Bears	Issued	Issue Price	Current Value
Sam	1993-94	$195	$195
Teddy Clown	1993-94	$225	$225

Stein Collectors
International, Inc.

281 Shore Drive
Burr Ridge, IL 60521
Director, Mrs. Pat Jahn
(708) 323-9283

Featured collectible: Beer steins, drinking vessels, and related items made of glass, porcelain, metals, wood, stoneware, etc.
Benefits: Subscription to quarterly magazine, access to local chapters, annual convention
Year club founded: 1965, collector sponsored
Membership size: 1,800 U.S.; also members in Germany, Canada, Australia, England, Belgium, Argentina, France and Japan
Local chapters available: 26, sponsored
Club publication: *Prosit* (quarterly, 30-40 pages, two-color)
Factory tours: Not available
Annual dues: $25   **Renewals:** $25
Extras: Back issues of *Prosit*, $2.50 each
Club year ends: December 31
No. of staff devoted to handling club: Seven volunteers
Also sponsors: Beer Stein Museum Library & Archive
Membership kits received: Four to six weeks after application submitted
How to join: By mail

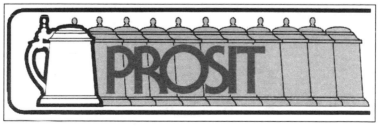

Masthead design for SCI's magazine

Cheers to Stein Collectors International, Inc. This collector-sponsored organization grabs a hefty mug of history and promotes the hobby of collecting steins, drinking vessels, and other related items without distinguishing a particular manufacturer.

Club members are encouraged to find out more about the culture and history of the people who made these varied items and to learn a bit about the countries where they were created.

With 1,800 members scattered across the globe, and 26 local chapters throughout the United States, Stein Collectors International has developed a loyal base since it was established in 1965. These local chapters host gatherings for members both locally and regionally and sponsor stein displays and exhibits. A five-day annual convention, hosted in the United States and occasionally in Germany, boasts an agenda of stein auctions and sales, lectures, workshops, and more — plus each attendee receives an annual convention stein to add to his or her collection.

Members are informed of club activities in the quarterly magazine, *Prosit*, which at 30-40 pages also is packed with articles on steins, chapter news, free-to-members stein exchange ads, and commercial ads listing steins for sale or auction.

The well-researched articles, complemented by black-and-white photos and renderings, bring these unique drinking vessels within hands' reach. Each stein has its own history, and *Prosit* will tell you where they originated and offer insight into what inspired the designs or subject matter depicted on each one.

If drinking vessels get your spirits going, this club may be the one worth toasting.

Director
Pat Jahn

Special Features

• Library and archives available for research.

• Videotaped lectures on various facets of stein collecting can be borrowed for a $3 charge, which covers postage to send and return the tape.

Stein Collectors International, Inc.

Members-Only Pieces

Steins	Issued	Issue Price	Current Value
Annual Convention Steins	1967-Present	$25-$90	$25-$90

Summerhill
Crystal Club

601 S. 23rd Street, P.O. Box 1479
Fairfield, IA 52556
Vice President, Imal Wagner
(515) 472-8279
Fax: (515) 472-8496

Featured collectible: Crystal figurines
Benefits: Members-only crystal paperweight, personalized certificate of membership, opportunity to purchase limited edition "Robbie Rabbit" crystal sculpture, personalized membership card entitling members to special offers, bi-annual newsletter
Year club founded: 1993
Membership size: 1,000
Annual dues: $25   **Renewals:** $25
How to join: Through authorized Summerhill Crystal retailers
How to redeem certificates: At an authorized Summerhill Crystal retailer

Summerhill Crystal Club

Members-Only Pieces

Item	Issued	Issue Price	Current Value
Robbie Rabbit	1993	$125	$125

"Robbie Rabbit"

A crystal droplet touched by a ray of light catches the eye so quickly with its spectral beauty. Think how much more radiant then a beautiful figurine crafted in crystal would be. The artists at Summerhill Crystal & Glass are immersed in the ongoing pursuit of unlocking age-old secrets that crystal possesses and capturing those secrets in the delicate sculptures they produce.

***Chief Designer
Imal Wagner***

The driving force behind this team of artists is chief designer Imal Wagner, who received two Awards of Excellence in 1992 from *Collector Editions Magazine* in two glass objects categories.

"The detail required to capture recognizable features of even the most demanding subject or character can be achieved," Imal says. "It takes a little magic, a lot of romance, and the ability to master crystal to forms we only dreamed of in the past."

Collectors of Summerhill Crystal are invited to be part of the magic as the Summerhill Crystal Club launches its charter year.

Charter members receive an exclusive crystal paperweight, a personalized certificate of membership, and a membership card that entitles them to special offers. They also have the opportunity to purchase the limited-edition crystal sculpture "Robbie Rabbit," signed and numbered by Imal Wagner. This sculpture is exclusively available to charter members. In addition, members will receive a bi-annual newsletter, which will inform them of club activities; new crystal introductions; and information that will help them maintain, enhance, and enjoy their Summerhill Crystal Collection.

"As we enjoy the special beauty crystal brings to our lives," Imal promises, "we pledge to bring you the most imaginative and challenging designs, always created with the magic of the medium, unequaled in quality and perfection."

> "We pledge to bring you the most imaginative and challenging designs, always created with the magic of the medium, unequaled in quality and perfection."
>
> — Imal Wagner

Swarovski Collectors Society

SCS

2 Slater Road
Cranston, RI 02920
Director, Ms. Frances Shipman
(800) 426-3088
Fax: (401) 463-8459

Featured collectible: Silver crystal figurines
Benefits: Subscription to bi-annual magazine, Silver Crystal product catalog, invitations to Swarovski events and European tours, access to limited editions; new member packet includes a certificate of membership in the form of a Swarovski paperweight, a membership card, a lapel pin, and a personal inventory list of pieces; renewal gifts
Year club founded: 1987
Sponsored by: Daniel Swarovski Corp., founded in 1895
Membership size: 155,000 in 18 markets; includes 80,000 U.S.
Club publication: *Swarovski Collector* (24 pages, bi-annual, four-color, published in seven languages)
Factory tours: Spring and fall European tours for members only. Members visit Austria and Switzerland
Annual dues: $30   **Renewals:** $20; 3-year renewal: $50
Club year ends: One year from date of joining
No. of staff devoted to handling club: Fifteen
Membership kits received: Four to six weeks after application submitted
How to join: By filling out applications available at SCS office or from authorized dealers and submitting membership fee
How to redeem certificates: At an authorized SCS dealer

1991 Annual Edition, "Save Me," the Seals

Nothing catches the eye quite like crystal does. Each ray of light that comes into contact with crystal transforms into a spectrum of color, delighting the eye with its elegant glow. The elegance and mastery of Swarovski Silver Crystal figurines has won a legion of admirers across the globe, and 155,000 of them in 18 markets are so fond of the pieces that they have joined together in the Swarovski Collectors Society.

Adi Stocker, designer

Although the Daniel Swarovski Corporation was founded in 1895, it took some 90 years before the formation of this Society in 1987. With the incredible number of requests and inquiries the company had received from collectors of Swarovski Silver Crystal all over the world, there was little else to do *but* form a Society for them.

These collectors were interested in crystal making in general and were eager to find out more about silver crystal and the new designs that Swarovski had in the works. More important, they were looking for an opportunity to meet other individuals who shared their passion for collecting crystal, so they could exchange views and ideas and forge closer links with the products that give them so much pleasure.

The pleasure and passion collectors derive from these glistening sculptures begin with the artists behind each Swarovski creation. Listen to a couple of them speak:

"I find crystal fascinating. It is as multifarious and beautiful as nature itself. Crystal challenges me to explore new avenues every time I work with it." — Adi Stocker

"If you consider anything beautiful or complex long enough, parallels with nature are bound to appear sooner or later." — Michael Stamey, *Collector Editions Magazine's* 1990 Award of Excellence winner for "Lead Me" (The Dolphins)

These same words could easily have come from the mouths of the Swarovski family, which founded its company nearly 100 years ago in Austria. After

Special Features

Customer Service Department fields all membership questions and concerns, as well as SCS-related questions.

years of supplying precision-cut crystal to jewelers and chandelier manufacturers, the Swarovskis began their line of crystal collectibles in 1976.

It was that autumn that a ball, a base stone, and two pear-shaped drops of faceted full lead crystal were joined together to form a mouse. As one craftsman remembers, "The whiskers were made of brass, trimmed to size and silver plated, and each and every aluminum foil tail had to be cut by hand!"

These unique gift items were a resounding success. The SCS official magazine, *Swarovski Collector* (Spring/Summer 1987), details what followed:

"Encouraged by the enthusiastic response of the public, a rapid development of the program took place. Elegant candleholders were added to the ornamental and decorative series and the crystal menagerie was steadily extended.

"Although initially the creations were composed of existing chandelier pendants and jewelry stones, within a short period of time the full lead crystal components were manufactured exclusively for the Silver Crystal line.

"Nowadays, the Original Silver Crystal range of products holds a coveted place in the collectible gift market and is available at selected retailers in over 70 countries around the world. Its fascination knows no boundaries. In fact, the magic beauty of each exquisitely rendered design has captured the hearts of many millions of people of different races, religions, cultures, and traditions."

A growing number of those people are the foundation of the Swarovski Collectors Society. As members, they enjoy the bi-annual *Swarovski Collector*, an annual Silver Crystal product catalog, and an annual Personal Inventory Listing. They also converge for corporate-sponsored museum exhibitions, European tours which draw members by the thousands, designer receptions, and SCS Design Celebrations (where SCS collectors meet in Orlando, Fla., to celebrate the first piece in a new series).

> The magic beauty of each exquisitely rendered design has captured the hearts of many millions of people of different races, religions, cultures and traditions.

The Swarovski Collectors Society is an endless source of information for collectors wanting to find out more about their Silver Crystal collections. The *Swarovski Collector*, for instance, provides helpful hints on how to display your favorite pieces — complete with items you will need and the exact measurements you should adhere to. These suggestions are great for holidays, parties, or just to enhance your collection.

Also, look for advice on how to care for your collection. As the *Collector* states, your crystal pieces "lose their captivating beauty in the moment when dust, fingerprints, air pollution, or oily particles leave their inevitable marks." SCS members learn how to clean their pieces, what to use, and what *not* to use: "Crystal should never be cleaned with hard, sharp objects."

For lovers of crystal figurines, the Swarovski Collectors Society offers the full spectrum of beauty, knowledge, and enjoyment.

> "If you consider anything beautiful or complex long enough, parallels with nature are bound to appear sooner or later."

Swarovski Collectors Society

Membership Gifts

Gifts	Years Available	Original Value	Current Value
Mini Crystal Cactus	1988	free	$20
Crystal key ring w/SCS logo	1989	free	$20
40mm crystal chaton paperweight	1990	free	$20
SCS crystal/gold pin	1991	free	$20
SCS pen w/crystal accent	1992	free	$20
SCS luggage tag w/ crystal accent	1993	free	$20

Members-Only Pieces

Crystal	Issued	Issue Price	Current Value
Togetherness (Lovebirds)	1987	$150	$3,000-$4,000
Sharing (Woodpeckers)	1988	$165	$1,500-$1,900
Amour (Turtledoves)	1989	$195	$995-$1,200
Lead Me (Dolphins)	1990	$225	$1,200-$1,550
Save Me (Seals)	1991	$225	$500-$750
Care for Me (Whales)	1992	$265	$374-$500
5th Anniversary SCS Birthday Cake	1992	$85	$125-$250
Inspiration Africa (Elephant)	1993	$325	$325

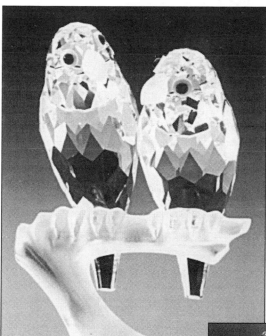

Clockwise from left: "Togetherness," "Sharing," "Inspiration Africa," "Care for Me," and "Amour"

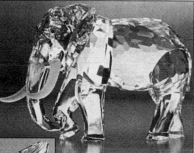

Swarovski members-only editions

The Toy Store's Collector Club for Steiff

P.O. Box 798
Holland, OH 43528
Director, Beth Benore Savino
(800) 862-TOYS, or (419) 473-9801
Fax: (419) 473-3947

Featured collectible: Plush teddy bears by German maker Steiff
Benefits: Membership card, enamel membership pin, color collector's catalog, price list and order form, newsletters, annual price list, and catalogs
Year club founded: 1985
Sponsored by: The Toy Store, founded in 1991 (the club was formerly sponsored by Hobby Center Toys)
Membership size: 2,000 U.S., 20 in Germany, 12 in Switzerland, 12 in England, 10 in Japan
Club publication: *Steiff Life* newsletter, quarterly, four to six pages, black and white with photos, art, some back issues available at $2 each. Includes Seekers and Sellers column
Annual dues: $8
Club year ends: December 31, membership ends one year after joining
No. of staff devoted to handling club: Two
Membership kits received: Six weeks after receipt of application
How to join: By contacting the club directly
How to redeem certificates: At The Toy Store
Special: Holds annual convention, Festival of Steiff, in Toledo, Ohio, each summer with Steiff founder's great-grandnephew, Jorg R. Jüngenger, as one of the guests. Includes auction, contests, and introduction of club piece for year. Club answers research questions on the phone or by mail

"Petsile" (or Little Petsy), sixth annual limited edition piece made for The Toy Store's Annual Festival of Steiff

Special Features

Holds annual convention, Festival of Steiff, in Toledo, Ohio, each summer with Steiff founder's great-grand-nephew, Jorg R. Jüngenger, as one of the guests.

The Toy Store's Collector Club for Steiff

Membership Gifts

Items	Years Available	Original Value	Current Value
Enamel pin	1989-92	free	n/a

Members-Only Items

Items[1]	Issued	Issue Price	Current Value
Gieng-Ling Panda, 5 ½", ed. 1,000, 0218/14	1988	$60	$275
Mr. Vanilla, 25 cm	1989	$140	$350
Teddy Bear Rosé, 7"	1990	$120	$250
Circus Dicky Set, ed. 1,000 (rose, mauve)	1991	$185	$250
Teddili, ed. 1,500 (1,000 produced), 7 ½"	1992	$99	$150
Petsile, ultra suede paws, 1,500 ed.	1993	$150	$150

[1] *Items are announced to club members first but not sold exclusively to them. All are made by Steiff.*

Muffy Vanderbear
Fan Club

401 North Wabash Suite 500
Chicago, IL 60611
Director, Marian E. Casey
(312) 329-0020
Fax: (312) 329-1417

Featured collectible: Muffy Vanderbear, a seven-inch, golden plush stuffed bear
Benefits: Muffy folder, membership card, membership certificate, photo album depicting all available Muffys, porcelain pendant and necklace with a full-color illustration of Muffy, set of Muffy stickers, set of Muffy stationery, a card from Muffy on your birthday, six newsletters (three *Fanfares*, three *NABCO News*)
Year club founded: 1990
Sponsored by: North American Bear Co., founded in 1978
Membership size: 17,000 U.S.; 800 members throughout Canada, Germany, Japan, Australia, Sweden, England, New Zealand
Club publication: *Fanfare* newsletter from Muffy (six-page, full color, received three times per year); *NABCO News* (details other products from North American Bear Co., three times per year)
Factory tours: Call (312) 329-0020 to reserve space in the weekly, one-hour tour
Annual dues: $20   **Renewals:** $12
Club year ends: One year after joining
No. of staff devoted to handling club: One
Membership kits received: Four weeks after request is submitted
How to join: Pick up application at select stores or send check or money order with name, address, phone, and age to club headquarters. Gift memberships also available
How to redeem certificates: At an authorized North American Bear Co. dealer

"Travels with Muffy"

Muffy Vanderbear is a seven-inch, golden plush teddy bear produced in high quality for the enjoyment of both adults and children.

Adult members love Muffy's cute expression and the quality clothes and accessories, while kids love Muffy because she's a warm, fun friend to play with.

The Fan Club keeps members informed of what's happening with Muffy, her friends, and family, as well as creating excitement and enthusiasm about Muffy and her bear counterparts.

Fanfare, one of the newsletters available to members, is a unique publication written by Muffy that includes games, puzzles, photos, fan mail, and information on the market. A special feature of the newsletter helps members buy and sell retired Muffys by providing free ad space. The *Fanfare* offers a pen pal exchange program that allows members from all over the world to communicate with one another.

The club also provides its members with the *NABCO News*, an additional newsletter that informs collectors about other products available from North American Bear Co., the maker of Muffy Vanderbear.

Barbara Isenberg, president and founder of North American Bear Co., set out to create a bear that would have the collectible quality to interest adults, and the warm, lovable quality to attract kids of all ages. The company recently was honored with *Teddy Bear Review's* "Golden Teddy Award" for the Best Dressed Bear.

Barbara attends the annual Walt Disney World Teddy Bear Convention in November. But Muffy can be seen far more often, appearing about 100 times annually at retail stores. And members can catch a glimpse of Muffy every year at the Macy's Thanksgiving Day Parade.

Members interested in a tour of the "teddy bear factory" can contact the club and arrange for a visit. Members also are notified by the club of all local appearances, and plans are in the works for the first Muffy Vanderbear Club Convention.

Special Features

• The newsletters are colorful and lots of fun, with handwritten letters from Muffy and original art throughout.

• A pen pal exchange program offers members the opportunity to communicate with collectors all over the world.

"Muffy Butterfly"

Look for
Muffy in
Macy's
Thanksgiving
Day parade.

Muffy Vanderbear Fan Club

Membership Gifts

Vanderbears	Years Available	Original Value	Current Value
Muffy Bandana, renewal	1992	$12	$12
Muffy Tote Bag, renewal	1993	$12	$12

Members-Only Pieces

Vanderbears	Issued	Issue Price	Current Value
Muffy Butterfly, 10,000 ed.	1992-93	$80	$120-180
Muffy Rose, 10,000 ed.	1993-94	$80	$80

One of the first Fanfare issues

The Windberg
Collectors Society

 1111 N. I-H 35, Ste. 220
Round Rock, TX 78664
Director, Evelyn Faye Windberg
(512) 218-8083
Fax: (512) 218-9093

Featured collectible: Limited edition Dalhart Windberg oil painting reproductions
Benefits: Membership card and kit, print reference guide of every Windberg print issued, acquisition certificates for each WCS members-only print offering, buyer/seller services, newsletter
Year club founded: 1992
Sponsored by: Windberg Enterprises Inc., founded in 1979
Membership size: 1,000-plus U.S.
Club publication: *Windberg Collectors Society* (four-page, full-color)
Annual dues: $30
No. of staff devoted to handling club: Three
Membership kits received: Three to six weeks after application submitted
How to join: Applications at authorized dealers
How to redeem certificates: At an authorized Windberg dealer

The Windberg Collectors Society
Membership Gifts

Gift offerings	Years Available	Original Value	Current Value
InformArt Magazine, one-year subscription	all	$21	$21

Members-Only Pieces

Oil painting reproductions	Issued	Issue Price	Current Value
Courtin' by Moonlight	1992-93	$120	$120

Texas artist Dalhart Windberg captures a world that is real and yet apart from reality through his oil paintings and prints.

Windberg is a self-described "romantic realist painter," presenting the world not necessarily as it is, but as we all would like it to be. He combines landscape, wildlife, still life, and nostalgic subject matter to create artwork that is soothing in its presence yet challenging in its depth. Having been featured in every major magazine covering the print art world, Dalhart also was selected by the Texas Legislature as an official Artist of Texas.

The Windberg Collectors Society offers hobbyists the unique opportunity to be a true part of the building of this collectors club. The society was founded in November 1992 and is in a state of rapid development and enthusiastic growth. The society has exciting plans for its members including the distribution of two different newsletters: the *Windberg Collectors Society Newsletter* plus the *Windberg ArtNews*, a color newsletter sent quarterly to all Windberg dealers and collectors.

Eventually, the society expects to be run by loyal Windberg collectors, independent but supported by Windberg Enterprises, Inc. Hoping to make the organization one that belongs to its members, the Windberg Collectors Society wants to serve as a focal point for long-term collectors of the artist's prints (and eventually collectors of other limited edition items based on Windberg art).

Artist Dalhart Windberg

Special Features

Detailed buyer/seller information is available to all members.

"Courtin' by Moonlight" for Windberg Collectors Society members

David Winter Cottages Collectors Guild

4456 Campbell Road
Houston, TX 77280
U.S. Chairman, Pia Colon
(713) 690-4477
Fax: (713) 462-7030

Featured collectible: Miniature cottages made of crystacal, a hard, durable gypsum plaster
Benefits: Yearly free membership piece, four Guild magazines, two redemption certificates for exclusive club pieces and an introductory magazine
Year club founded: 1987
Sponsoring company: John Hine Studios, founded in 1979
Membership size: 40,000-plus U.S., 5,000 U.K., 2,000 Canada, 1,000 Australia
Local chapters available: Thirty, independently organized
Club publication: *Cottage Country* magazine (four-color, 68 pages)
Factory tours: Contact John Hine Studios in advance at (0252) 334672, or write to John Hine Studios, 2 Hillside Road, Eggars Hill, Aldershot, Hampshire, England, GU113NB. Open seven days a week, tours begin at 10:30 a.m. and 2 p.m. weekdays, 1 p.m. weekends (must be pre-scheduled)
Annual dues: $40   **Renewals:** $40
Extras: Leather binder for Guild magazines, $15; sweatshirts, pins, buttons
Club year ends: December 31
No. of staff devoted to handling club: Four
Also sponsors: The Moe Head Club
Membership kits received: Six to eight weeks after application submitted
How to join: Applications at authorized John Hine Studios dealers, by phone, gift memberships, friend referral
How to redeem certificates: At an authorized dealer

1991 "Tomfool's Cottage"

The Guild is very spontaneous in approach, always looking for fresh and off-beat ways to serve members. Created to provide information, create excitement, and enhance the collectability of David Winter Cottages, the Guild attracts a loyal following of collectors who enjoy Winter's renditions of English cottages.

A fairly new breed, cottage collectors appreciate the detail of David Winter Cottages, each one sculpted by the popular English artist. Since 1987, the artist and John Hine Studios have received nearly two dozen awards for excellence in the collectibles field.

David Winter loves the natural beauty of the English countryside and tries to recapture its beauty through his art. A very private person, he enjoys the quiet and inspirational time of sculpting.

The Guild sponsors games and puzzles in the "Squeak!!!" section of *Cottage Country* along with contests that encourage members to write about specific series. Prizes might be cottages or signed books.

Cottage Country features new, retired, and Guild cottages; gives historical and political perspective on many designs; and profiles members and events around the world. "Letters to the Guild," "Peep at the Past," and "Inside..." (the story of an individual cottage) appear in each issue. Without ever visiting England, readers learn about the lives and livelihoods that built the country.

Company founder John Hine edits the magazine with his distinctive brand of humor and attention to detail. The lavish magazine appears quarterly in March, June, August, and November. Available back issues may be purchased by members for $7.50 each (plus shipping).

To learn more about David Winter cottages as well as the work of John Hine Studios' other artists (some of the world's finest sculptors), collectors may contact the studios in England to arrange tours.

David makes sporadic appearances at major

Sculptor
David Winter

Special Features

A colorful, well-written Guild magazine gives insights on the collection, artist, and England

trade shows, but when he does appear in a particular area, members receive a special mailing.

Local chapters have been formed by collectors in 30 cities, each one independent of John Hine Studios. The company provides information for meetings, as well as unscheduled mailings and giveaway items. Many local chapters have their own newsletters. The Guild office will assist new groups with general information on starting a club.

Members also receive special offers for magazine subscriptions, books, video tapes, a directory of cottages, and other items.

Don't forget to look for the mouse, hidden on some cottages.

David Winter Cottages Collectors Guild

Membership Gifts

Cottages	Years Available	Original Value	Current Value
Village Scene	1987-88	free	$241-$280
Street Scene (plaque)	1989	free	$150-$300
The Plucked Ducks	1990	free	$150-$270
Pershore Mill	1991	free	$95-$200
Irish Water Mill	1992	free	$75-$150
On the Riverbank (plaque)	1993	free	$40

Members-Only Pieces

Cottages	Issued	Issue Price	Current Value
Robin Hood's Hideaway[2]	1987	$54	$375-$625
Queen Elizabeth Slept Here[2]	1987	$183	$350-$600
Black Bess Inn[2]	1988	$60	$160-$360
The Pavilion[2]	1988	$52	$190-$375
Home Guard[2]	1989	$105	$225-$360
The Coal Shed[2]	1989	$112	$250-$350
The Cobbler[2]	1990	$40	$70-$150
The Pottery[2]	1990	$40	$75-$150
Cartwright's Cottage[3]	1990	$45	$80-$200
Tomfool's Cottage[1]	1991	$100	$145-$170
Will-o'-the wisp[1]	1991	$120	$150-$190
The Beekeeper's[1]	1992	$65	$90-$150
The Candlemaker's[1]	1992	$65	$90-$150
Thameside[1]	1993	n/a	$70-$140
Swan Upping Cottage[1]	1993	n/a	$69

[1] 1 yr.-certificate; [2] 2 yr.-certificate; [3] Proceeds donated to Ronald McDonald House

David Winter Cottages Collectors Guild

David Winter sculpts a Christmas cottage

"The Irish Water Mill" 1993

"The Beekeeper's" 1993

"Pershore Mill" 1991

"The Candlemaker's" 1993

Donald Zolan
Collector's Society

133 E. Carrillo St.
Santa Barbara, CA 93101
Director, John Hugunin
(805) 963-1371
Fax: (805) 962-0605

Featured collectible: Donald Zolan plates and lithographs — both full size and miniature

Benefits: Free miniature plate or miniature lithograph, quarterly newsletter, two members-only items for purchase, chance to win artist's proof plates, special prices on secondary market items, chance to win $100 for naming a painting, first news about all Zolan products, information about Zolan's public appearances

Year club founded: 1987

Sponsored by: Pemberton & Oakes, founded in 1977

Membership size: 35,000 U.S., 300 Canada

Club publication: *The Donald Zolan Collector's Quarterly* (eight-page newsletter)

Factory tours: Members are welcome to visit Zolan's home gallery, Pemberton & Oakes, in Santa Barbara, Calif. Gallery hours are 8:30 a.m. to 4:30 p.m., Monday through Friday

Annual dues: $17   **Renewals:** $17

Club year ends: December 31

No. of staff devoted to handling club: Three

Membership kits received: Six weeks after application is submitted

How to join: Collectors may join by writing to Pemberton & Oakes at the address above

"Brotherly Love" mini lithograph, 1992 membership gift

Donald Zolan's warm and realistic illustrations prompt collectors to enter the "Wonder of Childhood" world. Many Society members comment that Zolan's plate paintings remind them so much of their own children and grandchildren that they feel a personal bond with him. Having been voted the No. 1 favorite artist by *Plate World* magazine for five consecutive years, many of his limited edition collectibles also have won Awards of Excellence from *Collector Editions Magazine*. Some of his winners include "The Thinker" (mini plate), "Just We Two" (mini plate), "New Shoes" (full-size lithograph), and "Colors of Spring" (mini lithograph).

Artist Donald Zolan

Donald is devoted to bringing his "Wonder of Childhood" world to everyone who joins the society. His aim is to make all members feel part of the Zolan "family."

Members appreciate receiving full and comprehensive news on all new Zolan collectibles. They learn about what's new with his works and his lifestyle. In a recent edition of *The Donald Zolan Collector's Quarterly*, he spoke candidly about what inspires him to paint the beautiful and intriguing children that make up the *Wonder of Childhood Collection*: "Now that I've been painting for more than fifty years (my first drawing was when I was three), I thought Society members might be interested in some of my earliest memories and experiences of painting.

"I feel my first real work was when I copied Walt Disney's Donald Duck out of a comic book at age 4½. I spent a long time working on it up in my room, mixing the colors from the tins of colors I had, using a brush and a rag and a glass of water. When I showed it to Mother, she didn't realize at first that it was my painting and not from the comic because it was so accurately done.

"That work came shortly after I had a very profound experience out in the back yard when I was just four years old. It's as clear to me today as it was then. I was sitting out on a rock, sitting very quietly. I was wondering what I would do in my life when I heard what I refer to as my 'inner voice' talk to me. It said I would become an important artist. I wasn't at all frightened — I was open and accepting. The voice also said my signature would be very important and with me always, so right then I created how I sign my name today — a capital 'Z', a capital 'O' and lower case 'l,' 'a' and 'n.'

"It does seem strange, looking back, for such a little boy to have such a powerful and lasting experience, but at the time it seemed perfectly natural. No wonder I've never wanted to be anything but an artist. I knew the road I was to travel."

In working to keep Society members involved, the club sponsors plate-naming contests where collectors have the chance to win proof plates. In addition, unique special engagement dinners with the artist are offered. Society members, especially those who never have met Donald, will be interested in a videotape made during the society's five-year celebration party. It shows the artist discussing his work, signing collectibles, and conversing with members.

All members receive the Society newsletter, an eight-page publication that contains information about new Zolan products, special offers on Zolan

> **"No wonder I never wanted to be anything but an artist. I knew the road I was to travel."**
> **— Donald Zolan**

"New Shoes," free 1993 Zolan Society plate or lithograph

original paintings, news about collectible shows, secondary market prices, news about Trading Centers, notes of interest, and letters from members.

Also, The Pemberton & Oakes Client Services Department is happy to answer members' questions about current and past Zolan products. The Secondary Market Department buys and sells products released through 1990 and supports the network of Zolan Trading Centers. To date, there are more than fifty centers trading in all Zolan items, and a complete list is available to all members, free of charge.

> Zolan takes the long view as an artist — striving to equal work of the Old Masters.

Donald Zolan Collector's Society

Membership Gifts

Plates/Lithographs	Years Available	Original Value	Current Value
For You mini plate	1987	$12.50	$98
Making Friends mini plate	1988	$12.50	$76
Grandma's Garden mini plate	1989	$12.50	$69
A Christmas Prayer mini plate	1990	$14.40	$52
Golden Moment mini plate	1991	$16.60	$45
Brotherly Love mini plate	1992	$16.60	$44
Brotherly Love mini lithograph	1992	$18.00	$50
New Shoes mini plate	1993	$16.60	$17
New Shoes mini lithograph	1993	$18.00	$18

Members-Only Pieces

Plates	Issued	Issue Price	Current Value
By Myself mini plate	1990	$14.40	$63

"A Christmas Prayer"

"Golden Moment"

"Summer's Child"

Local Chapters

Below is a sampling of local chapters available across the United States and Canada. New chapters may have formed since these lists were compiled, so contact club headquarters for additional information on any clubs in which you are interested.

Enesco Memories of Yesterday Collectors' Society

Accent Flowers & Gifts
114 E. Broadway
West Memphis, AR 72301
Doris Nichols, (501) 735-0550

Crown Card
8180 Wiles Rd.
Coral Springs, FL 33067
Paul & Barb Trubatch, (305) 344-2666

Fans of Mabel Lucie Attwell
Edelweiss
55 N. Main St.
P.O. Box 61
Minster, OH 45863
Susan Krieg, (419) 628-4155

Emily's Memories & Moments
Emily's Hallmark
14855 Clayton Rd.
Chesterfield, MO 63017
Ramona Gillespie, (314) 391-8755

Friendship Has No Boundaries
European Imports
7900 N. Milwaukee
Niles, IL 60648
Valerie Serafini, (708) 967-5253

Collecting Memories
Jayne Ann's
3229 E. Broadway
Pearland, TX 77581
Jayne Ann Miller, (713) 485-9877

Hoping to See You Soon
Lawrence's Gifts Inc.
2415 W. Jefferson
Joliet, IL 60435
Larry Lardi

Welcome to Your New Home
Linda's Hallmark
125 N. Saginaw St.
Durand, MI 48429
Linda Johnson, (517) 288-6554

Remembering When
North Pole City
4201 S. Interstate 44
Oklahoma City, OK 73119
David Green, (405) 685-6635

Remembering
Shirley's Hallmark
1745 Highway, #138
Conyers, GA 30208
Barbara Stokes, (404) 483-1806

Memories of Special Occasions
Special Occasions
515 Lansing Street
Charlotte, MI 48813
Charlie Maines, (517) 543-6050

We Belong Together
Stone's Hallmark
2508 S. Alpine
Rockford, IL 61108
Claudette Amdal, (815) 397-5558

Gateway to Memories
West Coast Collectibles
8424 4th St. N.
St. Petersburg, FL 33702
Jo Waterman, (813) 577-1651

Forever Friends Collectors' Club

Pettaways Doll Hospital
12323 Glen River Drive
Houston, TX 77058-2009
Gloria, (713) 695-1066

Jan Hagara Collectors Club

Yesterday's Children
c/o Deborah's Hallmark
5154 Conway Rd., Store D
Orlando, FL 32812
Ginger Funsch, (407) 851-5229

Love at First Sight
c/o The Card Cupboard
116 W. Main St.
Coldwater, OH 45828
Julie or Mary, (419) 678-2417

We Fell in Love Again
c/o Dell's
14124 N. State Rd.
Otisville, MI 48463
Pat O'Dell, (517) 871-3490

Rural Rooster
RR 1, Box 172
McPherson, KS 67460
Virginia, (316) 241-1959

Yesterday's Future
1529 N. Cotner Blvd.
Lincoln, NE 68505
Deloris, Aubryn, or Audrey, (402) 464-7359

Heirlooms and Romance
c/o Patches
3927 S. 48th
Lincoln, NE 68506
Donna Welch, (402) 488-8062

Greater Rockwall Collectors Club
c/o Eloise's
722 S. Goliad
Rockwall, TX 75087
Sue Reeves, (214) 771-6971

My Heart's Desire
c/o Jan Hagara Collectables
1804 Koenig Lane
Austin, TX 78756
Joanne Elam, (512) 258-1140

Club Directory and Price Guide

Somewhere in Time
c/o Grandma's Cupboard
5701 E. Santa Ana Canyon Rd.
Anaheim, CA 92807
Jean or Linda, (714) 974-1030

Victorian Romance in the City of Roses
c/o Accent on Collectibles
9738 SE Washington St.
Portland, OR 97216
Cathy, (503) 253-0841

Cherished Memories of Times Gone By
c/o De Poppen Huis
4686 Portland Rd., NE
Salem, OR 97305
Mr. Ponder, (503) 393-6001

Mary's Collectibles
229 Viewpoint Dr.
Danville, CA 94506
Mary De Cesare, (510) 736-4737

Doll World
214 Buchanan
Breman, GA 90110
Clara Bailey, (706) 537-4039

Ron Lee Greatest Clown Collector's Club

Deckers Custom Jewelry & Collectibles
777 South Main Street,
  Suite 9
Orange, CA 92668-46-6
(714) 541-4746
Local Chapter dues: $10

P. Buckley Moss Society

ARIZONA
Arizona Friends
Phoenix
Kate Cummings, (602) 944-4901

CALIFORNIA
Central California
Fresno
Elaine Mau, (209) 435-1035

Mossaholics
La Verne
Jean Howell, (714) 593-5656

San Jose
Bill Maly, (408) 448-2147

COLORADO
Denver
Cathy Gunderson, (303) 477-7548

FLORIDA
Central Florida
Winter Park
John Kowalski, (305) 671-4682

Tampa Bay
Clearwater
Carol Culbertson, (813) 447-1082

GEORGIA
Mossaphile
Atlanta
Emily Bracewell, (404) 325-5804

Pat's Peaches
Duluth
Cathy Woolen, (404) 441-2642

Rome
Rome
Cathy Adams, (404) 232-2029

ILLINOIS
Pat's Lambs
Waukegan
Rosita Villarreal, (708) 244-6663

INDIANA

2240 N. Winton Avenue
Speedway
Margaret Layne, (317) 243-0049

Michiana Moss
Mishawaka
Pat Palmer, (219) 255-7469

Pat's Happy Hoosiers
Columbia City
Arlis Gamble, (219) 244-6353

Wabash Friends
West Lafayette
Phyllis Williams, (317) 463-6346

IOWA
For the Love of Moss
Osage
Marlene Ham, (515) 732-3008

Hartland Moss
Bettendorf
Joann Pomeroy, (319) 355-3017

Louisa
Columbus Junction
Thelma Rutt, (319) 728-2049

Mississippi Moss
Maquoketa
Cathy Krieger, (515) 424-6019

Moss For All Seasons
Newton
Barbara Starrett, (515) 792-6536

Moss Heaven
Ottumwa
Judy Switala (515) 682-8906

Plum Grove
Iowa City
Linda Randell, (319) 338-0590

Tri-County Southeast Iowa
Bloomfield
Carolyn Wirtanen, (515) 664-1251

KANSAS
Over the Rainbow with Moss
Overland
Cynthia Vatcher, (913) 469-4001

KENTUCKY
Central Kentucky
Lexington
Mimi Lawson, (606) 278-7815

LOUISIANA
Pat's Blue Goose
Gordonsville
Dorothy Hiter, (703) 832-3887

MICHIGAN
First Michi-ganders
Utica
Noreen Johnson, (313) 726-9639

Mid-Michigan
Saginaw
Patricia Hess, (517) 790-1728

MINNESOTA
Moss Appeal
Fairmont
Judi Woodward, (507) 235-6867

Pat's Friends
Roseville
Marjorie Kuhl, (612) 484-7367

MISSOURI
Hog Hollow
Chesterfield
Darleen Walsh, (314) 532-5752

P.B.'s Pals
Fenton
Kathy Lyons, (314) 3443-9240

Moss Shows Children
Odessa
Bonnie Shyrock, (816) 885-4060

Show Me Moss
Clinton
Debbie Sieger, (816) 885-4060

NEBRASKA
Geese and Ganders
Omaha
Joan Weber, (402) 493-0339

NEW JERSEY
New Jersey Friends of Moss
Landing
Lynn Holden, (201) 770-0557

NEW YORK
Gathering Moss
Amhurst
Leslie Greene, (716) 836-4879

OHIO
Buckeye Blossoms
Westerville
Marilyn Machosky, (614) 891-1857

Cuyahoga Valley
Akron
William Swain, (216) 867-7942

Essence of Moss
Canfield
Elaine Klempay, (216) 533-6046

Flag City Moss
Findlay
Rita Kreinbihl, (419) 424-3017

Heart of Ohio
Canton
Patricia Bird, (216) 494-0183

Maid Marion Chapter
Caledonia
Judy Smith, (614) 389-2791

Miami Valley Moss
Union
JoAnn Schindler, (513) 836-8045

Springfield-Ohio Star
Dayton
Debbie Callahan, (513) 236-0166

Waynesville - Friends Meeting
Springfield
Mary Peirano, (513) 323-4726

Western Reserve
Cortland
Anita Stocz, (216) 637-9814

OREGON
Columbia River Moss Collectors
Lake Oswego
Patricia Vroman, (504) 635-9487

PENNSYLVANIA
Allegheny Moss
Pittsburgh
Linda Pelkofer, (412) 963-7361

Lake Marburg Moss
Dover
Annetta Almoney, (717) 292-6024

Moss Roses
York
Tullia Hydinger, (717) 767-5111

Moss-A-Teers
Elverson
Esther Stoner, (215) 286-5280

Three Rivers Moss
Pittsburgh
Carol Megill, (412) 364-3415

TENNESSEE
First P.B. Moss Society
Jonesborough
Carolyn Mauk, (615) 753-5454

TEXAS
To Pat, With Love
Dallas
Donna Sherf, (214) 739-2868

VIRGINIA
Allegheny Highlands
Covington
Calvin Davis, (703) 962-5733

Apple Valley
Middletown
Lynette Dalton, (703) 869-5519

Daughter of the Stars Chapter
Woodstock
Sharon Funk, (703) 459-5470

Moss in the Valley
Roanoke
June Simmons, (703) 342-4194

Moss Tideawater Flock
Virginia Beach
Marjorie Powers, (804) 467-5431

Richmond Friends
Richmond
Suzanne Boothe, (804) 282-7230

Shenandoah Valley
Greenville
Jean Harris, (703) 337-4231

WASHINGTON
Northwest Moss Society
Oak Harbor
Kathy Sparks, (206) 679-1240

WISCONSIN
Dairylanders of Wisconsin
Muskego
Mary O'Neil, (414) 679-2218

M.I. Hummel Club

To join an M.I. Hummel local chapter, contact Cheryl Gorski, Local Chapter Correspondent, and she'll put you in touch with a nearby group. If there is no chapter nearby, or if you would like to start your own, the club will be glad to help you get up and running. For information, call 1-800-666-CLUB (2382), or write to: M.I. Hummel Club, Dept. LC, Goebel Plaza, P.O. Box 11, Pennington, NJ 08534-0011.

ARIZONA
Northwest Valley (Sun City)

ARKANSAS
Arkansas Traveler (Harrison)

CALIFORNIA
Bumble Bee (Burbank)
Camarillo
Central Coast (Santa Maria)

Club Directory and Price Guide

Fresno
Hollywood
San Bernardino (Yucaipa)
San Diego
San Gabriel (Camarillo)
San Jose
Whittier (Orange)

COLORADO
Loveland
Mile Hi (Denver)
Pikes Peak (Colorado Springs)

CONNECTICUT
Rose City (Norwich)

FLORIDA
Broward County (Hollywood)
Daytona Beach
Fivay (Hudson)
Greater Zephyrhills
Jacksonville
Ocala
Orlando Area
Palm Beach (Lake Park)
St. Petersburg
Seven Rivers (Beverly Hills)
Suncoast (Palm Harbor)
Tampa Area

ILLINOIS
Chicago/Niles
Greater Peoria Area
Gateway East
LaGrange Park (Bridgeview)
N.W. Suburban (Palatine)
Springfield
Southern Illinois (Irvington)

INDIANA
Illiana (Crown Point)
Danville

IOWA
Quint Cities (Rock Island)
Siouxland Bees (Sioux City)

KANSAS
Mo-Kan (Kansas City)
Flint Hills (Americus)

LOUISIANA
Cajun Collectors (Baton Rouge)

MAINE
Nor'Easter (Lewiston)

MARYLAND
Silver Spring
Frederick

MASSACHUSETTS
Cape Cod (Sandwich)
Pioneer Valley (Springfield)
Neponset Velley (Dedham)
Quabbin (Belchertown)

MICHIGAN
Dearborn
Great Lakes (Dearborn)
Mid-Michigan (Flushing)
Niles
Saginaw Valley (Bay City)
Tri-County (Shelby Township)

MINNESOTA
Minneapolis/St. Paul (Eagan)
St. Cloud

MISSOURI
Gateway City (St. Peters)
St. Louis Area

MONTANA
Big Sky (Great Falls)

NEBRASKA
Lincoln
Omaha

NEVADA
High Sierra (Reno)

NEW HAMPSHIRE
The Graniteer (Manchester)

NEW JERSEY
Garden State (Maplewood)
Ocean Pines (Whiting)
Raritan Valley (Piscataway)

NEW YORK
Brookhaven (Babylon)
Great South Bay (Amityville)
Nassau-Suffolk (Centereach)
Paumanok (Babylon)
Rochester (Hilton)
Western NY (Buffalo)

NORTH CAROLINA
Carolina Mountain Region (Hendersonville)

OHIO
Greater Cleveland (Parma)
Firelands Area (Sandusky)
Miami Valley (Dayton)
Toledo
Western Reserve (Cleveland)
Youngstown/Hubbard

OKLAHOMA
OK Chapter (Oklahoma City)

OREGON
Cascade (Eugene)
Portland (West Linn)

PENNSYLVANIA
Antietam Valley (Waynesboro)
Berks County (West Lawn)
Central (Muncy)
Pocono (Stroudsburg)
Perkasie (Doylestown)
Philadelphia
Pittsburgh
Schuykill County (Pottsville)
York County (Spring Grove)

PUERTO RICO
El Coqui (Guaynoba)

RHODE ISLAND
Bristol County

SOUTH CAROLINA
Piedmont Carolinas (Fort Mill)

TEXAS
Alamo (San Antonio)
Brazosport (Lake Jackson)
Fort Worth
Heart of Texas (Waco)
Gulf Coast (Houston)
Metroplex (McKinney)

UTAH
Beehive (West Jordan)

VERMONT
Burlington

VIRGINIA
Northern Virginia (Fairfax,
Tidewater Area (Virginia Beach)

WASHINGTON
Bellevue
Puget Sound (Kirkland)
Seattle-Tacoma (Brier)

WISCONSIN
Fox Valley (Fond du Lac)

CANADA

ALBERTA
Calgary
Edmonton (Sherwood Park)

BRITISH COLUMBIA
Greater Vancouver (Langley)

MANCHESTER
Manitoba (Winnipeg)

Sources and Resources

N.A.L.E.D.
Limited Edition Dealers
are
The Best in the Business

#1

With Collectibles · With Quality · With Product Knowledge · With Service

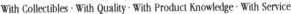

ALABAMA
CHRISTMAS TOWN, Mobile, AL, 205-661-3608
COLLECTIBLE COTTAGE, Birmingham, AL, 205-988-8551
COLLECTIBLE COTTAGE, Gardendale, AL, 205-631-2413
LIBERTY LANE, Huntsville, AL, 205-837-7012
LIBERTY LANE, Huntsville, AL, 205-880-9033
OLD COUNTRY STORE, Gadsen, AL, 205-492-7659
OLDE POST OFFICE, Trussville, AL, 205-655-7292
TREASURE CHEST, Brewton, AL, 205-867-9757

ARIZONA
BONA'S CHRISTMAS ETC, Tucson, AZ, 602-885-3755
CAROUSEL GIFTS, Phoenix, AZ, 602-997-6488
CROWN SHOP, Little Rock, AZ, 501-227-8442
FOX'S GIFTS & COL, Scottsdale, AZ, 602-947-0560
LAWTON'S GIFTS & COL, Chandler, AZ, 602-899-7977
MARYLN'S COLLECTIBLES, Tucson, AZ, 602-742-1501
MUSIC BOX & CLOCK SHOP, Mesa, AZ, 602-833-6943
RUTH'S HALLMARK SHOP, Cottonwood, AZ, 602-634-8050

CALIFORNIA
BLEVINS PLATES 'N THINGS, Vallejo, CA, 707-642-7505
CAMEO GIFTS & COLLECTIBLES, Temecula, CA, 909-676-1635
CARDTOWNE HALLMARK, Garden Grove, CA, 714-537-5240
CAROL'S GIFT SHOP *, Artesia, CA, 310-924-6335
COLLECTIBLE CORNER, Placentia, CA, 714-528-3079
COLLECTIBLES UNLIMITED, Tarzana, CA, 818-757-7250
COLLECTOR'S WORLD, Montrose, CA, 818-248-9451
CRYSTAL AERIE, Fremont, CA, 510-820-9133
DE WITTS GIFTS OF ELEGANCE, Oceanside, CA, 619-722-3084
DODIE'S FINE GIFTS, Woodland, CA, 916-668-1909
EASTERN ART, Victorville, CA, 619-241-0166
ELEGANT TOUCH, Arcadia, CA, 818-445-8868
ENCORE CARDS & GIFTS, Cypress, CA, 714-761-1266

CALIFORNIA (con't)
EVA MARIE DRY GROCER, Redondo Beach, CA, 310-375-8422
FORTE OLIVIA GIFTS, West Covina, CA, 818-962-2588
FRAME GALLERY, THE, Chula Vista, CA, 619-422-1700
FRIENDS COLLECTIBLES, Canyon Country, CA, 805-298-2232
GALLERIA GIFTS, Reedley, CA, 209-638-4060
KENNEDY'S COL & GIFTS, Sacramento, CA, 916-973-8754
LENA'S GIFT GALLERY *, San Mateo, CA, 415-342-1304
LIEBERG'S, Alhambra, CA, 818-282-8454
LOU'S HALLMARK, Ridgecrest, CA, 619-446-5100
LOUISE MARIE'S FINE GIFTS, Livermore, CA, 510-449-5757
MAC KINNONS STATIONARY, La Habra, CA, 310-691-9322
MARGIE'S GIFTS & COL, Torrance, CA, 310-378-2526
MARY ANN'S CARDS, GIFTS, Yorba Linda, CA, 714-777-0999
MUSICAL MOMENTS & COL, Shingle Spgs, CA, 916-677-2221
NORTHERN LIGHTS, San Rafael, CA, 415-457-2884
NYBORG CASTLE GIFTS & COL *, Martinez, CA, 510-930-0200
P M COLLECTABLES, Cupertino, CA, 408-725-8858
REFLECTIONS AT BLACKHAWK, Danville, CA, 510-736-9050
RUMMEL'S VILLAGE GUILD, Montebello, CA, 213-722-2691
RYSTAD'S LIMITED EDITIONS, San Jose, CA, 408-279-1960
SUTTER STREET EMPORIUM, Folsom, CA, 916-985-4647
TOMORROW'S TREASURES, Riverside, CA, 909-354-5731
TOWNEND'S CARD ATTACK, Moreno Valley, CA, 909-788-3989
VILLAGE PEDDLER, La Habra, CA, 310-694-6111
WEE HOUSE FINE COLLECTIBLES, Irvine, CA, 714-552-3228
WILSON GALLERIES, Fresno, CA, 209-224-2223

COLORADO
KENT COLLECTION, Englewood, CO, 303-761-0059
KING'S GALLERY OF COL, Col Springs, CO, 719-636-2228
NOEL - THE CHRISTMAS SHOP, Vail, CO, 303-476-6544
PLATES ETC, Arvada, CO, 303-420-0752

COLORADO (con't)
QUALITY GIFTS & COL, Colorado Springs, CO, 719-599-0051
SWISS MISS SHOP, Cascade, CO, 719-684-9679
TOBACCO LEAF, Lakewood, CO, 303-274-8720

CONNECTICUT
CARDS & GIFTS ETC, Danbury, CT, 203-743-6515
CELIA'S HALLMARK, Riverside, CT, 203-698-2509
CRICKET'S HALLMARK, North Haven, CT, 203-239-0135
FIFTH AVENUE, Trumbull, CT, 203-261-7592
J B'S COLLECTIBLES, Danbury, CT, 203-790-1011
MAURICE NASSER *, New London, CT, 203-443-6523
PERIWINKLE, Vernon, CT, 203-872-2904
REVAY'S GARDERNS & GIFT, East Windsor, CT, 203-623-9068
THE TAYLOR'D TOUCH, Marlborough, CT, 203-295-9377
THREE CHEERS HALLMARK, Meriden, CT, 203-634-7509
UTOPIA COLLECTIABLES, Oxford, CT, 203-264-0419
WINDSOR SHOPPE, North Haven, CT, 203-239-4644

DELAWARE
GIFT DESIGN GALLERIES, Dover, DE, 302-734-3002
PEREGOY'S GIFTS, Wilmington, DE, 302-999-1155
TULL BROTHERS, Seaford, DE, 302-629-3071

FLORIDA
CAROL'S HALLMARK SHOP, Tampa, FL, 813-960-8807
CHRISTMAS COL, Altamonte Springs, FL, 407-862-5383
CHRISTMAS COTTAGE & GIFT, Melbourne, FL, 407-725-0270
CHRISTMAS SHOPPE, Miami, FL, 305-255-5414
CLASSIC CARGO, Destin, FL, 904-837-8171
CORNER GIFTS, Pembroke Pines, FL, 305-432-3739
ENTERTAINER, THE, Jacksonville, FL, 904-725-1166
GAIL'S HALLMARK, Miami, FL, 305-666-6038
HEIRLOOMS OF TOMORROW, North Miami, FL, 305-899-0920

FLORIDA (con't)
HUNT'S COLLECTIBLES, Satellite Beach, FL, 407-777-1313
METHODIST FOUNDATION, Jacksonville, FL, 904-798-8210
PAPER MOON, West Palm Beach, FL, 407-684-2668
SUN ROSE GIFTS, Indian Harbor Beach, FL, 407-773-0550
VILLAGE PLATE COLLECTOR *, Cocoa, FL, 407-636-6914

GEORGIA
BECKY'S SMALL WONDERS, Helen, GA, 706-878-3108
CHAMBERHOUSE, Canton, GA, 404-479-9115
COTTAGE GARDEN, Macon, GA, 912-743-9897
CREATIVE GIFTS, Augusta, GA, 706-796-8794
GALLERY II, Atlanta, GA, 404-872-7272
GIFTS & SUCH, Augusta, GA, 706-738-4574
GLASS ETC, Atlanta, GA, 404-493-7936
IMPRESSIONS, Brunswick, GA, 912-265-1624
MARTHA JANE'S, Cave Springs, GA, 706-777-3608
MTN CHRISTMAS-MTN MEMORIES, Dahlonega, GA, 706-864-9115
PAM'S HALLMARK SHOP, Fayetteville, GA, 404-461-3041
PARSONS, Cumming, GA, 404-887-9991
PIKE'S PICKS FINE GIFTS, Roswell, GA, 404-998-7828
PLUM TREE, Tucker, GA, 404-491-9433
SPECIAL EFFECTS GIFTS, Blue Ridge, GA, 706-632-6950
SWAN GALLERIES, Stone Mountain, GA, 404-498-1324
TINDER BOX AT LENOX, Atlanta, GA, 404-231-9853
WESSON'S, Helen, GA, 706-878-3644
WHIMSEY MANOR, Warner Robins, GA, 912-328-2500

HAWAII
OUR HOUSE COL GALLERY, Honolulu, HI, 808-593-1999

ILLINOIS
BITS OF GOLD JEWELRY, Nashville, IL, 618-327-4261
C A JENSEN, LaSalle, IL, 815-223-0377
CHRYSLER BOUTIQUE, Effingham, IL, 217-342-4864
CLASS ACT, LAKE ZURICH, IL, 708-540-7700
COLLECTOR'S PARADISE, Monmouth, IL, 309-734-3690
COUNTRY OAK COLLECTABLES, Schaumburg, IL, 708-529-0290
COVE GIFTS, Bloomingdale, IL, 708-980-9020
CROWN CARD & GIFT SHOP, Chicago, IL, 312-282-6771
DORIS COLLECTIBLES, St Peter, IL, 618-349-8780
EUROPEAN IMPORTS & GIFTS, Niles, IL, 708-967-5253
GATZ COLLECTABLES, Wheeling, IL, 708-541-4033
GIFTIQUE ONE OF LONG GROVE, Long Grove, IL, 708-634-9171

ILLINOIS (con't)
GRIMM'S HALLMARK, St Charles, IL, 708-513-7008
GUZZARDO'S HALLMARK, Kewanee, IL, 309-852-5621
HALL JEWELERS & GIFTS LTD, Moweaqua, IL, 217-768-4990
HAWK HOLLOW, Galena, IL, 815-777-3616
JBJ THE COLLECTORS SHOP, Champaign, IL, 217-352-9610
KIEFER'S GALLERIES LTD, LaGrange, IL, 708-354-1888
KIEFER'S GALLERY/CRST HILL, Plainfield, IL, 815-436-5444
KRIS KRINGLE HAUS, Geneva, IL, 708-208-0400
LYNN'S & COMPANY, Arlington Heights, IL, 708-870-1188
MAY HALLMARK SHOP, Woodridge, IL, 708-985-1008
MC HUGH'S GIFTS & COL, Rock Island, IL, 309-788-9525
PAINTED PLATE LTD EDITION, O'Fallon, IL, 618-624-6987
RANDALL DRUG & GIFTS, Aurora, IL, 708-907-8700
ROYALE IMPORTS, Lisle, IL, 708-357-7002

ILLINOIS (con't)
RUTH'S HALLMARK, Bloomingdale, IL, 708-894-7890
SANDY'S DOLLS & COL, Palos Hills, IL, 708-423-0070
SOMETHING SO SPECIAL, Rockford, IL, 815-226-1331
STONE'S HALLMARK SHOPS, Rockford, IL, 815-399-4481
STONE'S ON THE SQUARE, Woodstock, IL, 815-338-0072
STRAWBERRY HOUSE, Libertyville, IL, 708-816-6129
STROHL'S LIMITED EDITIONS, Shelbyville, IL, 217-774-5222
TOWER SHOP, Riverside, IL, 708-447-5258
TRICIA'S TREASURES, Fairview Hgts, IL, 618-624-6334
WHYDE'S HAUS, Canton, IL, 309-647-8823

INDIANA
BEA'S HALLMARK, Indianapolis, IN, 317-898-8408
BEAS'S HALLMARK, Rushville, IN, 317-932-3328
CAROL'S CRAFTS, Nashville, IN, 812-988-6388
CURIO SHOPPE, Greensburg, IN, 812-663-6914
GNOME CROSSING, Carmel, IN, 317-846-5577
LANDMARK GIFTS & ANTIQUES, Kokomo, IN, 317-456-3488
NANA'S STICHIN STATION, Butler, IN, 219-868-5634
ROSE MARIE'S, Evansville, IN, 812-423-7557
ROSIE'S CARD & GIFT SHOP, Newburgh, IN, 812-853-3059
SMUCKER DRUGS, Middlebury, IN, 219-825-2485
STUNTZ & HOCH PINES, Walkerton, IN, 219-586-2663
TEMPTATIONS GIFTS, Valparaiso, IN, 219-462-1000

INDIANA (con't)
TOMORROW'S TREASURES, Muncie, IN, 317-284-6355
WALTER'S COLLECTIBLES, Princeton, IN, 812-386-3992
WATSON'S *, New Carlisle, IN, 219-654-8600

IOWA
COLLECTION CONNECTION, Des Moines, IA, 515-276-7766
DAVE & JANELLE'S, Mason City, IA, 515-423-6377
DAVIS COLLECTIBLES, Waterloo, IA, 319-232-0050
HAWK HOLLOW, Bellevue, IA, 319-872-5467
HEIRLOOM JEWELERS, Centerville, IA, 515-856-5715
VAN DEN BERG'S, Pella, IA, 515-628-3266

KANSAS
CAROL'S DECOR, Salina, KS, 913-823-1739 Ext 186
HOURGLASS, Wichita, KS, 316-942-0562

KENTUCKY
ANN'S HALLMARK, Lexington, KY, 606-266-9101
KAREN'S GIFTS, Louisville, KY, 502-425-3310
SCHWAB'S COLLECTIBLES, Lexington, KY, 606-266-2433
STORY BOOK KIDS, Florence, KY, 606-525-7743

LOUISIANA
AD LIB GIFTS, Metairie, LA, 504-835-8755
GALILEAN, THE, Leesville, LA, 318-239-6248
LA TIENDA, Lafayette, LA, 318-984-5920
PARTRIDGE CHRISTMAS SHOPS, Covington, LA, 504-892-4477
PLATES AND THINGS, Baton Rouge, LA, 504-753-2885
PONTALBA COLLECTIBLES, New Orleans, LA, 504-524-8068

MAINE
CHRISTMAS SHOPPE, Bangor, ME, 207-945-0805
GIMBEL & SONS COUNTRY, Boothbay Harbor, ME, 207-633-5088
HERITAGE GIFTS, Oakland, ME, 207-465-3910

MARYLAND
BODZER'S COLLECTIBLES, Baltimore, MD, 410-931-9222
CALICO MOUSE, Glen Burnie, MD, 410-760-2757
CALICO MOUSE, Annapolis, MD, 301-261-2441
CHERRY TREE CARDS & GIFTS, Laurel, MD, 301-498-8528
EDWARDS STORES, Ocean City, MD, 410-289-7000
FIGURINE WORLD, Gaithersburg, MD, 301-977-3997
GREETINGS & READINGS, Towson, MD, 410-825-4225
KEEPSAKES & COLLECTIBLES, Baltimore, MD, 410-727-0444
PENN DEN, Bowie, MD, 301-262-2430
PLATE NICHE, Davidsonville, MD, 410-798-5864

MARYLAND (con't)
PRECIOUS GIFTS, Ellicott City, MD, 410-461-6813
TIARA GIFTS, Wheaton, MD, 301-949-0210
TOMORROW'S TREASURES, Bel Air, MD, 410-893-7965
WANG'S GIFTS & COL, White Marsh, MD, 410-931-7388
WANG'S GIFTS & COLLECTIBLE, Bel Air, MD, 410-838-2626

MASSACHUSETTS
GIFT BARN, North Eastham, MA, 508-255-7000
GIFT GALLERY, Webster, MA, 508-943-4402
HONEYCOMB GIFT SHOPPE, Wakefield, MA, 617-245-2448
LEONARD GALLERY, Springfield, MA, 413-733-9492
LINDA'S ORIGINALS, Brewster, MA, 508-385-4758
MERRY CHRISTMAS SHOPPE, Whitman, MA, 617-447-6677
SHROPSHIRE CURIOSITY I, Shrewsbury, MA, 508-842-4202
SHROPSHIRE CURIOSITY II, Shrewsbury, MA, 508-842-5001
STACY'S GIFTS & COL, East Walpole, MA, 508-668-4212
WARD'S, Medford, MA, 617-395-2420

MICHIGAN
CARAVAN GIFTS & COLLECTIBLES, Fenton, MI, 313-629-4212
COPPER CRICKET, Westland, MI, 313-425-6977
COUNTRY CLASSIC COLLECTIBLES, Lapeer, MI, 313-667-4080
CURIO CABINET COL & XMAS, Lexington, MI, 313-359-5040
DEE'S HALLMARK, Clinton Twp, MI, 313-792-5510
ELLE STEVENS JEWELERS, Ironwood, MI, 906-932-5679
ELSIE'S HALLMARK SHOP, Petoskey, MI, 616-347-5270
EMILY'S GIFTS, COL, St Clair Shores, MI, 313-777-5250
FOUR SEASONS GIFT SHOP, Grand Ledge, MI, 517-627-7469
FRITZ CHINA & GIFTS, Monroe, MI, 313-241-6760
GEORGIA'S GIFT GALLERY, Plymouth, MI, 313-453-7733
HARPOLD'S, South Haven, MI, 616-637-3522
HAUG'S JWEWLRY & COL, Houghton, MI, 906-482-3430
HOUSE OF CARDS & COLLECTIBLES, Macomb, MI, 313-247-2000
HOUSE OF CARDS & COL, Rochester Hills, MI, 313-375-5600
JACQUELYNS GIFTS, Warren, MI, 313-296-9211
KEEPSAKE GIFTS, Kimball, MI, 313-985-5855
KNIBLOE GIFT CORNER, Jackson, MI, 517-782-6846
LAKEVIEW CARD & GIFT, Battle Creek, MI, 616-962-0650
MARION'S COLLECTIBLES, Livonia, MI, 313-522-8620

MICHIGAN (con't)
MOMBER PHARMACY & GIFTS, Sparta, MI, 616-887-7323
PAST & PRESENT SHOP, Wyoming, MI, 616-532-7848
PINOCCHIO'S INC, Frankenmuth, MI, 517-652-2751
PLATE LADY, Livonia, MI, 313-261-5220
RAY'S MART, Clinton Twp, MI, 313-791-2265
ROSEMARY'S COLLECTIBLES, Riverview, MI, 313-479-0494
SALLY ANN'S COLLECTIBLES, Waterford, MI, 313-623-6441
SCHULTZ GIFT GALLERY, Pinconning, MI, 517-879-3110
SPECIAL THINGS, Sterling Heights, MI, 313-739-4030
THEN & NOW GIFT SHOP, Union Lake, MI, 313-363-1360
TROY STAMP & COIN EXCHANGE, Troy, MI, 313-528-1181
YOUNG'S CHRISTMAS FANTASY, Warren, MI, 313-573-0230

MINNESOTA
ANDERSEN HALLMARK, Albert Lea, MN, 507-373-0996
BJORNSON IMPORTS, Mound, MN, 612-474-3957
COLLECTIBLES SHOWCASE, Bloomington, MN, 612-854-1668
COMMEMORATIVE IMPORTS, Stillwater, MN, 612-439-8772
GUSTAF'S, Lindstrom, MN, 612-257-6688
HELGA'S HALLMARK, Cambridge, MN, 612-689-5000
HUNT HALLMARK CARD & GIFT, Rochester, MN, 507-289-5152
HUNT SILVER LAKE DRUG, Rochester, MN, 507-289-0749
KOPPEN KOLLECTIBLES & DRUG, Pine City, MN, 612-629-6708
MARY D'S DOLLS & BEARS, Minneapolis, MN, 612-424-4375
ODYSSEY, Rochester, MN, 507-288-6629
ODYSSEY, Mankato, MN, 507-388-2004
SEEFELDT'S GALLERY, Roseville, MN, 612-631-1397

MISSISSIPPI
CHRISTMAS WORLD, Gulfport, MS, 601-896-9080
DOLL FANTASY & COL, Hattiesburg, MS, 601-545-3655

MISSOURI
DICKENS GIFT SHOPPE, Branson, MO, 417-334-2992
ELLY'S, Kimmswick, MO, 314-467-5019
EMILY'S HALLMARK, Ballwin, MO, 314-391-8755
HELEN'S GIFTS & ACCESSORIES, Rolla, MO, 314-341-2300
JOHNNIE BROCK'S, St Louis, MO, 314-481-8900
JOHNNIE BROCK'S, St Louis, MO, 314-481-5252 K C
COLLECTIBLES & GIFTS, Kansas City, MO, 816-741-2448
OAK LEAF GIFTS, Osage Beach, MO, 314-348-0190
SHIRLOCK II, Joplin, MO, 417-781-6345
TOBACCO LANE, Cape Girardeau, MO, 314-651-3414

MISSOURI (con't)
UNIQUE GIFT SHOPPE, Springfield, MO, 417-887-5476
MISSOURI (con't)
YE COBBLESTONE SHOPPE, Sikeston, MO, 314-471-8683

MONTANA
TRADITIONS, Missoula, MT, 406-543-3177

NEBRASKA
GERBER'S FINE COLLECTIBLES, Kearney, NE, 308-237-5139
L & L GIFTS, Fremont, NE, 402-727-7275
MARIANNE K FESTERSEN *, Omaha, NE, 402-393-4454
MARIANNE K FESTERSEN*, Omaha, NE, 402-393-4454
SHARRON SHOP, Omaha, NE, 402-393-8311

NEW HAMPSHIRE
STAINED GLASS FANTASY, Bedford, NH, 603-625-2314
STRAW CELLAR, Wolfeboro, NH, 603-569-1516

NEW JERSEY
CHINA ROYALE INC, Englewood, NJ, 201-568-1005
CHRISTMAS CAROL, Flemington, NJ, 908-782-0700
CLASSIC COLLECTIONS, Livingston, NJ, 201-992-8605
COLLECTORS CELLAR, Pine Beach, NJ, 908-341-4107
COLLECTORS EMPORIUM, Secaucus, NJ, 201-863-2977
CRAFT EMPORIUM, Waldwick, NJ, 201-670-0022
EMJAY SHOP, Stone Harbor, NJ, 609-368-1227
EXTRA SPECIAL TOUCH INC, Pompton Lakes, NJ, 201-835-5441
GIFT CARAVAN, North Arlington, NJ, 201-997-1055
GIFT GALLERY, Paramus, NJ, 201-845-0940
GIFT WORLD, Pennsauken, NJ, 609-663-2000
J C'S HALLMARK, Old Bridge, NJ, 908-826-8208
JIANA, Union, NJ, 201-492-1728
KATHE LUCEY GIFTS & COL, Kenvil, NJ, 201-584-3848
LIL BIT OF COUNTRY GIFT SHOP, Richwood, NJ, 608-256-0099
LITTLE TREASURES, Rutherford, NJ, 201-460-9353
MEMORY LANE, Union, NJ, 908-687-2071
MOLK BROS, Elmwood Park, NJ, 201-796-8377
NOTES-A-PLENTY GIFT SHOPPE, Flemington, NJ, 908-782-0700
OAKWOOD CARD & GIFT SHOP, Edison, NJ, 908-549-9494
OLD WAGON GIFTS, Colts Neck, NJ, 908-780-6656
SOMEONE SPECIAL, Cherry Hill, NJ, 609-424-1914
SOMEONE SPECIAL, W Berlin, NJ, 609-768-7171
STATION GIFT EMP, Whitehouse Station, NJ, 908-534-1212

NEW JERSEY (con't)
TOM'S GARDEN WORLD, McKee City, NJ, 609-641-4522
WESTON'S LIMITED EDITIONS, Eatontown, NJ, 908-542-3550
ZASLOW'S FINE COLLECTIBLES, Middletown, NJ, 908-957-9560
ZASLOW'S FINE COLLECTIBLES *, Matawan, NJ, 908-583-1499

NEW MEXICO
LORRIE'S COLLECTIBLES, Albuquerque, NM, 505-292-0020

NEW YORK
A LITTLE BIT OF CAMELOT, Warwick, NY, 914-986-4438
ALBERT'S ATTIC, Clarence, NY, 716-759-2231
ANN'S HALLMARK CARDS & GIFTS, Newburgh, NY, 914-564-5585
ANN'S HALLMARK SHOPPE, Newburgh, NY, 914-562-3149
CANAL TOWN COUNTRY STORE, Rochester, NY, 716-424-4120
CANAL TOWN COUNTRY STORE, Irondequoit, NY, 716-338-3670
CANAL TOWN COUNTRY STORE, Rochester, NY, 716-225-5070
CERAMICA GIFT GALLERY, New York, NY, 212-354-9216
CLASSIC GIFT GALLERY, Centereach, NY, 516-467-4813
CLIFTON PK COUNTRY STORE, Clifton Park, NY, 518-371-0585
CLOCK MAN GALLERY, Poughkeepsie, NY, 914-473-9055
COLLECTIBLY YOURS, Spring Valley, NY, 914-425-9244
CORNER COLLECTIONS, Hunter, NY, 518-263-4141
COUNTRY GALLERY, Fishkill, NY, 914-897-2008
CROMPOND COUNTRY STORE, Crompond, NY, 914-737-4937
ELLIE'S LTD ED & COLLECTIBLES, Selden, NY, 516-698-3467
ELLIE'S LTD ED & COL, Miller Place, NY, 516-744-5606
ISLAND TREASURES, Staten Island, NY, 718-698-1234
J R'S COLLECTIBLES, Poughkeepsie, NY, 914-298-0226
JOY'S LAMPLIGHT SHOPPE, Avon, NY, 716-226-3341
LIMITED COLLECTOR, Corning, NY, 607-936-6195
LIMITED EDITION, THE *, Merrick, NY, 516-623-4400
MARESA'S CANDELIGHT GIFT, Pt Jefferson, NY, 516-331-6245
PAUL'S ECONOMY PHARMACY, Staten Island, NY, 718-442-2924
PLATE COTTAGE, St James, NY, 516-862-7171
PORTS OF THE ORIENT, Cheektowaga, NY, 716-681-3020
PRECIOUS GIFT GALLERY, Levittlawn, NY, 516-579-3562
PRECIOUS GIFT GALLERY, Franklin Square, NY, 516-352-8900
PREMIO, Massapequa, NY, 516-795-3050
SIX SIXTEEN GIFT SHOPS, Bellmore, NY, 516-221-5829

NEW YORK (con't)
TODAY'S PLEAS.TOM.TREASURE, Jeffersonville, 914-482-3690
VILLAGE GIFT SHOP, Tonawanda, NY, 716-695-6589

NORTH CAROLINA
GIFT ATTIC, Raleigh, NC, 919-781-1822
MC NAMARA'S *, Highlands, NC, 704-526-5551
OLDE WORLD CHRISTMAS SHOPPE, Asheville, NC, 704-274-4819
TINDER BOX, Charlotte, NC, 704-366-5164
TINDER BOX/WINSTN-SALEM, Winston-Salem, NC, 919-765-9511

NORTH DAKOTA
BJORNSON IMPORTS, Grand Forks, ND, 701-775-2618
HATCH'S COLLECTORS GALLERY, Fargo, ND, 701-282-4457
HATCH'S COLLECTORS GALLERY, Minot, ND, 701-852-4666
HATCH'S COLLECTORS GALLERY, Bismarck, ND, 701-255-4821
JUNIQUE'S, Bismarck, ND, 701-258-3542

OHIO
ALADDIN LAMP, Lima,, OH, 419-224-5612
ANN'S HALLMARK, Cincinnati, OH, 513-662-2021
BELLFAIR COUNTRY STORES, Dayton, OH, 513-426-3921
CABBAGES & KINGS, Grand Rapids, OH, 419-832-2709
CELLAR CACHE, Put-in-Bay, OH, 419-285-2738
CHRISTMAS TREASURE CHEST, Ashland, OH, 419-289-2831
COLLECTION CONNECTION, Piqua, OH, 513-773-6788
COLLECTOR'S GALLERY, Marion, OH, 614-387-0602
COLLECTOR'S OUTLET, Mentor On The Lake, OH, 216-257-1141
COMSTOCK'S COLLECTIBLES, Medina, OH, 216-725-4656
CURIO CABINET, Worthington, OH, 614-885-1986
EASTERN ART, Parma, OH, 216-888-0277
EXCALIBUR GIFT, Sandusky, OH, 216-572-1322
GIFT GARDEN, No Olmsted, OH, 216-777-0116
GIFT GARDEN, Euclid, OH, 216-289-0116
GIFTS & TREASURES, North Canton, OH, 216-494-5511
GINGERBREAD HOUSE GIFTS, West Milton, OH, 513-698-3477
HARTVILLE COLLECTIBLES, Hartville, OH, 216-877-2172
HIDDEN TREASURES, Huron, OH, 419-433-2585
HOUSE OF TRADITION, Perrysburg, OH, 419-874-1151
KATHRYN'S GALLERY OF GIFTS, Solon, OH, 216-498-0234
LAKESHORE LTD, Huron, OH, 419-433-6168
LITTLE RED GIFT HOUSE, Birmingham, OH, 216-965-5420
LITTLE SHOP ON THE PORTAGE, Woodville, OH, 419-849-3742
LOLA & DALE GIFTS & COL, Parma Heights, OH, 216-885-0444

OHIO (con't)
MC KENZIE SQUARE, Hubbard, OH, 216-534-1166
MUSIK BOX HAUS, Vermilion, OH, 216-967-4744
NORTH HILL GIFT SHOP, Akron, OH, 216-535-4811
OLDE TYME CLOCKS, Cincinnati, OH, 513-741-9188
PORCELLANA LTD, Hamilton, OH, 513-868-1511
ROCHELLE'S FINE GIFTS, Toledo, OH, 419-472-7673
SANDY'S FAMILY COLLECTIBLES, Elyria, OH, 216-365-9999
SAXONY IMPORTS, Cincinnati, OH, 513-621-7800
SCHUMM PHARMACY HALLMARK, Rockford, OH, 419-363-3630
SETTLER'S FARM, Middlefield, OH, 216-632-1009
STORY BOOK KIDS, Cincinnati, OH, 513-769-5437
STRAWBERRY PATCH, Brunswick, OH, 216-225-7796
STRUBLE'S DRUG INC OF SHELBY, Shelby, OH, 419-342-2136
STUHLDREHER FLORAL CO, Mansfield, OH, 419-524-5911
TOWNE CENTRE SHOPPE, Streetsboro, OH, 216-626-3106

OKLAHOMA
COLONIAL FLORISTS, Stillwater, OK, 405-372-9166

OKLAHOMA (con't)
DODY'S HALLMARK, Lawton, OK, 405-353-8379
NORTH POLE CITY, Oklahoma City, OK, 405-685-6635
RATHBONES FLAIR FLOWERS, Tulsa, OK, 918-747-8491
SHIRLEY'S GIFTS, Ardmore, OK, 405-223-2116
SUZANNE'S COLLECTORS GALLERY *, Miami, OK, 918-542-3808
W D GIFTS, Okmulgee, OK, 918-756-2229

OREGON
ACCENT ON COLLECTIBLES, Portland, OR, 503-253-0841
CROWN SHOWCASE # 2, Portland, OR, 503-280-0669
DAS HAUS-AM-BERG, Salem, OR, 503-363-0669
MANCKE'S COLLECTIBLES, Salem, OR, 503-371-3157
PRESENT PEDDLER, Portland, OR, 503-639-2325
TREASURE CHEST GIFT SHOP, Gresham, OR, 503-667-2999

PENNSYLVANIA
BANKUS GIFTS, Pocono Lake, PA, 717-646-9528
BOB'S CARDS & GIFTS, Southampton, PA, 215-364-2872
CARGO WEST CHRISTMAS BARN, Scotrun, PA, 717-629-3122
COLLECTOR'S CHOICE, Pittsburgh, PA, 412-366-4477
COLLECTOR'S MARKETPLACE, Montrose, PA, 717-278-4094
DEN, THE, Lahaska, PA, 215-794-8493
DUTCH INDOOR VILLGE, Lancaster, PA, 717-299-2348

Club Directory and Price Guide

PENNSYLVANIA (con't)
EMPORIUM COLLECTIBLES GALLERY, Erie, PA, 814-833-2895
EUROPEAN TREASURES, Pittsburgh, PA, 412-421-8660
GIFT DESIGN GALLERIES, Whitehall, PA, 215-266-1266
GIFT DESIGN GALLERIES, Strouesburg, PA, 717-424-7530
GIFT DESIGN GALLERIES, Wilkes-Barre, PA, 717-822-6704
GILLESPIE JEWELER COL *, Northampton, PA, 215-261-0882
LAUCHNOR'S GIFTS & COL, Trexlertown, PA, 215-398-3008
LE COLLECTION, Belle Vernon, PA, 412-483-5330
LIMITED EDITIONS, Forty Fort, PA, 717-288-0940
LIMITED PLATES, Collegeville, PA, 215-489-7799
LINDENBAUM'S COL SHOWCASE, Pittsburgh, PA, 412-367-1980
MOLE HOLE OF PEDDLERS VILLAGE, Lahaska, PA, 215-794-7572
PICCADILLY CENTRE, Duncanville, PA, 814-695-6297
RED CARDINAL, THE, Ambler, PA, 215-628-2524
ROBERTS GALLERY, Pittsburgh, PA, 412-279-4223
SAVILLE'S LIMITED EDITIONS, Pittsburgh, PA, 412-366-5458
SIDE DOOR *, McMurray, PA, 412-941-3750
SOMEONE SPECIAL, Bensalem, PA, 215-245-0919
SPECIAL ATTRACTIONS, Sayre, PA, 717-888-9433
TODAY'S COLLECTABLES, Philadelphia, PA, 215-331-3993
TODAY'S TREASURES, Pittsburgh, PA, 412-341-5233
VILLAGE OF COLONIAL PEDDLERS, Carlisle, PA, 717-243-9350
WISHING WELL, Reading, PA, 215-921-2566
YEAGLE'S, Lahaska, PA, 215-794-7756

RHODE ISLAND
GOLDEN GOOSE, Smithfield, RI, 401-232-2310

SOUTH CAROLINA
ABRAMS DOLLS & COLLECTIBLES, Conway, SC, 803-248-9198
CHRISTMAS CELEBRATION, Mauldin, SC, 803-277-7373
CURIOSITY SHOP, Florence, SC, 803-665-8686
DUANE'S HALLMARK CARD & GIFT, Columbia, SC, 803-772-2624

SOUTH DAKOTA
AKERS GIFTS & COL, Sioux Falls, SD, 605-339-1325
GIFT GALLERY, Brookings, SD, 605-692-9405

TENNESSEE
BARBARA'S ELEGANTS, Gatlinburg, TN, 615-436-3454
CALICO BUTTERFLY, Memphis, TN, 901-362-8121
COX'S BAZAAR, Maryville, TN, 615-982-0421

TENNESSEE (con't)
HOUR GLASS II, Chattanooga, TN, 615-877-2328
LEMON TREE, Gatlinburg, TN, 615-436-4602
OLD COUNTRY STORE, Jackson, TN, 901-668-1223
ORANGE BLOSSOM, Martin, TN, 901-587-5091
PAPILLON INC, Chatanooga, TN, 615-499-2997
PATTY'S HALLMARK, Murfreesboro, TN, 615-890-8310
PIANO'S FLOWERS & GIFTS, Memphis, TN, 901-345-7670
STAGE CROSSING GIFTS & COL, Bartlett, TN, 901-372-4438

TEXAS
BETTY'S COLLECTABLES LTD *, Harlingen, TX, 210-423-8234
CHRISTMAS TREASURES, Baytown, TX, 713-421-1581
COLLECTIBLE HEIRLOOMS, Friendswood, TX, 713-486-5023
COLLECTOR'S COVE, Greenville, TX, 903-454-2572
ELOISE'S COLLECTIBLES, Houston, TX, 713-783-3611
ELOISE'S COLLECTIBLES, Katy, TX, 713-578-6655
ELOISE'S GIFTS & ANTIQUES, Rockwall, TX, 214-771-6371
GIFTS CARTOONS COLLECTIBLES, Hurst, TX, 817-590-0324
HOLIDAY HOUSE, Huntsville, TX, 409-295-7338
KEEPSAKES & KOLLECTIBLES, Spring, TX, 713-353-9233
LADYBUG LANE, Dallas, TX, 214-661-3692
LOUJON'S GIFTS, Sugar Land, TX, 713-980-1245
MR C COLLECTIBLE CENTER, Carrollton, TX, 214-242-5100
OPA'S HAUS, New Brauwfels, TX, 512-629-1191
SHEPHERD'S SHOPPE, THE, San Antonio, TX, 210-342-4811
SUNSHINE HOUSE GALLERY, Plano, TX, 214-424-5015
TIS THE SEASON, Ft Worth, TX, 817-877-5244

VERMONT
CHRISTMAS LOFT, Jay, VT, 802-988-4358

VIRGINIA
BIGGS LIMITED EDITIONS, Richmond, VA, 804-266-7744
CREEKSIDE COLLECTIBLS, Winchester, VA, 703-662-0270
GAZEBO GIFTS, Newport News, VA, 804-595-0331

WASHINGTON
CHALET COLLECTORS GALLERY, Tacoma, WA, 206-564-0326
GOLD SHOPPE, Tacoma, WA, 206-473-4653
JANSEN FLOWERS INC, Longview, WA, 206-423-0450
NATALIA'S COLLECTIBLES, Woodinville, WA, 206-481-4575
SLUYS GIFTS, Poulsbo, WA, 206-779-7171

WEST VIRGINIA (con't)
STEFAN'S EUROPEAN GIFTS, Yakima, WA, 509-457-5503
TANNENBAUM SHOPPE, Leavenworth, WA, 509-548-7014

WEST VIRGINIA
ARACOMA DRUG GIFT GALLERY, Logan, WV, 304-752-3812
EASTERN ART, Charleston, WV, 304-345-4786
FENTON GIFT SHOP, Williamstown, WV, 304-375-7772

WISCONSIN
A COUNTRY MOUSE, Milwaukee, WI, 414-281-4210
BEAUCHENE'S LTD ED, Thiensville, WI, 414-242-0170
BOOK & GIFT COLLECTIBLES, Manitowoc, WI, 414-684-4300
CENTURY COIN SERVICE, Green Bay, WI, 414-494-2719
COLLECTIBLES ETC INC, Brown Deer, WI, 414-355-4545
KIE'S PHARMACY, Racine, WI, 414-886-8160
KRIEGER JEWELERS INC, Green Bay, WI, 414-468-7071
KRISTMAS KRINGLE SHOPPE, Fond Du Lac, WI, 414-923-8210
MAXINE'S CARD'S & GIFTS, Beaver Dam, WI, 414-887-8289
NUTCRACKER GIFT HOUSE, Delavan, WI, 414-728-8447
P J'S COLLECTIBLES, Green Bay, WI, 414-437-3443
P J'S HALLMARK SHOP, Marinette, WI, 715-735-3940
SANSONE DRUGS & GIFTS, Hubertus, WI, 414-628-3550
SANSONE DRUGS & GIFTS, Slinger, WI, 414-644-5246
SANSONE GIFT & CARD, Mequon, WI, 414-241-3633
TIVOLI IMPORTS, Milwaukee, WI, 414-774-7590

INTERNATIONAL MEMBERS

AUSTRALIA
LIBERTY LANE, Sydney, NSW, Aust, 011-61-2-261-3595

CANADA
BAKEROSA COLLECTIBLES, London, Ont, 519-472-0827
CHARLES' HOUSE/PLATES, Bloomfield, Ont, 613-393-2249
CHORNYJS' - HADKE, Sault Ste Marie, Ont, 705-253-0315
DURAND'S LTD ED, Calgary, Alberta, CAN, 403-277-0008
HAPPINESS IS, Durham, Ont, CAN, 519-369-2115
HOMESTEAD GIFT SHOP, Lennoxville, Quebec, 819-569-2671
MIDDAUGH'S COLLECTIBLES, Goderich, Ont, 519-524-5540
OVER/RAINBOW GALLERY, Streetsville, Ont, 416-821-2131
PLATE CONNECTION, Sherwood Park, Alberta, 403-467-0008
PLATEFINDERS, Edmonton, Alberta, 403-435-3603
TOMORROW'S TREASURES, Bobcaygeon, Ont, 705-738-2147

*J*oin two clubs that are filled with loving, caring and sharing!

The Enesco Precious Moments Collectors' Club^{SM}
and
The Enesco Precious Moments Birthday Club^{SM}

With membership in The Precious Moments Collectors' Club, you'll receive these spectacular benefits:

◆ Symbol of Membership figurine
◆ Four issues of *The Goodnewsletter,* the club's official magazine
◆ Official Gift Registry
◆ Full color Pocket Guide to The Precious Moments® Collection
◆ Official club binder for storing member materials
◆ Official Membership Card
◆ Special mailings throughout the year
◆ Opportunity to purchase two limited edition Members Only figurines

---

With membership in The Precious Moments Birthday Club, you'll receive these exciting benefits:

◆ Symbol of Membership figurine
◆ Full color certificate with easel
◆ Official welcome letter from Club Headquarters
◆ Subscription to the Club's official newsletter, *Good News Parade*
◆ Birthday Card mailed to you from Club Headquarters
◆ Opportunity to acquire Members Only offerings

ENESCO
CORPORATION

Become a member of either collectors' club by calling (708) 640-5228!

enjoyment from your collectible line...

organization today!

features fantastic benefits:

Enesco Musical Society^{SM}

(708) 640-3190

◆ Special gift designed exclusively for members
◆ Subscription to *Musical Notes,* the Society's quarterly newsletter
◆ Welcome Letter from the Society
◆ Pocket folder to hold material received from Society Headquarters
◆ Opportunity to purchase Members Only offerings

Sports Impressions Collectors' Club^{SM}

(708) 956-5400

◆ Symbol of Membership collectible
◆ Current Sports Impressions catalog
◆ Member Services Directory
◆ Subscription to *The Lineup,* the Club's quarterly publication
◆ Opportunity to purchase exceptional sports collectibles available only to members

Edna Hibel Society

The Edna Hibel Society is one of the world's oldest non-profit international fellowships honoring an artist. We are dedicated to sharing and propagating the rich treasures of Love, Beauty and Humanity expressed in Edna Hibel's timeless art.

"Harmony" 29⅛″ × 22½″

"Melody" 29⅛″ × 22½″

"Harmony" and "Melody"

Limited edition framed reproductions of original paintings by Edna Hibel. Exclusively for members of the Edna Hibel Society.
(407) 848-9663

Have You Forgotten. . .

all the wonderful things a Toy Store Steiff Club membership brings you? Quarterly informative newsletter; the newest catalog & price list available; membership card; members only discounts once a year; an enameled pin authorized by Steiff — this year a brand new design designed by Jörg R Junginger; information on all Steiff related events; and the first opportunity to purchase our 1993 limited edition piece, "Petsile".

To join or renew, send $8.00 U.S., $12.00 all other countries, to: The Toy Store, P.O. Box 798, Holland, OH 43528

Announcing our Steiff Collector's Pin ★

Wear it with pride. . . or add it to your collection. It's yours when you join or renew your Club membership.

As a Toy Store Steiff Club member, you'll receive our quarterly newsletter, Steiff Collection Catalog, membership card and a beautiful full-color enamel pin — designed by Jörg R. Junginger of the Steiff Company.

If you've already renewed your membership, you'll receive your Steiff Collector's pin from The Toy Store automatically. If you haven't joined or renewed, do so now — and your pin will soon be on its way.

Designed by
Jörg R. Junginger
of the Steiff Company

YES. . . Please enter my Steiff Club membership. And, send my Steiff Club Collector's Pin — and all the exciting news throughout the year. My check is enclosed.

Name _____

Street Address _____

City _____ State _____ Zip _____
(Province/Country)

Annual Membership Fee $8.00 U.S.; $12.00 all other countries.

Clip and mail coupon today!

The Specialists

◆ **Bear's Den**
Joyce Harper
Wycoff, New Jersey
(201) 444-9133

A dealer of teddy bears

◆ **Carol's Gift Shop**
Marge Rosenberg
17601 S. Pioneer Blvd.
Artesia, California 90701
(310) 924-6335

A full service collectible and limited edition dealer in business for more than 25 years

◆ **Carousel Fantasy**
Atlantic City, New Jersey
(609) 441-8542

A dealer of carousel horses

◆ **Collectible Exchange, Inc.**
6621 Columbia Road
New Middletown, Ohio 44442
(800) 752-3208

A secondary market collectible exchange and listing service

◆ **Collector's Marketplace**
Russ Wood and Reneé Tyler
RR1, Box 213B
Montrose, Pennsylvania 18801
(800) 755-3123

A secondary market collectible exchange and listing service

◆ **The Cottage Collector**
Pat Cantrell
6211 Oakmont Blvd., #381
Fort Worth, Texas 76132
(817) 294-1961

Secondary market specialist in cottages and architectural designs, publisher, author

◆ **Finishing Touch**
James Wetherbee
4020 Rhea Road
Wichita Falls, Texas 76308
(800) 877-0070

Dealer of 42 lines of collectibles and limited editions. Specialist in Cairn gnomes

◆ The Greenbook
Louise Patterson
Old Coach at Main, Box 515
East Setauket, New York 11733
(516) 689-8466

Publisher of secondary market price guides on Precious Moments, Hallmark and other collectibles

◆ Lorrie's Collectibles
Lorrie Church
3107 Eubank, NE
Albuquerque, New Mexico 87111
(800) 945-0020

A full service collectible and limited edition dealer

◆ Janet Gale Mauro's
550 Harbor Cove Circle
Longboat Key, FL 34228-3544
(813) 387-0102

Lladró secondary market specialist

◆ Miller's Hallmark & Gift Gallery
Dean A. Genth
Northedge Mall
1322 North Barron Street
Eaton, Ohio 45320
(513) 456-4151

A secondary market Hummel and Swarovski specialist, publisher, author

◆ Opa's Haus, OHI Exchange
Ken Armke
1600 River Road
New Braunfels, Texas 78132
(512) 629-1191

A secondary market collectibles exchange and secondary market specialist in steins

◆ Secondary Market Scene
Helga Grasher
Metamora, Michigan
(313) 724-0893

A secondary market publisher

◆ Shropshire Curiosity Shoppe
Edna and George Samara
500 Main Street
Shrewsbury, Massachusetts 01545
(508) 845-6317 or 842-4202

Full service collectibles retailers specializing in retired pieces, club editions and artist events

◆ Rosie Wells Enterprises, Inc.
Rosie Wells
RR#1
Canton, Ohio 61520
(800) 445-8745

A secondary market specialist in Precious Moments, Lowell Davis, Hallmark ornaments; a secondary market collectibles listing service; publisher

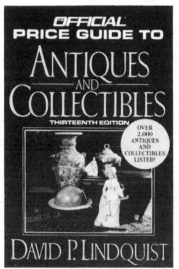

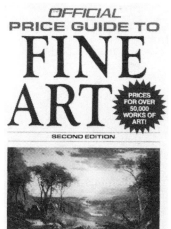

Index

◆ Clubs by Category

Club Directory and Price Guide

About the Authors

Susan K. Elliott lives in Dallas, where she writes about various aspects of collectibles, specializing in artists. She grew up in a family of collectors and began writing about antiques and collectibles in the early 1970s as a high school senior working for her family's collectibles publishing business.

Editor of *Plate Collector* magazine from 1975 to 1986, she covered the evolution of limited edition collectibles from a hobby focused primarily on blue-and-white plates to today's present diversity of cottages, dolls, ornaments, figurines, musicals, and lithographs. She has traveled widely in the United States, Canada, and Europe for artist interviews, publishing more than 150 profiles in the last two decades.

Editorial Director of *Collector's mart* magazine for three years and now a regular contributor, she also edits two newsletters for the National Association of Limited Edition Dealers and serves on the board of directors of NALED.

Susan is currently Managing Editor of Special Projects for Beckett Publications, a publisher of sports card magazines based in Dallas, and is engaged to be married to Jerry Hamm.

Kevin Samara was born and raised in central Massachusetts. He received his MBA from Clark University in 1975. He has been married to his wife, Phyllis, for 17 years and has two daughters, Nicole and Elizabeth.

Kevin has been associated with the gift and collectible business for the past 23 years. While he was still in college, his parents opened the Shropshire Curiosity Shop in Shrewsbury, Mass. Today, Kevin is co-owner of the Shropshire Shop, one of the nation's leading collectible galleries.

Kevin has served the collectible industry as a member of the NALED board of directors for the past eight years. He is currently serving a third term as president of NALED. Kevin has been instrumental in developing a number of innovative retail programs that enable the collectibles dealer to effectively serve the collector.

A frequent speaker on collectibles to various industry groups. He is on the board of directors for the Collectibles and Platemakers and the advisory committee for the International Collectible shows. Producer of the Eastern States Plate and Collectible Show, and a professional restorer of fine art and collectibles.